"For the first time director, this book offers ideas a [...] guage and illustrations. But of even greater import [...] ..orking with producers, technicians, and actors in the usual a [...] .ension and chaos. This valuable book by an experienced director demystifies filmmaking."

> — Irvin Kershner, Director, *Star Wars: Episode V–The Empire
> Strikes Back, Never Say Never Again, Robocop II, The Return
> of a Man Called Horse*

"Gil Bettman has brilliantly written a terrific insider's introduction to the filmmaking process. All the terrific tricks and techniques that make modern movies special are excitingly explained. Young filmmakers can put Gil's ideas to work right away."

> — John Badham, Director, *The Shield* (TV), *Saturday Night
> Fever, War Games, Blue Thunder, Stakeout, Short Circuit, Bird
> on a Wire, Point of No Return, Drop Zone*

"For the aspiring breakthrough director, Gil's book deftly steers you around the frequent and cavernous pitfalls of professional filmmaking. Filled with experiences and examples from contemporary models, his advice is invaluable for the practical artist. If you're just starting out or even an experienced filmmaker, you need this book!"

> — Donald Petrie, Director, *How to Lose a Guy in 10 Days, Miss
> Congeniality, Grumpy Old Men, Mystic Pizza*

"Aspiring directors owe Gil Bettman a debt of thanks. Mr. Bettman has spared nothing in pursuit of his goal: grooming the first timer so thoroughly that he or she can actually live their movie before they shoot it. The book is stuffed with hardcore practicality, from rude awakenings (your first film will be under-budgeted) to Bettman's take on cinematography (move the camera a lot if you want to have any credibility in low budget features or series television)."

> — Thomas Ackerman, ASC, Cinematographer, *Snow Dogs, Rat Race,
> The Muse, Beetlejuice, George of the Jungle, Dennis the Menace*

"Gil Bettman has written the most detailed and informative guide to directing that I've seen, and the only one that effectively tackles the problem of script development. For the aspiring director, *First Time Director* is a wonderful roadmap, for the experienced director, an invaluable refresher course."

> — David S. Ward, Academy Award-Winning Screenwriter, *The
> Sting*; Academy Award-Nominated Screenwriter, *Sleepless in
> Seattle*; Screenwriter, *The Mask of Zorro, Major League, The
> Milagro Beanfield War*; Director: *Down Periscope, Major League
> I & II, The Program, King Ralph, Cannery Row*

"This book is a must-have for all down-and-dirty guerrilla filmmakers."

> — Penelope Spheeris, Director, *The Crooked E: The Unshredded Truth About Enron* (TV), *Wayne's World, The Little Rascals, The Beverly Hillbillies, Black Sheep, The Decline of Western Civilization, Parts I, II & III*

"With wit, insight, and three decades of experience in the motion picture and television industry, Professor Gil Bettman is giving back. His textbook, *First Time Director*, is invaluable for the aspiring director. Aside from covering the technical issues in depth, Bettman stresses knowing and trusting oneself, probably the most important issue a director must learn. In my career as an editor, I always gravitated toward directors who were secure enough with their own creativity to allow them to interact and collaborate with others. Gil Bettman knows this, he knows himself, and he has written a terrific book."

> — Robert C. Jones, Academy Award-Winning Screenwriter, *Coming Home;* Editor, *Crazy in Alabama, Bulworth, Heaven Can Wait, Bound for Glory, Shampoo, The Last Detail, Love Story, Ship of Fools, Guess Who's Coming to Dinner*

"If you can get Dad to give you a budget of $30,000, the only other thing you need is this book and you're ready to make your breakthrough movie."

> — Leonard Schrader, Academy Award-Nominated Screenwriter, *Kiss of the Spider Woman;* Screenwriter, *The Yakuza, Blue Collar*

"*First Time Director* is an extremely pragmatic and useful guide that all aspiring filmmakers should read. Gil Bettman offers clever solutions to common directorial problems, among them, improving weak performances."

> — Delia Salvi, Professor, UCLA School of Film, Television and Theater; Author, *Friendly Enemies: Maximizing the Director–Actor Relationship;* Professional Actor, Director, and Coach

"Bettman's book is packed with information from cover to cover, no fat or easy fillers, very little anecdotes — just solid points of reference about the craft and art of directing. It takes the director firmly by the hand and guides him or her through the minefield of potential disasters. It makes no promises of enduring success, but it certainly lightens the deep shadows in what can often appear a vale of tears. In short, the book is the rocket engine that can help launch the career of any aspiring director. Of the endless books analyzing films already made, this is one of the precious few that deal with the reality of directing. This is the 'survival guide' for directors, a textbook which should be required reading for every film student."

> — Dick Ross, formerly Co-Chair, Graduate Film Department, Columbia University in the City of New York; Chairman, Graduate Film Department, New York University; Deputy Director, National Film and TV School, Beaconsfield, U.K.

MICHAEL WIESE PRODUCTIONS
www.mwp.com

We are delighted that you have found, and are enjoying, our books.

Since 1981, we've been all about providing filmmakers with the very best information on the craft of filmmaking: from screenwriting to funding, from directing to camera, acting, editing, distribution, and new media.

It is our goal to inspire and empower a generation (or two) of film and videomakers like yourself. But we want to go beyond providing you with just the basics. We want to shake you and inspire you to reach for your dreams and go beyond what's been done before. Most films that come out each year waste our time and enslave our imaginations. We want to give you the confidence to create from your authentic center, to bring something from your own experience that will truly inspire others and bring humanity to its full potential — avoiding those urges to manufacture derivative work in order to be accepted.

Movies, television, the Internet, and new media all have incredible power to transform. As you prepare your next project, know that it is in your hands to choose to create something magnificent and enduring for generations to come.

This is not an impossible goal because you've got a little help. Our authors are some of the most creative mentors in the business, willing to share their hard-earned insights with you. Their books will point you in the right direction but, ultimately, it's up to you to seek that authentic something on which to spend your precious time.

We applaud your efforts and are here to support you. Let us hear from you.

Sincerely,

Michael Wiese
Filmmaker, Publisher

first time director:
how to make your breakthrough movie

gil bettman

Published by Michael Wiese Productions
11288 Ventura Blvd, Suite 621
Studio City CA 91604
Tel. (818) 379-8799
Fax (818) 986-3408
mw@mwp.com
www.mwp.com

Cover Design: agdesign.com
Cover Photography: Ryan Ngyuen
Layout: Gina Mansfield
Editor: Brett Jay Markel

Printed by McNaughton & Gunn, Inc., Saline, Michigan
Manufactured in the United States of America

The author would especially like to thank the following writers and copyright holders for permission to use examples from their scripts and/or images from their films:

Back to the Future written by Robert Zemeckis & Bob Gale ©1985 Universal City Studios Inc. All Rights Reserved.

What Lies Beneath screenplay by Clark Gregg © 2000 DreamWorks LLC and Twentieth Century Fox Film Corporation.

Chasing Amy ©1997 Buena Vista Pictures Distribution.

Never Too Young to Die ©1986 Paul Entertainment.

Pulp Fiction ©1994 Miramax Films.

Shine ©1996 Fine Line Features. All Rights Reserved.

The Untouchables ©1987 Paramount Pictures Corporation. All Rights Reserved.

Library of Congress Cataloging-in-Publication Data

Bettman, Gil, 1948-
  First time director : how to make your breakthrough movie / Gil
Bettman.
     p. cm.
  ISBN 0-941188-77-9
  1. Motion pictures--Production and direction. 2. Cinematography. I.
Title.
  PN1995.9.P7B45 2003
  791.4302'33--dc22

                                                    2003017743

ACKNOWLEDGEMENTS

Since undertaking the writing of this book, I have discovered that — up to a certain point — book writing, like filmmaking, is a collaborative venture. Yes, for the most part, it is a solitary pursuit, but you cannot do it all by yourself, and I am grateful for that. For me, a large part of the thrill of directing comes from the collaborative requirements of filmmaking. Nothing is more exhilarating than allowing your ideas to be shaped by the thinking of your collaborators — writers, actors, cinematographers, editors, etc. — and then discovering that the results exceed your expectations. That happy scenario has repeated itself at various junctures in the writing of this book, and I would like to acknowledge and thank those individuals who have tempered my ideas with their own energy and imagination.

I would like to thank Bob Zemeckis for sharing his incisive thinking with me throughout the years, and for allowing me to quote him extensively in this book.

When I started teaching in the School of Film and Television at Chapman University in the fall of 1995, I had been working as a freelance director for 15 years. I knew a fair amount about directing but very little about how to teach what I knew. My students at Chapman have inspired and required me to shape my knowledge so that they could grasp it and make it their own. This is an ongoing process. I am still learning and I thank them for continuing to demand that I give them the best of what I have got to give in the most palatable, comprehensible form possible.

Along the way, other artists, filmmakers, and teachers have guided and inspired me. Robert Lowell convinced me I had some creative gifts. Brooke Hopkins is to blame for firing my interest in film. Ed Brokaw and Delia Salvi shared some of their vast understanding of the directing process with me when I was a graduate student at UCLA. While at UCLA, my path crossed that of David S. Ward. Since then he has regularly shared with me flashes of his laser-precise thinking about scriptwriting, directing, and the film business, and in so doing provided me with some of the best material in this book. Richard Walter helped me build a bridge from Hollywood to the Ivory Tower of academia. Arthur Hiller helped me sustain that bridge once I crossed it. Through Arthur, I met Robert C. Jones and John Badham. Their ability to articulate their shared mastery of the art and craft of filmmaking helped me to clarify many of the lessons in this book. Fortunately for me, Leonard Schrader joined the faculty of the film school at Chapman shortly after I did, and since then I have sought him out regularly and let him shower me with his genius. Throughout all of the above, I have been privileged to count

David E. James as a close friend and to be regularly exposed to his brilliant thinking. His thoughts have inspired me to clarify and verify my thinking, and given me an inkling of the demands of true scholarship.

No one has made a greater creative contribution to this book than my former student, Michael Kendrick. Although he is half as old as I am, he is twice as talented. His ample gifts are on display in the drawings in this book. Another former student, Byron Werner, put his expertise as a cinematographer to work for me and shot the photos in Chapter 5 that illustrate the different properties of different lenses. All of the other photographic images in the book were gathered and up-rezzed by Tod Withey. Thanks to his patience and cyber-prowess, this book has pictures that far exceed the eloquence of my words.

I am also indebted to the generosity of the film studios and production companies that allowed me to use still images from their films: Dreamworks SKG, Miramax, Pandora, Paramount Pictures, and Universal Studios.

Some of those rights I could never have secured without the help of my lawyer and long-standing ally, Alan Grodin. Many times in the course of my Hollywood career I have felt the same as Michael Ontkean in the film *Slap Shot*, when he stated, "My fan club meets in a phone booth." In my case, Alan has yet to exit that phone booth.

If, when writing a book, you have a friend who will take the time to read what you write and wordsmith it, then you are truly blessed. I was so blessed by Janell Shearer. Her steadfastness as a friend is only outstripped by her gifts as a wordsmith. The other master wordsmith in my life, my old friend, Daryl Henry, was kind enough to put his own writing projects aside from time to time and help me rewrite some key passages

I came up for tenure at Chapman University in the middle of writing this book. After many years of climbing the greasy pole of Hollywood, I could not pass up the possibility of a job for life. So I shelved the book for a year while I applied myself fulltime to making sure I got my tenure. As a result, it was completed years after the date I had originally promised it to my publisher, Michael Weise. Yet Michael was forever patient and a steady source of constructive criticism and empowering advice. Along with his associate, Ken Lee, he provided a gentle, strong hand that guided this project from an idea to a manuscript to a book.

On the Use of Personal Pronouns
In the interest of clarity and economy, the personal pronouns "he," "him," and "his" as used in this book often may be taken also to mean "he or she," "him or her," and "his or hers."

To Ron Thronson:
an aristocrat of the soul

TABLE OF CONTENTS

PART FOUR – SET POLITICS

PART FIVE – POSTPRODUCTION

FOREWORD

by Robert Zemeckis, Director, *Cast Away*; *What Lies Beneath*; *Contact*; *Forrest Gump*; *Back to the Future I, II & III*; *Who Framed Roger Rabbit*; *Romancing the Stone*

By writing *First Time Director*, Gil Bettman has done for directing what Lajos Egri did for screenwriting when he wrote *The Art of Dramatic Writing*: put out the first book which explains how the craft is practiced professionally. Until I picked up *First Time Director*, I had never read anything that went right to the heart of what a director must do to succeed. Most texts on directing are filled with information about things that most directors never concern themselves with — not the case with Gil's book. He has lucidly set down the ABCs of directing so that dedicated students can learn exactly what will be required of them when they step onto a set.

Better yet, the book is tailored specifically for the director taking on his or her first professional assignment — the only logical approach for a textbook on directing. Success on the first assignment is crucial. Without it, it's effectively impossible to launch a career. Since no textbook can teach like on-the-job experience, especially in a three-dimensional medium like directing, you don't need a textbook after you have survived your first professional assignment. The fact that Gil Bettman has built this truth into the approach of his book is both brilliant and good common sense.

I always knew Gil could write and direct. I set up a deal for him to write and direct a film for Universal, and later on, one for Warner Bros. As is often the case, neither project made it onto the screen. But *First Time Director* proves that he has found a great way to put his talents as a writer and a director to good use. People who are as good as Gil is at writing and directing are usually too preoccupied making Hollywood movies. But in Gil's case, the film industry's loss has been the film student's gain. *First Time Director* reveals to those still on the outside what's going to be expected of them when they get on the inside, and it is spot-on accurate, because it has been written by somebody who has been there and done that. I wish somebody had handed me this book the day I got out of USC.

PREFACE

When I first started teaching directing, I read every "how to" book on the subject that I could find. I knew what I was looking for: a text that taught what I had learned during my 20-year career as a director in Hollywood. My plan was to draw on those lessons in order to provide my students with the information they wanted above all else. I had gone through the M.F.A. program at UCLA when I was an aspiring director. I could remember what I had wanted then, and I could not imagine it being any different today. I wanted my professors to teach me the directing skills that I needed to know to break through and start a career in Hollywood. Now, 25 years later, I knew that the particular nature of my industry experience made me especially qualified to teach them this. After all, I had broken into the business not once, but three times — first as an episodic television director, then as a rock video director, and finally as a director of low budget features. But as hard as I tried, I could not find a book that would serve as a companion text for the course I envisioned. Ironically, almost all the books I read contained a wealth of well-articulated, accurate information. But my experience had taught me that most of this information was useless to a first time director. Even those passages that were invaluable could not be learned from — because they were indistinguishably mixed in with those which were of no use. That was when I decided I had to write this book.

How can it be that the other books on directing do not contain these crucial lessons? As far as I can tell, it is because they were written by very intelligent, knowledgeable people who have never really broken into the business and maintained a viable directing career. These individuals may have had an ancillary role on some mainstream Hollywood projects, or done some directing on the periphery of the industry. But, unlike myself, they have never really once kicked down the door to direct a project which opened nationwide in theaters or was aired on primetime network television. Their knowledge of filmmaking was encyclopedic and academic, but due to their lack of practical experience, they burdened the first time director with superfluous information. What a first time director needs is a survival guide, not an encyclopedia. I intend this book to be that survival guide.

Unless you are an established Hollywood scriptwriter or cinematographer — someone like a Larry Kasdan or a Jan DeBont — it is highly unlikely that a major studio is going to put up the money for your first feature film. Inevitably, your big break is going to be a day late and a dollar short. You are going to have to endure that which Spike Lee, Kevin Smith, Doug Liman, Neil LaBute, the

Wachowski brothers, and all of the hot young directors working in today's Hollywood endured when they started out: You are going to be charged with making a film in record time, on a minimal budget, with a shorthanded, inexperienced crew. Even if the funds to make your breakthrough movie or TV show or rock video are ultimately coming from a big name studio, network, or record label with deep pockets, the fact remains that you are not yet bankable. And until you are, you can be sure that the bean counters at those big companies will be doling out those funds to you in nickels and dimes. No matter whether the money is coming from you or your Uncle Harry or MCA Inc., the budgetary restrictions are going to be equally constraining.

Under these circumstances, things are bound to go wrong on a regular basis. The atmosphere is going to be chaotic. The crew and the production support are going to be under stress. And yet, as first time director, you are going to have to rise to the occasion and do that which a director must do in order to make the film he wants to make. You are going to have to be so self-assured and so capable that you manage to allay everyone's fears and pull form out of the chaos. If you seem hesitant, or if your solutions are not up to the problems, those on whom you are depending for support — the assistant director, the cinematographer, or the producer — will not hesitate to supercede you and take control of the film, whether out of jealousy, fear, or necessity. In order to prevent this from happening, and to be certain that you get to make the film that you want to make, you are going to need a very specific kind of understanding of the director's craft — an understanding tailored to these unusual circumstances. That is what this book provides.

This book focuses on what a director must know to control the set, because this is the key to his success as a first time director. I am amazed at the amount of pages devoted to a director's responsibilities in preproduction and postproduction in the existing books on directing. As a director, I always looked forward to preproduction and especially postproduction because, when compared to the chaos of the production, they were utterly stress-free. If, during these phases in the making of a film, I ever found that I did not know something that was required of me, I simply told those who were expecting me to make a well-informed decision that I would "think it over and get back to them tomorrow." Then I would go home and call a friend who was an expert in the field and get him to fill in the gaps in my knowledge. The next day, I would return and casually deliver the word from on high.

On the set there is no tomorrow. Directing on the set is like being at the helm of a river raft going through increasingly precipitous rapids. There is no stopping, no turning back, and every decision must be instantaneous and correct, otherwise disaster is imminent. The smaller the budget, the smaller the raft, the fewer the oars, the greater the likelihood that — if you make a wrong turn — the boat will flip or smash on the rocks. To continue the metaphor, preproduction is the planning which takes place before the raft is put in the water and postproduction is like rowing across a calm lake at the bottom of the rapids. The existing books focus about 90% on what comes before and after that white water and about 10% on what it takes to get through that critical phase. It should be the other way around. This book will fill this need.

It will tell you everything you need to know about the easy stuff — preproduction and postproduction — so you can convincingly discharge your duties as a director in those areas. It is going to tell how, while the set is being lit, you can take a bad performance and make it respectable, or a respectable performance and make it good. If you are lucky enough to actually have an actor on the set who is capable of delivering a good performance, this book will teach you what you will need to know to take the good performance and make it great. (I am not going to burn up pages with sense memory exercises and lengthy rehearsal techniques; you will never get to use them. Because unless your actors are sufficiently committed to your film to donate their time gratis, there will be no money for rehearsals.) All the time you are going to get is that which elapses between the first walk through and when the set is lit. You may not be able to bring forth miracles in that span, but this book will enable you to come as close to such alchemy as is humanly possible.

Will this book teach you how to move your camera like John Woo or Michael Bay? Actually, yes. By extrapolation you can take my approach to camera blocking and, budget permitting, move your camera all the time, in every imaginable way, like Woo and Bay. But it is unlikely your budget will permit you to do this. So this book is intended to teach how, within the constraints of your peanut-sized budget, you can emulate the camera technique of all those directors who are now setting the trends in the realm of mis en scene.

This book will arm you with the "silver bullets" which you are going to need to kill the demons which will be coming at you right and left on the set. Time and money are going to be in such short supply, all your solutions to all your problems are going to have to be lightning fast and deadly — instantaneous and spot-on. These silver bullets may not be the most elegant. They may not be Academy Award-winning examples of a director's craft. But they get the job done. You can worry about the Academy Award on your second film, or better still, your third. When you get to that level, you can read all the other books on directing. At that point, elegant solutions are going to be expected of you. Then you will able to afford them. For now, your goal should be to survive your directorial debut in the best shape possible. This book is your guide to survival. It will enable you to pull form from chaos and make the best film possible within the limited resources provided to you.

PART ONE:
BEFORE THE BATTLE

CHAPTER 1 | PREPRODUCTION

Soaking Up the Atmosphere

Yes, preproduction is a picnic compared to production! Preproduction is the honeymoon. Production is the day-to-day grind of a difficult marriage. As a first time director, or a neophyte director, you're going to be a little nervous, but relax. You should be pinching yourself to make sure you are not dreaming. Nobody gets to direct without chewing glass for the privilege. Some just have to chew more than others. It is a well-established fact that for every available directing position there are dozens if not hundreds of individuals equally capable of expertly discharging the responsibility. The fortunate ones who manage to claw their way over the herd, slip through it, or somehow remarkably stand out from it, have got to congratulate themselves. It doesn't matter if they are going to get to direct a feature film or an infomercial. In their own world, big or small, they have made it to the top. There is no way they could have been anointed the chosen ones without an extraordinary effort, for — with a few exceptions — the director is king.

Because you are the director, you are going to have to be Solomon: a fount of knowledge, imagination, and reason. From now until the project is shipped, everyone is going to be hitting on you for answers. You are going to have to come up with more solutions to more problems than you ever imagined existed. You had better be a take-charge person, the kind who gets off on dispensing wisdom and likes being challenged. Otherwise you had better get out of the directing game.

I'm that kind of take-charge person. I like being the boss, so for me, preproduction has always been a blast. I am not fatheaded. It doesn't become a director to be so. I have my doubts about myself, as probably do all those who aspire to a career in the arts. Still, there has always been a part of me that thought I should be king of the world. Such is human nature. We all embody many contradictions. But I would guess that there is a little bit of that arrogance in everyone who aspires to direct. When you are the director, you get to be king of your own little world. Your producer, the bonding company, the investors, or the studio are the power behind the throne. They don't have the guts or the energy to direct. It can be a dirty, thankless job, so they have hired you to do it. A line producer whom I worked with on *Knight Rider* confessed to me that in his youth he had been a director but had given it up, because "You wake up in the middle of the night. You drive millions of miles to the location. As soon as it's light you start working. You work and you work and you work. Then, you look at your watch, and it's 10:00 a.m.! The guys at the studio are just getting in to work. You can have it!"

But almost all those standing behind the throne, in their heart of hearts, *think* they are a director, and a better director than you. So they will meddle in your business and second-guess you, especially if you are a first time director. But for whatever reason, they have put you on the throne, and when you stand on high you call the shots. As a first time director, many of the crucial decisions will not be left solely up to you — especially those that impact the budget. But if it's purely a matter of taste and doesn't dramatically affect the budget, it should be your call. If it is *your* movie, it will be a better movie. It won't become a mishmash of what you want to do and what those who stand behind the throne want. For better or for worse, it will hang together as a coherent reflection of your vision and taste, and if you have any talent, then it will be a better film. Or at least so says a guy named Frank Capra. If you don't believe me, read his autobiography, *The Name Above the Title*. In fact, don't even *think* about becoming a director until you have read that book.

Preproduction is a blast because now you finally get to be king of your own little kingdom and work with your capable minions on planning a great military campaign. I am not particularly partial to war, but I compare making a film to a military campaign because, once the shooting starts, it always *feels* like it's matter of life and death. Of course, nobody actually dies, and only the greatest films have any impact on history. Making a movie is probably more comparable to building a bridge, but it's *your* bridge, and, for some reason, you always tend to approach it the same way Alec Guiness did when it came to building his *Bridge on the River Kwai*. Your film, in the big scheme of things, may be of no more consequence than a bridge, but it always feels like Guiness' bridge — like something worth fighting and dying for, so when you take it on you are well served to gird yourself as if it were a War of the Worlds. The beauty of preproduction — the most delightful aspect of planning this great military campaign — is that everyone you are working with is certain that it is going to be a great success. You are going to win every battle, conquer new lands, and come back heroes. The powers behind the throne always have their doubts. But I have always found film crews and film support staff to be almost universally positive, energetic, and resourceful people. They have to be, otherwise they could never put up with the hours, the working conditions, and the stress. When I was directing rock videos, my favorite production manager wore a T-shirt that said it all: "Sleep is for beginners." My experience has always been that the level of dedication of the average film crew is right up there with firefighters, though they do have to get some sleep. (Although a producer from the Philippines once asked me to direct a feature for him in 12 days, working

20 hours a day.) But what I love about that T-shirt is the attitude behind it. To me it says that if you want to make movies, you have got to be willing to sacrifice in some way to get the job done right.

The director sets the tone of the workplace. Stay positive, because you are going to need every bit of optimism to make it through the battle ahead. Be your own best cheerleader. Exude confidence. Take all the positive energy film people bring to the workplace and jack it up even higher. There is no such thing as going into production with too much hope and optimism. You want to plan for every contingency, but you had best go in feeling like a winner.

Decisions! Decisions!

Throughout the preproduction period you are going to have to make dozens of decisions every day. This book is *not* going to take you through *all* those decisions, because my experience has convinced me that anyone smart and capable enough to get themselves hired as a director can make all the decisions he needs to make in preproduction simply by relying on good taste, reason, and common sense. If you have the force of personality and the poise to get hired as a director, you ought to be capable of vamping convincingly whenever called upon to make a decision that you are incapable of making because you lack some piece of hard knowledge or technical expertise. Whenever such a moment arises, every director has the prerogative to put the decision off until tomorrow, think about it, and come back with the answer. Take advantage of that prerogative; get a reprieve until tomorrow, and then simply get on the phone and download the missing bit of expertise from a friend or an associate who is knowledgeable in the field. This method has never failed me either in preproduction or postproduction because in either, you should have the right to put any decision off until tomorrow. Once on the set, there is no tomorrow.

Yet it is wise to anticipate such occasions. If you are going to direct a film which relies heavily on some realm of filmmaking that you are new to — whether it's something as old hat as song and dance numbers or stunts, or something as cutting edge as 3-D CGI graphics — then before you ever set foot in the office, study the nuts and bolts of that process so you can walk the walk and talk the talk. Most of these specialty realms of filmmaking are best learned through observation. Get hold of a director who is in the middle of doing a stunt film or a film that's heavy on CGI and tag around after him for as many days as possible.

You are not actually expected to know everything going in. Everyone — both the money people and your minions — would certainly prefer that you did, because it would take the burden off them. If anything goes wrong, there will always be someone to blame: you. The general assumption is that you are so smart and such a fast learner, you will pick up everything you need to know in a couple of days, if not a couple of hours. This position presumes a great deal, but such is the burden of a director. Bob Zemeckis (whom I will quote throughout this book, since I know him well and I think he can safely be cited as an authority on directing) has a saying: "The director is responsible for everything, even that which he has no control over." Again, the beauty of the saying lies in the figurative interpretation — the attitude. It challenges the director to step up to and face his burden. If you want to be king, and have everyone look up to you and obey you as if you were a god, then you had best seem to have the power of a god. The director should never be heard laying blame or making excuses. It is not his place. He should have anticipated everything and made all the right decisions. Even if disaster befalls him, he should have had a back-up plan that saves the day. If everything comes up lemons, he makes lemonade. If the situation was truly beyond his control, it's not for him to say. His collaborators should be the ones to step in and let him off the hook.

Work, Work, Work

For a first time director, this burden of appearing infallible is even greater. Without the mandate of a proven track record, he is going to have to work that much harder to instill confidence in everyone around him. Yes, you may not be expected to know everything going in, but from the minute you land your first directing gig until the minute you step on the set, you should do all in your power to prepare yourself to make every one of your decisions well-informed. There is an old Hollywood saying which best expresses the logic behind overestimating what is expected of you as a first time director: "You are only given a couple of chits in this business. You've got to make every one of them count." You've had to chew glass to get this first directing gig, so make it count. Prepare and then prepare some more. There is no such thing as being over-prepared.

As I pointed out in the preface, because you are not, as yet, a bankable director, your breakthrough directing gig is going to inevitably be a day late and a dollar short. The bean counters are going to force you to make do with a little less of everything, and that includes preproduction time. None of your principal collaborators or the crew will be put on salary until the last possible minute. This means that you, as well as all your staff, are not going to have enough time to adequately prepare before you start shooting. Since the director is responsible for everything, you, all by yourself, will have to compensate for the fact that your support staff are going to be flying along by the seats of their pants. The only way to do this is to work tirelessly day and night, weekends and weekdays, from the moment you even think that you might land this directing job until the first day of shooting.

Even though you are actually starting too late when you first come on board as the director, the start of principal photography will seem to be an eternity in the future. The natural inclination will be to put off making final decisions. Don't. Start nailing anything down, provided it won't cost you real money if in the end it does not come to pass. Half of what you nail down will have to be ripped out, but half will stay. As the start of production nears, and it seems as if almost every important decision has been left until the last moment, you will be very glad that you finalized any chunk of business early on.

Filmmaking is a collaborative art. So it follows logically that in filmmaking, relationships are everything. Some of the most crucial relationships for a first time director are with those individuals who precede him onto the project. Generally speaking, the producer, if he is not going to act as his own line producer, will hire a **line producer** and perhaps even a **Unit Production Manager** (a **UPM**) before he hires a director — if he's smart. Why? Because more than anything else, the producer wants the line producer and the UPM to make the movie for the money in the budget, and to squeeze the most out of every dollar in the pot. The line producer and the UPM are the budget watchdogs. They are in charge of the money side of the film. (Ideally, you are in charge of the creative side.) It is impossible for them to do their job well unless you cooperate with them. If you are too artistically inclined to respect the constraints of the budget, theirs is a lost cause. The only way they can relax and do their jobs well is if they can trust you to be the kind of director who can fit the square peg in the square hole — who can make the movie for the money he is given.

I have always found that those who are just expeditors — namely the line producer and the UPM — will not venture into your territory and impinge on your creativity, if you do not venture into their territory and impinge on their efforts to stay within the budget. And the converse of this axiom is also true. If you seem to put your creativity ahead of their budget, then they will put their budget ahead of your creativity. Avoid this situation at all costs. Their reputations — their ability to get hired and rehired on a regular basis — are almost solely dependent on their ability to bring the movie in on budget. It is human nature that they will strive to preserve that reputation at all costs. Sure, they want to make a well reviewed, well received film. But more than that, they want to work again. Beware! If, in the course of trying to realize your artistic aspirations, you threaten their budget, then you threaten their very livelihood.

Many first time directors, myself included, are determined from the day they are hired to make a film that is so amazing, so stellar, so earth-shattering in its brilliance, it will immediately catapult them into the top tier of living directors. That is an admirable ambition and one that the first time director should hang onto it with all his might. He will need that purpose to power himself over some of the huge obstacles he is going to encounter on the road to making a film which succeeds just enough to get him hired to direct a second film. The problem with this towering desire to become the next Spielberg or Tarantino is that it becomes so overpowering, the first time director is ready to sacrifice anything and everything to make it happen, including the budget which the line producer and the UPM hand him when he comes in for his first day of work. He does so at his own peril.

The first budget and schedule that come out in preproduction are never the last. Everything constantly changes throughout the preproduction period because you keep revising your game plan. The day-out-of-days changes, the schedule changes, and the construction costs go up and down as shoot days on practical locations are swapped with work to be done on sound stages. If you have inadvertently put the line producer or the UPM in an adversarial position, the next time they revise the budget and the schedule they will give you less of all that you wanted more of. And if you fight back, the next time you will get even less. If you keep it up, when you start shooting, they are going to be breathing down your neck. They will force your **first assistant director** (1st AD) to work against you, instead of for you. They will consult with you about your production needs in a cursory way or, even worse, they will start dictating to you what they are going to dole out in time, money, and material. This attitude will keep you from making the film you want to make. Whatever they unilaterally decide to give you will in fact not really be tailored to what you actually need to realize your vision. So, in the end, you will be able to do *less* artistically.

From the day you start to work, show the utmost respect for the budget. Study the **budget** and the **schedule** in the form that relates most directly to you: the **production board**. If you do not understand how to read "the board," talk to a director friend who is an expert, and learn how — immediately. It is boring work, not very glamorous, but you have got to do it if you want to realize your vision. Unless you are a science nerd or a policy wonk, the budget and, to a lesser extent, the "one-line" schedule, will confuse you a little. When you get confused, take notes and then ask the line producer or the UPM to explain whatever you don't understand. Let them clarify the logic of the way they have structured their guidelines. Everybody likes to talk about what they do best, so by asking these questions you ingratiate yourself with these key players. More importantly, you give them the impression that you are the kind of director who will tailor his artistic vision so that it can be realized for the money in the budget.

If you have nurtured these key relationships throughout preproduction, then when you start shooting, the line producer and the UPM will feel that they can take you at your word. You have done yourself a huge favor. If they trust you, they will give you enough slack in the reins so that, when disaster strikes (as it inevitably will), you have enough room to wriggle out of trouble. If they don't trust you, they'll keep you on a short leash and when disaster strikes, they will limit your options for rectifying the problem; your chances of recovering successfully will be compromised. You will end up even more over budget, as well as less successful in realizing your artistic vision, than if you had been allowed the freedom to create your own solutions.

When I was fresh out of UCLA film school and working at Universal Studios as an associate producer on *McCloud* — certain that any day I would get a break and be tapped to direct an episode of *Marcus Welby, M.D.*, like the great Spielberg or the lesser known Randal Kleiser (who went on to direct *Grease* and have a long and successful career as a feature director) before me — if I had read any of the above, I probably would have rejected it all as overly cautious and artistically unambitious. At that time, I remember I had once heard it said, "The only reason a director gets fired off a picture is if his dailies aren't good enough." I think whoever made this point to me backed it up by noting that Spielberg, who had just finished shooting *Jaws*, had spent 120 days and some astronomical amount (at the time), like $10 million, to complete the picture — even though the initial schedule and budget gave him 60 days and half the money. Whoever was watching the dailies, probably Sid Sheinberg and Lew Wasserman, had loved every day of them, and wisely decided to let Spielberg finish the picture at his own pace, spending whatever it cost to get it done the way he wanted. Young and arrogant as I was, I was inclined to believe that the best way to catapult myself into the top tier of working directors was to shoot artistically or technologically inspired footage on my breakthrough directing job (whenever it came along) and trust that the producer, the studio, and whoever was paying the bills and could fire me, would be so impressed with my directorial virtuosity, they would let me complete the picture — no matter what it cost.

Any first time director who thinks he can get away with this kind of fiscal irresponsibility on his breakthrough directing gig is going to be digging himself an early grave. *Jaws* was not, by any means, Spielberg's first directing job. He got his break on the TV show *Night Gallery*. After that, he directed a special episode of the fore-mentioned *Welby*, an episode of *Columbo*, and another half dozen episodes for Universal Television. He was a "very good boy" and did all these shows on schedule and for the budget. But the directing job which made almost everyone stand up and take notice and say, "This kid is a *director*, a *talent*!" was the TV movie *Duel*, starring Dennis Weaver. With *Duel*, Spielberg established that the innovative way he set up and moved his camera enabled him to make cinema, in general, and action, in particular, more visually dynamic, more hard-hitting and suspenseful than it had ever been done before. He also shot *Duel* on a shoestring budget in record time. All of the old studio hands, the UPMs and the line producers whom I later worked with as a director on *BJ and the Bear* and *Knight Rider*, could not stop marveling at how he had gone to the Mojave desert with a scaled down crew made up of a bunch of journeymen Hollywood technicians and come back, in something like 15 days, with an undeniably brilliant film in the can. Yet his earlier success on *Welby, Night Gallery,* and the other episodic TV shows were the priceless chits with which he had built up enough credibility as a director. By the time he took on *Jaws,* he was the hot young thing. It had become accepted that he could take a script and turn it into a blockbuster piece of entertainment. So he went ahead and blew his budget on *Jaws* and survived to work another day, but only because he had already broken through and established himself as a bankable director.

I cannot think of a single name director in Hollywood who was not a model of fiscal propriety on his breakthrough gig. Even those who, as their directing careers progressed, became notorious for always falling behind schedule and going over budget — such as James Cameron, Francis Coppola, or Stanley Kubrick — all, when they were young and starting out, played by the budgetary rules. Cameron did it on *Piranha* and again on *Terminator.* Coppola did it on *Finian's Rainbow.* Kubrick did it on *The Killing* and *Paths of Glory.*

There is another path. Many directors of note were chosen to direct their breakthrough films the same way that Napoleon became the Emperor of the French Republic — they anointed themselves. They actually had more of a right than Napoleon, because, unlike the French Emperor, their breakthrough films never would have happened if they had not *made* them happen by raising the money themselves. In most cases, they also wrote the script (which is another way in which they made the film happen). This cadre of directors includes almost all of those who are thought of as independent and artistically gifted and inclined: Spike Lee, Jim Jarmusch, John Sayles, Robert Townsend, the Coen brothers, Doug Liman, Whit Stillman, Neil LaBute, Robert Rodriquez, Kevin Smith, Todd Solondz, John Paul Anderson, and whoever else is going to break through this year at Sundance.

Generally speaking, these directors were the producers of their own first films and so were the power behind their own thrones. In most cases they hired all the production staff — the line producer, the UPM, and the 1st AD — and worked together with all of them to craft the budget. These circumstances made it unnecessary for them to forge a successful working relationship with the budget watchdogs. In reality, they had to act as their own budget watchdog. If they had gotten careless and spent too much money on the first half of their film, there would not have been enough money to finish. If the film had not been finished, it never would have made its way into a festival, never would have won a prize, never garnered glowing reviews, and never been distributed in theaters. In short, it would not have done what it was intended to do: launch that director's career. Instead, it would have ended up being an exercise in futility.

With this sword hanging over their heads, most of these gifted directors were able to sacrifice their artistic aspirations to whatever extent was needed to stay on schedule and under budget. This is not surprising. It was very much in their interest to do so. Very few first time directors get a second chance if they cannot get into the mindset of being a budget hawk. It is fundamentally irrelevant whether they do so out of necessity — as in the case of all the directors who raised the money themselves — or whether they do so naturally or out of common sense, as in the case of those first time directors who were picked up as a hired gun by a producer or a studio. In either case, they had to show respect for the budget.

Producer and Director – 'Til Death Do Them Part

The director's relationship with his producer is rarely trouble-free. This is especially true in the case of a first time director, because, more often than not, the producer is a wannabe director. So if the producer wants to direct, why doesn't he just go out and raise the money to make his breakthrough film and then direct it himself? The answer holds the source of all the trouble and strife between producers and directors: Most producers are wannabe directors who lack the confidence to direct. They know they can sail and they want to sail across the Atlantic, but they are not quite sure they can make it all by themselves. So they hire the director. The director is perfectly capable of sailing across the Atlantic all by himself. In some cases, he has actually done it — once, twice, even a half a dozen times. If the producer would just let the director do what he has hired him to do, they would both make it to port safe and sound.

It rarely works that way. Most producers want to direct so badly, they have to "help" the director, even though the director does not want or need their help. The worst of the wannabe director-producers have no taste for the dirty or difficult part of directing. They tend to let the director do all the grunt work and get everything moving in one direction, whereupon they step in and second-guess him and tell him he has to move in the opposite direction. The worst of them will do this every step of the way. Every pivotal creative decision the director has to make, the producer is likely to either veto outright or dabble with to suit his fancy. And it is all perfectly unnecessary.

The hell of it for the director, especially the first time director, is that he has to *let* them muck about and get in the way. The reason for this was made abundantly clear to me over and over again by the Spanish producer who hired me to direct my first feature film. It was a little low budget rock 'n' roll love story which, when it was released briefly in this country, was called *Crystal Heart*. It actually enjoyed a long run in the Spanish-speaking world, where it was known as *Corazon de Crystal*. The producer, I'll call him Pedro, was a semi-articulate but fairly bright businessman who at one time had been the heavyweight champion of Spain. (He had the physique and the flattened nose to attest to his accomplishments in the ring.) He and his business partner were actually funding this million-dollar venture themselves. There was no studio, no bank loan, no investors. All the funds to make the picture were coming out of their own bank accounts.

From day one Pedro did not let me take creative control of the picture. For starters, the script desperately needed another draft. It was a love story that conveniently omitted the process by which the boy and girl fall in love. Boy and girl meet. They have a little spat. They make up and, the next thing you know, they are in love. I tried desperately to convince Pedro that this little omission required a little rewrite. He equivocated. He stalled. He entered into negotiations with the writer. The negotiations fell apart. Then I offered to do the rewrite myself for free. But it was too late. Pedro declared that we were too close to the start of production and a rewrite would complicate the preproduction process and generate overages. When I tried to convince him he was cutting off his nose to spite his face, he would pick up the script and wave at me for emphasis declaring, "Dees eez de script. We shoot dees." When I protested one time too many, he reminded me, ""Oooh, but Meester Bettman, eez so seemple. Eez *myyyyyyy* mooonie, eez *myyyyyy* mooovie!"

And he was 100% correct. He was writing the checks. He was going to call the shots. Determined artist that I was, I continued to fight with him, sometimes openly, in front of the crew. The Mexican sound mixer, Manuelito, took pity on me and tried to clarify the futility of railing against the producer's *droight de seigneur*. One day he took me aside and counseled, "*Con dinero, baille el pero,*" which loosely translated means: "If he's paid, the dog dances." This was very wise advice that I was just too young and full of myself to heed. I kept on fighting with Pedro, which simply compounded the situation. The problem with the love story in the script was a real one. I was right to see it and right to want to correct it. But once Pedro had told me in no uncertain terms that he had made his final decision to leave the script unchanged, it was stupid of me to continue to fight. It was a battle I could never win. By entering into it, I had much to lose and comparatively little to gain.

When I started out as a director, I was inclined to fight with producers over creative directorial decisions for the same reason that I was inclined to fight with line producers and UPMs over budgets. If anything came between me and the fulfillment of my ambition, I was going to attack it. Again, such passion is useful. Nobody becomes a successful director without it. But, as a first time or neophyte director, you should never risk one iota of whatever trust and goodwill exists between you and your producer. You must quell your desire to make that stellar breakthrough film if you run even the smallest risk of getting into an adversarial relationship.

When you get into a disagreement with the producer, it is usually because he is trying to do your job for you. He is trying to "help" you sail the boat, by making a key creative decision about the script or the casting or the art direction or the mis en scene or some other realm of creative endeavor. Unless you are very lucky and happen to land a truly imaginative and gifted producer, his decision is going to suck.

And yet you are going to have to pretend that it's great, or somehow, miraculously, trick him into changing his mind. If you are a trickster, if you are adept at manipulating people into doing things you want them to do without being up front about it, go for it! The goal is to avoid being confrontational. If there had been some way I could have gotten Pedro, all by himself, to arrive at the decision that the script needed a rewrite... if I could have made him believe that it was *his* decision, the decision would have been implemented. We would have made a better movie.

As a first time director, the only way for you to get ahead with your producer is by getting along. Without the money, there is no movie, and the producer brings the money to the table. But there can still be a film, even a fine film, without you as the director. The producer always knows this dirty fact.

The harder you struggle against the producer's right to meddle in the creative decision-making process, the more frequently and the more vehemently he will assert that right. I found this axiom out the hard way with Pedro. I was too inexperienced to recognize the irrefutable logic of "eez *myyyyyy* mooonie, eez *myyyyyy* mooovie!" When Pedro refused to let me rewrite the script to clarify exactly why the boy and the girl fall in love, I simply went ahead and did it, and then talked the male and female leads into playing it the way I had rewritten it, rather than the way it was in the script. In retrospect, I'm amazed that I was naïve enough to think that I could pull this subterfuge off without Pedro detecting it. His English was self-taught, and somewhat spotty. I guess I was hoping that this would keep him from picking up on my little rewrite. I hoped wrong. He figured it out and was furious.

The next day on the set, after we had finished shooting, he drew me aside into a quiet, darkened corner for a little tete à tete. We were seated opposite each other. He leaned in close and lowered his voice for emphasis and told me, "Meester Bettman (pause) what chu do today...(long pause)....EEZ SHIEET!!! EEZ SHIEET, WHAT CHU DO!!! My partner see deece...E SAY I CRAZY HIRE CHU!!!!@@@@!!!!!!"

That became his constant refrain. It seemed like practically everyday he told me in so many words that, in his mind, what I had done up until that point, "Eez shit!" All the same, he never fired me. I kept on coming to the set, day after day, and doing what the director has to do.

But when the picture was wrapped, Pedro shut me out of the editing room. I was banished from the entire postproduction process. When I called him to protest, he told me, "You no need come to the editing room. I do everything." All in all, the postproduction job did not hurt what I had done, nor did it help. I am certain that the picture would have played better if I had had a hand in the post. But enough things had been done right on the set, so that, even though all the pieces were put together without much inspiration, the picture sometimes *almost* takes flight. The post was a missed opportunity.

Crystal Heart was distributed in the U.S. by New World. It had a very brief run on the coasts and then folded. Pedro had much better luck distributing it internationally, especially in Spanish-speaking markets. Amazingly, about a year and a half after the last time Pedro informed me, "What you do today eez shit," I had lunch with him and he asked me to direct another picture for him. It was a boxing movie called *Fist Fighter*. Or "Feeeast Fiiighter" as he would say, drawing out the vowels with anticipatory relish. When I politely declined, he actually begged me to do the picture.

What this proves is that we both had provoked an intense conflict and had driven each other mad with anxiety throughout the production of *Crystal Heart* for no good reason. If we could trust each other and anticipate working together in a constructive fashion on *Fist Fighter*, we could have done it a couple of years earlier on

Crystal Heart. If I had known then what I know now, when Pedro pronounced "dees eez da script!" I would have said, "Okay. Fine. Whatever you say." By trying to sneak another version past him, I put him on the defensive and incited a conflict that ultimately hurt the film more than the revision of the script ever could have helped it. Yes, he did not fire me. But I had poisoned the well. I had threatened Pedro's authority. His response was to rattle my cage about everything and anything. After that, it became impossible for me to do my best work.

You have a great deal to lose and not much to gain by alienating your producer. As the director you get to sit on the throne and act like the king. Still, the producer is above you. He is god. And no king, in his right mind, ever defied god and came out ahead. If the wisdom of the Old Testament can be boiled down to one line, I would say that line would be, "Respect the Almighty, even when he deals with you capriciously or unjustly." As a first time director, that is how you have to treat your producer.

One way to make sure you have a productive relationship with your producer is to socialize with him as much as possible. Do whatever he suggests that you do together, right up to having sex with him. Sex overcomplicates matters and can do more harm than good. Common sense dictates against it, but, under the right circumstances, even sex, or something like it, is worth engaging in with your producer if it's certain to solidify your relationship.

The validity of this truism was borne out in the best preproduction experience I ever had with a producer — one which I would hold up as model to be replicated as often as possible. It was with a British producer. I will call him Reg. He was a founding partner of one of the first little production companies to get a start in rock videos and then move into producing high-end commercials and feature films. We got started on the right foot and built up enough momentum so that we did not start to feud until the last day of production. This was because Reg came on the project after I had already sold it to the record company and band. Through a series of fortunate coincidences, the Vice President of Promotions at Warner Records, Jeff Ayeroff, took me into a pitch meeting with the band, Chicago, without a clue as to what I was going to try to sell to them. All he knew was that I had followed his instructions to listen to the cut, *Stay the Night*, and come up with a concept for the video that featured a wall-to-wall car chase.

I came to the pitch meeting so completely over-prepared I even had gone to the trouble to have a storyboard artist who was a buddy of mine storyboard the entire pitch. Having never done a rock video before, and wanting very much to get into that game, I recognized that meeting for what it was: one of those rare chits you get offered to get ahead in Hollywood. So I made sure if I was going to miss out on this opportunity, it wasn't going to be due to lack of preparation. Hence the storyboards.

The band and their manager loved the storyboards and the pitch, and so I got the gig. Ayeroff and Warner Records then contracted with Reg and his company to produce the piece. This made Reg the only producer I ever came to with the project and the money in hand — probably one of the big reasons why Reg and I got along so famously all through preproduction. Because I was on the project before Reg, and because Warners and Chicago were putting up their money to have Reg produce my idea from my storyboards, I had more status and clout than a director usually has on his breakthrough gig.

But even taking that into consideration, my relationship with Reg was exceptionally harmonious. To a large extent I think this was because Reg had a kind of an English schoolboy crush on me. I don't mean to imply that Reg was gay. A touch kinky, maybe, but by no means gay. The whole time we were in prep, Reg seemed much more interested in getting together with me to party than in working on the video. In the office, he was polite and charming in a coy, Brit-like way. He had dated Madonna briefly and clearly could not avoid giving himself a little ego boost by dropping her name and telling stories, out of school, about their little fling. Ironically, it turned out I was something of an old friend of the actress who he was sleeping with when we were prepping the video. I will call her Sally. She was a tall, strong, fresh-faced Valley girl who was one of the seven lady truckers whom the TV network guru of the hour, Fred Silverman, had added to the cast of *B.J. and the Bear* in the second season of the show. Silverman's theory was that their collective cup sizes would give some lift to our sagging ratings. It did not work. The show was cancelled after the second season, but in the meantime, Sally and I had had a lot of fun flirting with each other when I directed the show. When I was prepping *Stay the Night*, it seemed as if, at least once or twice a week, Reg would call me up late at night when he was with Sally. They always seemed very high on something. They would be laughing and making wisecracks and between the jokes and the giggles, Reg would let it drop that we should all get together. I would look at my watch. It would be almost midnight, if not later. "What, now?" I would ask, slightly incredulous. "C'mon, don't be a party pooper!" they would shout.

I never went, but I should have. Never pass up an opportunity to socialize with your producer, or for that matter, with any of your key collaborators on your breakthrough directing gig. The stars, the DP, the UPM, the line producer, the department heads, even the studio people or the bonding company — hang out with any and all of them at every available opportunity. Do whatever you need to do to get loose and have a good time with them. It doesn't matter if they want to play croquet or footsie — as seemed to be the case with Reg and Sally. Play their little game, because it is money in the bank. We humans are all naturally inclined to be much more patient and trusting with those that we like. If they like you, or if they think you are funny, or if they respect you for your intelligence or your uncanny ability to recite the batting averages of the 1955 Brooklyn Dodgers, then, when you are working to bend them to agree with you on some matter which could significantly improve your movie, like a story point or a casting decision or the choice of a location, instead of feeling threatened and going on the defensive, they will try a little harder to see it your way. Nothing could be more valuable. A little friendship can go a long way in getting your key collaborators to work with you and allow you to realize your vision. If you have some doubts about the validity of this truism, read Budd Schulberg's immortal tale of the importance of schmoozing in Hollywood, *What Makes Sammy Run?* Yes, it was published in 1941, but it is still as accurate as if it had been written yesterday.

Even if you find that you have nothing in common with the higher-ups or your key collaborators — even if you find them, for some reason, loathsome and despicable, turn on the charm! Make them like you! If this groveling is beneath you, if you are such a Boy Scout and an honest Abe that you cannot artfully dissemble in order to ingratiate yourself with people you secretly despise, you are going to be at a distinct disadvantage in the Hollywood film business. The simple fact of the matter is that in Hollywood relationships are everything. No sane person with a significant amount of experience in the business would deny that. To a great extent your success will be determined by the extent to which you can charm everyone and get them all to like you. On your breakthrough directing gig, this axiom is especially true when applied to your key collaborators and those above you who have the power to make or break your film. In America, the culture of the workplace demands that working relationships be non-confrontational. In Hollywood, relationships are everything. The combined weight of these two truths is what leads me to tell every film student in every class I have ever taught that the best training for the film business they can get while in film school is to find a classmate who they loath and detest and then make that classmate like them. It won't be fun or easy, but as Zemeckis used to tell me whenever I would start to whine about the difficulties of getting ahead in the film business: "If it were easy to get in the club, Gil, everybody would be in the club."

Crewing Up

Though making a film is like fighting a war, it can also be compared to building a cathedral. As the director, you should be the driving force behind the construction of the cathedral. So you, as director, could be likened to a bishop who has convinced a king to put up the money to convert your vision into a physical reality. In this context, the king is the producer or the studio. The writer is the architect. He draws up the plans. The cinematographer is the head mason. The line producer and the production manager are the construction bosses. But the actual building is done by a myriad of laborers, most of them stone masons of one sort or another. Although you, the director, are charged with the responsibility of making the cathedral a work of art, the actual work is not done by your hands. As anyone who has studied the glass or the stonework of any great cathedral can tell you, to a large extent, the beauty of the whole is dependent on the beauty of each individual part. The cathedral could never be considered a work of art unless all those on whom the bishop depended to carry out his vision — from the architect down to each individual stonemason and glass worker — was, in his own right, a great artist.

I have always found that the first time director buys himself some very valuable insurance if he makes some key contributions to the process by which the crew for his film is hired. Sometimes this is not an option. In episodic TV, the series usually is run by the producer and/or the star. They hire the crew for the duration of the series. The directors rotate in and out every second, third, or fourth show. Under these circumstances, the director is a kind of queen for a day and the cinematographer may actually run the set. Hollywood or New York directors who work out of the country or out of their home state (unless they do so on a regular basis) are not going to know crew people in Texas, Canada, or the Philippines.

But my experience breaking in as a rock video director and then later as a low budget feature director in Los Angeles taught me that those who were hiring the crew, whether it was the producer or the line producer or the UPM, were always happy to have me lend a hand when it came time to hire all the department heads as well as all the "little people." The logic of this approach is undeniable. Most of the great directors who are so thoroughly bankable they get everything they want to make a film — who never have to compromise on anything — never compromise when it comes to hiring department heads and/or crew. They know that their film will not be great unless they get great people on their team to attend to all the details that they cannot attend to. The director is responsible for everything, but he cannot actually do everything. He has to delegate. All those directors who have the power to do so, delegate strictly to those whom they know they can trust. As a first time director you will not be given this kind of veto power over the crewing-up process. But you should do your best to have as much influence as possible.

Since hiring crew falls under the job description of the line producer or the UPM, they always have a roster of their own people to draw from. But if their people are good (and you better hope that they are), then many of them will be working and unavailable. Or they may not be willing to compromise and accept the wages of your budgetarily compromised film. Under these circumstances, suggestions are usually welcomed. To this end, I have always saved all my crew sheets from every shoot I ever worked on. And if I had the good fortune to work with any crew person who was a standout at what he did, whether he was a PA or a cinematographer, I have always entered his name and phone number in my Rolodex, under his job title.

As soon as you come on board as the director, sit down with whoever is hiring the crew and casually suggest that you go over his choices for the department heads: the director of photography, the art director, the editor, the wardrobe department head, the hair and makeup person, the prop master, the special effects man, the stunt coordinator, and the graphic effects designer. Try to feel out how open he is to your suggestions. He may welcome your input or he may be completely opposed to it. Whichever, follow his lead. Yes, crewing up is important, and a first time director can only help his cause if he provides some key input into the process. Yet it is definitely not so important that the first time director should risk getting into an adversarial relationship with the line producer or the UPM or whichever one of the higher-ups is doing the hiring.

In almost all instances, the director participates in the hiring of the cinematographer. This only makes sense. The harmony and efficiency of the production is almost entirely dependent on whether or not the director and the cinematographer can get along with each other as human beings while collaborating as artists. Truly, it is as if the cinematographer and the director paint a picture together. The director must rely on words to tell the cinematographer what to paint. The producer and the higher-ups would be buying themselves some very cheap insurance guaranteeing that their set will be a happy and productive place if they hire a DP with whom you, the director, have collaborated with successfully in the past. You have got to hope that they understand the special nature of your relationship with the DP, and will respect your wishes when it comes hiring time. If they can't, or don't, politely and persistently try to enlighten them. If they are beyond being enlightened, after a week or ten days, you have to give up, even though your relationship with the DP is arguably more important than your relationship with the producer.

As a rule, successful cinematographers get ahead by getting along. Their careers are not going to flourish unless they have the people skills to amicably resolve differences of opinion between themselves and the many different directors — all with different work habits and personalities — with whom they are going to have to collaborate on their way up the ladder. Pedro never even introduced me to the DP on *Crystal Heart*. He just told me his nickname, Vasaleo, which means vaseline in Spanish. The nickname said it all. This guy was as smooth as they come. He was cheerful, completely unflappable, flexible, always full of ideas, but ready to incorporate mine. I had no trouble working with him, and it was to Pedro's credit as a producer that he knew filmmaking and Vasaleo well enough to know in advance that this would be the outcome.

If the producers are so incompetent they are going to force you to work with an intractable DP, this is going to be the least of your worries. If they blow it at this important juncture, then it is (tragically) more than likely that they are going to make bad decisions in two other areas that happen to be much more crucial to the success of the film: the rewriting of the script and the casting of the actors. Unfortunately, there is very little you can do to remedy this situation.

CHAPTER 1 | SUMMARY POINTS

■ As a first time director, many of the crucial decisions will not be left solely up to you — especially those that impact the budget. But if it's purely a matter of taste and doesn't dramatically affect the budget, it should be your call. If it is *your* movie, it will be a better movie.

■ The director sets the tone of the workplace. Stay positive, because you are going to need every bit of optimism to make it through the battle ahead. Be your own best cheerleader.

■ The director is responsible for everything, even that which he has no control over.

■ The director should never be heard laying blame or making excuses. It is not his place. He should have anticipated everything and made all the right decisions. Even if disaster befalls him, he should have had a back-up plan that saves the day.

■ Prepare and then prepare some more. There is no such thing as being over-prepared.

■ If you are going to direct a film which relies heavily on some realm of filmmaking that you are new to — whether it's something as old hat as song and dance numbers or stunts, or something as cutting edge as 3-D CGI graphics — then before you ever set foot in the office, study the nuts and bolts of that process so you can walk the walk and talk the talk.

■ As a first time director, you should never risk one iota of whatever trust and goodwill exists between you and your producer. The only way for you to get ahead with your producer is by getting along.

■ Very few first time directors get a second chance if they cannot get into the mindset of being a budget hawk.

■ The director is responsible for everything, but he cannot actually do everything. Crew up well and delegate.

CHAPTER 2 | CONTENT IS EVERYTHING

Casting and Scripting

You cannot make a great movie without a great script and a great cast. This truism is well known and well supported. Anyone who aspires to direct has probably heard it bandied about repeatedly. And yet, most aspiring directors neither understand how true this theory is, nor do they grasp the full ramifications of that truth. I certainly did not when I was starting out as a director. In fact, only recently, after 25 years as a working director, have I come to actually embrace and internalize this truth.

The reason for this is that in the last 30 years or so, pretty much since Spielberg set a new standard for how movies should look, the "look" of the film has become conspicuously more important than the content of the film. All big movies must *look* big. Ideally, they should unveil some technological breakthrough that the film makers have harnessed to give that film a whole new look. Advances in CGI graphics have paved the way. Lucas used them to give us space battles such as we had never seen before in *Star Wars*. Zemeckis used new graphic technology to integrate live action and two-dimensional animation in *Who Framed Roger Rabbit*. Spielberg's dinosaurs in *Jurassic Park* showed us how CGI technology could produce three-dimensional animated dinosaurs and seamlessly place them in the real world. Then Zemeckis had to top that by using the same technology to seamlessly integrate the fictitious main character of *Forrest Gump* into actual documentary footage of three past presidents. Today when teenage boys, who are the target audience for every big Hollywood film, discuss which films are worth seeing and why, they rate "the effects" on par with and of equal importance to the story or the cast.

No big film can pull a big audience without a big look, and so only those directors who are most adept at generating the big look are big successes. Lucas, Spielberg, and Zemeckis launched this trend. Today it is carried on by John Woo, Michael Bay, David Fincher, and every director whose career is launched with a big action film produced by Jerry Bruckheimer. One never hears these directors discussed in the same breath with those directors who deal with character or plot-driven movies. In a way, the directors who do the smaller budget, independent films — the Coen brothers, Spike Lee, Jim Jarmusch, John Sayles, Whit Stillman, Neil LaBute, Todd Solondz, Kevin Smith, etc. — will forever be relegated to a kind of second-string status. On a big Hollywood film, probably 90%, if not more, of the director's energy is consumed by the process of making the technology work to generate the desired big look. As a result, the biggest directors — the ones who get the big bucks and their name in big lights — are those who have been most successful at mastering the big look. The significance of this situation is not lost on aspiring young directors. To make it big, you have to be a master of the technology.

In this atmosphere, it is all too understandable why most directors today, when lightning strikes and they get their big breakthrough gig, can only think about how they can best use the peanut-sized budget for their film to make it look as much as possible like Spielberg's or Michael Bay's latest multimillion dollar extravaganza. This is clearly a big mistake. It is definitely a case of putting the cart before the horse. On his breakthrough gig, the first time director should be ready to move heaven and earth to assure that the content of his film is of the highest caliber — the content being the script and the cast.

If you equate making a movie to sculpting a statue, then the quality of the script and the cast are like the quality of the marble or whatever stone is used to make the statue. For the finished product to be of the highest quality, the marble has to be of the highest quality. If the stone is flawed or somehow inherently unattractive, no matter how skillful the sculptor, no matter how refined his technique, the end product will be similarly unattractive.

The big look costs big money. It should be left to big studio films with unlimited budgets. There are numerous examples of great films which were visually unadorned and low-tech, but which achieved critical and popular success because they had the right fundamental components: (1) a great story that was well told and (2) universally excellent performances. Most first time directors who made it to the top with a breakthrough film relied on great content to make their debut films stand out. They gave their films as good a look as they could muster on a shoestring budget. But, as a rule, these directors skyrocketed to the top because they had the script savvy to write or recognize a great script, and they had the eye and the drive to unearth movie stars at casting calls. Collectively, over the last 30 years, these directors actually initiated and carried out most of the trends of the independent film market.

The films which fall into this elite category are *Easy Rider*; *What's Up, Tiger Lily?*; *Mean Streets*; *Sisters*; and *The Return of the Secaucus Seven*. This initial wave of low budget successes was continued by *She's Gotta Have It*, *Stranger Than Paradise*, and *Blood Simple*. In the last few years, the most notable examples are probably *Clerks*, *Welcome to the Dollhouse*, *In the Company of Men*, and *The Blair Witch Project*.

These films all had the desired end result of a breakthrough film: They created an ongoing directing career for their writer-directors (with the possible exception of Dennis Hopper, who wrote and directed *Easy Rider* and was handed a franchise which he immediately trashed by making *The Last Movie*).

Much of this book will be devoted to explaining how the first time director can best go about giving his breakthrough film a contemporary, hip look. If you know what you're doing, even on a peanut-sized budget, you can make your camera dance like Tinker Bell in the hyperkinetic style which has been popularized by Spielberg, Bay, Woo, et al. But the hard truth is that style alone — style slavishly adhered to — will never make your film great. Style is a necessary condition for greatness, but it is not sufficient. Good script and good casting are both necessary and sufficient.

This undeniable fact is rooted in the moviegoing experience. Most people go to the movies to be transported in space and time into the lives of Indiana Jones or Forrest Gump or Michael Corleone. They want to spend two hours in the dark experiencing everything that these mythic beings encounter in their fictional lives on screen — thrilling to all the impending dangers, tasting all the joys, enduring all the hardships. The story and the actors are the vehicle that transports the viewers out of themselves and into the drama of the film. The actors, if they are good, do not seem to be acting. They are real and compelling, if not attractive, so we identify with them. The story, if it is good, is both fascinating and believable. We are sucked into the illusion that something crucial is happening to these characters with whom we are identifying. We sit there for two hours, eagerly anticipating what is going to happen next. The extent to which this transportational effect takes hold of an audience is the extent to which a film succeeds.

The first time director must understand and take to heart the fundamental truth that, if the audience is transported into the drama of the film, they will sit there happily for the entire two hours with their eyes riveted on the screen, even if the look of the film is decidedly low-tech. The lighting can be hit or miss, the set almost bare, the focus in and out, the camera forever rooted in one place; there might be no effects, no quick cutting, no glitz, no big look, but if the story and the acting are consistently convincing and compelling, most people will enjoy the film. *Stranger than Paradise, Clerks, In the Company of Men, She's Gotta Have It,* and *Blair Witch* are five films that succeeded in this manner. They were all made for under $50,000. They have virtually no look, or at least, no big look. But they made money and were critically acclaimed, and most important, they made their writer-director's career — because when it came to the story and the acting, they hit a home run.

This immutable truth offers the first time director an extraordinary opportunity. He can count on the fact that his film, like all breakthrough films, is inevitably going to be a day late and a dollar short. But, during preproduction he has an opportunity to make his film screw-up proof. If during preproduction he takes to heart the truth that a great movie can be made from a great script and a great cast, and, accordingly, slavishly devotes himself to writing and rewriting the script until he has made it as close to perfect as is humanly possible; if he simultaneously launches himself on a never-ending quest for, not just good actors, but the very best actors which money can buy on the face of the planet for all of the key parts in his film; then, when he goes into production, he can rest assured that, no matter how budgetarily compromised his film is, no matter what disasters strike during filming, he can still make a great film. If he has a great script and a great cast, all he has to do is to get them to say the lines in the script while the camera is rolling. That's it.

A Few Examples from the World According to Bob

I developed two feature scripts with Zemeckis for studio movies that I was to direct. Neither project ever got made, but going through script development with a master like Zemeckis was enlightening. Bob used to say, "The script is never finished." He meant that only perfection is good enough, so you have to keep on rewriting and improving the script until it is too late — because you just finished filming the scene. On every film Zemeckis has made, even after the studio had approved the script and it was being prepared for production, Bob continued to work with the writer. This may seem obsessive to some, but Zemeckis looks on it as the most productive use of preproduction.

He knows that nothing done during the preproduction process will have as great an effect on the quality of the finished product as the script. During the preproduction for a huge scene like the one in *Forrest Gump* at the anti-war rally in front of the Lincoln Memorial, where Forrest reunites with Jennie after a separation of many years, Zemeckis understood that everything which takes so much time and money to prepare — securing the location, hiring the hundreds of extras who will make up the crowd, working with the effects artists to prepare the CGI graphics that will add tens of thousands of additional people to the crowd, renting all the period costumes, renting all the additional camera and lighting equipment, transporting all the men and material to the location, catering, and the like — would make the movie a little bit better. But none would contribute one-tenth as much to the overall quality of the film as the script and the cast. What makes the scene in front of the Lincoln Memorial moving and great is the way it was written and the way that Tom Hanks and Robin Wright played it.

You should not begin to shoot a film without the right cast. Ironically, the most concrete proof of this axiom is a Zemeckis film which made that very mistake. The film, *Back to the Future*, put Zemeckis over the top and made him a director of note. What most people don't know about this film is that Bob first cast Eric Stoltz over Michael J. Fox as the main character, Marty McFly. In retrospect, this seems surprising. In the years that have passed since *Back to the Future* came out, Eric Stoltz has gone on to deliver many fine performances, almost always playing a mercurial, quirky, slightly oddball type, and Michael J. Fox has built a successful career (cut tragically short by his illness) with the help of some respectable actor chops, but relying mostly on that which God gave him: earnest likeability, pluck, puckish charm, and deft comic timing. Twenty-five years later it's obvious — Eric Stoltz is an excellent actor, but Michael J. Fox is the definition of Marty McFly.

Back in 1984, when Zemeckis went into production on *Back to the Future*, Stoltz and Fox were young actors, just starting out and largely unknown. Bob shot for three weeks with Stoltz before he realized he had made a crucial mistake. Eric was a good actor, but he could never do justice to the role of Marty McFly. Because Spielberg was the executive producer, and the film was being made at Universal — where Spielberg was, de facto, the most powerful man on the lot — Zemeckis was allowed to shut down the production for several weeks, recast Marty, and finish the picture with Michael J. Fox in the lead. And the rest is history. We now can see clearly that without the perfect actor in the role of Marty — Michael J. Fox — the film would have never achieved greatness. It would have a good film. The script was great. Christopher Lloyd was perfectly cast as Doc Brown. The rest of the cast was solid down to the bit parts. But with Eric Stoltz playing Marty McFly? No one can say for sure, but it seems highly likely *Back to the Future* would not have been the film that launched a franchise.

Perfecting Your Script –
Getting the Audience into the Movie

A first time director is wasting valuable time and energy during preproduction if he concerns himself with questions such as how many days, if any, he will get to have a steadicam. Instead, he should focus on what will yield the greatest results: perfecting the script and securing a dream cast. How does he go about doing this? It is incredibly difficult. If it were simple or easy, great first films would be a dime a dozen, instead of one in a hundred.

All first time directors, before they undertake their big breakthrough gig, should have spent a reasonable amount of time trying to understand and incorporate the wisdom of one of the great screenwriting gurus. Zemeckis swears by Lajos Egri.

According to Bob, everything you need to know about screenwriting is in Egri's book, *The Rules of Dramatic Writing*. I personally found the approach of Frank Daniel, who ruled the USC School of Cinema when Zemeckis was a student there, to be the most enlightening. His teachings are memorialized in a book written by two of his disciples, David Howard and Edward Mabley, called *The Tools of Screenwriting*. Many of my colleagues at the School of Film and Television at Chapman University think the best book on screenwriting is Chris Vogler's *The Writer's Journey*. You are well advised to read and take to heart the teachings of one of these books (or one of comparable greatness) before you direct your breakthrough film. Your understanding of what a director must do to make his breakthrough film great will be seriously compromised if you do not.

That said, I personally think the easiest way to get a handle on how to perfect your script is to understand exactly how an imperfect script ruins the experience of watching a film. As mentioned earlier, I am adamantly convinced that people go to the movies because they want to be transported in space and time into the action of the film. They want to identify with the main character and live in his skin for the two hours they are in the theater. Again, the extent to which the film allows them to do this is the extent to which the film succeeds. This explains why different films have different audiences. Generally speaking, those under 30 get off on spending two hours being Batman or Spider-Man, while those over 30 prefer being transported in space and time to somewhere like Jane Austen's England, or present-day America courtesy of the Coen Brothers, where they witness a series of events which provides some insight into our current collective consciousness. In a movie made from a script that is flawed, the transportational effect will be weak, even for its target audience — perhaps so weak as to be nonexistent — or it will be intermittent. In either case, the audience's appreciation of the film will be diminished.

There are a number of reasons why the transportational effect of the script might be weak. Usually it is because the script fails to give the audience the basic information they need to enter the action of the film. The audience must know who the main character of the film is. They must know what the main character wants, and they must want him to get it. Often this essential component of a good script is referred to as the **protagonist** and **objective**. The audience has to know who the protagonist is and what his objective is. Sometimes the main character or the protagonist is embodied in two characters. The protagonist of *The Godfather* could accurately be said to be the joint character of Vito and Michael Corleone. The godfather of the Corleone family is the main character, and throughout the film this role is passed from the father, Vito, to his heir, Michael. In the case of an ensemble film, like *Diner* or *American Graffiti*, there is no single protagonist. It is easiest to think of ensemble films as being a number of shorter films woven into one longer film. Each shorter film has its individual protagonist. This is whom the audience identifies with and enters the action through, each time the film shifts to the story centered on that particular protagonist.

If somebody is going to put up the money to have a first time director direct a script, hopefully they know enough about filmmaking to have made sure that the script has a clear protagonist and objective. Where most scripts are flawed and could be improved is in the extent to which the audience wants the protagonist to realize his objective. Do they really care? If I have heard Zemeckis ask me once, I have heard him ask me a thousand times, "Who cares, Gil? Who really cares?" This is the acid test. This is the hard question every first time director should ask himself when he starts the preproduction on his breakthrough film. Will your audience have an *intense* desire to see your hero succeed? The more the audience cares, the more fully they enter the action of the film.

So when he reads the script that he is to direct, the first time director should put it to this acid test on every page. When the audience is watching action described on the page, will they care if the hero gets what he wants? How much will they care? The answer should be: a lot. If not, the director is advised to immediately go to work on the rewrite.

The Hero

If the answer to the acid test question is that the audience does not care a great deal, then the problem either lies in the nature of the main character or in his objective. Either the hero is not sufficiently heroic or his quest is not truly a worthy quest — one that the audience sees as valid and is eager to participate in. Or it could be a bit of both. You have to determine this and then attack the problem.

If the problem is with the hero, it is most often because he does not establish himself early on as being of truly heroic proportions. Entire books have been written on what makes a hero a true hero. The best of these are by the scholar Joseph Campbell. Every first time director would be advised to have read Campbell's definitive *The Hero with a Thousand Faces* before taking on the task of rewriting the script for his breakthrough film. The defining quality of a true hero is self-sacrifice and selflessness. All the heroes of all the Capra movies did the right thing at the crucial moment, in spite of the fact that by so doing they had everything to lose and nothing to gain. Somebody who does something rash or risky when the bad guy has a gun to his head is being brave, but nowhere nearly as brave or heroic as somebody who puts his life on the line in a situation where he could walk away with his head held high. This is the key to the heroism of the final moment of

Saving Private Ryan. Neither Captain John Miller (Tom Hanks) nor Private James Ryan (Matt Damon) has to defend that bridge. In fact, by defending it, they are both disobeying orders. Likewise, at the end of *Casablanca*, Rick, the Humphrey Bogart character, could use the letters of transit and fly off with Ilsa, the Ingrid Bergman character, and we know that they would be happily in love for the rest of their days on this earth. Rick has spent the entire movie obsessed about having lost Ilsa, and desiring nothing but to get her back. But when he has the chance, he walks away from it, surrendering Ilsa to Victor Laszlo for the good of mankind. Described in those terms it seems implausible and corny. True cynics would say it is. But 99 % of the human populace who have seen that film are moved to tears (or have to fight them back) when they witness Rick's act of selflessness.

These examples of heroic action are taken from the *conclusion* of two classic films. It is best if, early on in the film, the hero performs such a selfless act. This will initiate the process by which the audience identifies with the main character. The more selfless this initial act of heroism, the better. If the audience themselves wants everything that the hero is giving up, then they will know in their heart of hearts that they would never be so selfless, so strong, and so heroic to sacrifice what he is sacrificing. This intensifies their admiration for the main character. The more intense their admiration, the more complete their identification. This is the process by which the audience is transported out of themselves and into the action of the film.

One of the best examples of such a defining moment early on in a film can be found in *The Godfather*. It comes after the Tattaglia family has tried, unsuccessfully, to assassinate Vito Corleone. Vito lies mortally wounded in the hospital. Sonny, played by James Caan, and the capos of the Corleone family are plotting how best to strike back at the Tattaglias. They want to stage a hit on two key players: Captain McCluskey and Sollozzo, known as the Turk. McCluskey is the crooked NYPD captain protecting the Tattaglias. Sollozzo, a heroin importer, is pushing the Tattaglias into a turf war with the Corleones. He obviously put out the hit on Vito Corleone. Sonny and his capos are trying to figure out who in their family is so trusted by the Tattaglias that he could get close enough to Sollozzo and McCluskey to put a bullet in their heads.

Michael Corleone, played by Al Pacino, volunteers to do the hit. Nobody can believe it. Sonny even starts baiting Michael, asking him, "Whaddya gonna do, nice college boy, huh?....You think this is the army where you shoot them from a mile away? You gotta get 'em up close. BUDDABING! You blow their brains all over your nice Ivy League suit.."

No one in the family would ever think of Michael as a candidate to do this hit. Why? Because Michael is the only Corleone who is clean. He has never sullied himself in the family business. He has an Ivy League education. He is a war hero. He has lovely Diane Keaton waiting to marry him, move to New Hampshire, raise a family, and lead the clean version of the American dream. But he turns his back on it all. He volunteers to give it all up and commit a murder. Why? Out of loyalty and love. He is a member of the Corleone family first, and an individual second. The extent of this selfless act makes him a gigantic hero. This is his peak. It is one of the defining moments of the *Godfather* trilogy. When ordered in a linear chronology, unlike the films themselves, everything from this moment on until the end of *The Godfather: Part III* is about the fall of this hero.

I would advise every first time director to compare the main character of his breakthrough film to Michael Corleone. Ask yourself if your protagonist does something early on in the script that proves that he has the strength to make such a sacrifice. If not, your script needs a rewrite. Your main character does not have what it takes to get the audience rooting for him to the extent that they can enter the action of the film.

You must bear in mind that there are heroes, like Michael Corleone, who act out their heroism, and there are anti-heroes, like Rick in *Casablanca*, who are as strong and self-sacrificing as a Michael Corleone, but either deny it, like Rick, or are unaware of it, like Marty McFly. Rick claims that he "sticks his neck out for no one." But the script makes it clear that this is a pose. The audience can tell from early on in the film that underneath Rick's cynical, alcoholic, Euro-trash façade beats the heart of a lion. In the opening scenes we learn that Rick ran guns to the Ethiopians defending their country from the Axis invasion. Then Rick hides Ugarte, played by Peter Lorre, from the Gestapo. It would seem he has an ulterior motive for doing so: This is how he gets his hands on precious letters of transit out of Casablanca, which become the MacGuffin of the film. But when he tells the bandleader to play *La Marseillaise* so as to drown out the Nazi's beer hall anthem, we know that he has the heroic capacity for self-sacrifice of a Michael Corleone... he just has to get back in touch with it.

At the beginning of *Back to the Future*, Marty is on the verge of being screwed up by his screwed-up parents. Like all teenagers, he knows that his parents are geeks. His purpose in life is to somehow become the antithesis of everything they are. Everything in Marty's existence seems to be conspiring against him and working to turn him into as big a loser as his Dad. Everything except Doc Brown. So Marty sneaks out in the middle of the night to the Twin Pines Mall to bear witness to the unveiling of Doc Brown's time machine. Then, by a series of freak accidents, Marty ends up getting sent back into the past in the time machine.

There is little self-sacrifice in hanging out with Doc Brown. At this stage, Marty is not very heroic. But the target under-30 audience, and for that matter, anyone who can remember being a teenager, can clearly see the outlines of a true hero in the making underneath Marty's slightly callow, wise-cracking, self-deprecating exterior. For Marty to have both the good sense to recognize his parents' deficiencies and the intense need (it could even be called courage) to defy them, makes him extremely sympathetic — if not heroic — in the eyes of the target audience.

When putting his main character to the acid test of heroism, the first time director must keep in mind the size and the scope of the target audience for his breakthrough film. Some audiences will never be able to care intensely about the fate of a specific main character because that character is from a world that is completely alien to them. The hero of *Trainspotting*, Retten, is a heroin addict. The hero of *Boys Don't Cry*, Brandon Teena, is a lesbian who crossdresses as a man. These movies are not for everyone. They were made for a younger, urban audience that is acquainted with, if not accepting of, heroin addiction and/or gender bending.

The studios prefer to make movies aimed at a wide audience because there is a greater risk involved in making an edgy movie with a morally ambiguous hero. For that reason, such movies are usually made by independent companies who are looking for their audience *outside* of the boundaries proscribed by studio films. This audience, along with the critics, will embrace a film that takes these chances. So if, as a first time director, you are hired to make an edgy film about a character like Retten or Teena, then allow your main character to be as much of an outsider, as weird, as flawed as possible. Do not pull your punches. Go for the limit. The films of Pedro Almodóvar have proved that, in the new millennium, educated urban audiences will gladly identify with characters whose lifestyles are totally divorced from all societal norms. And, it could be argued, that the more bizarre, the more sexually deviant and morally ambiguous they are, the better. It would seem that, for an educated urban audience, there is a certain radical chic in embracing films like Almodóvar's that feature societal outcasts in the main roles. It takes guts to live as they do, in defiance of societal norms. In almost all Almodóvar films, these outcasts/heroes invariably undertake a daunting quest early on — a quest which is made that much more difficult, because, in trying to reach their goals, Almodóvar's heroes must overcome the additional obstacles thrown in their way by those who are prejudiced against them and intent on denying their fundamental humanity. Rebels always make good heroes and Almodóvar's rebels are usually rebels burning with a cause.

The Heroic Quest

Yet a main character of truly heroic proportions alone does not a great script make. If the audience is going to enter the action of the film, they have to have an intense admiration for the main character and an equally intense desire for him to achieve his objective. What the main character wants has to be something they see as worth wanting very much.

A good rule of thumb to make sure that the audience will very much want the main character to achieve his objective is to simply require that the objective is either one of two things: (1) love, because we never get enough love or the right kind of love and so we see love as supremely desirable, or (2) a matter of life and death — something the hero is willing to give up his life to get. It can be a matter of life and death even if it isn't an action movie. The hero's life doesn't have to actually be on the line. If it is clear that he will die either physically or spiritually if he doesn't achieve his objective at the climax of the film, like Lester Burnham (Kevin Spacey) in *American Beauty*, then the audience, given that they admire the hero, will find reason enough to root for him with enough passion to transport themselves into the action of the film.

Though the scripts of almost all successful films conform to this rule of thumb, many bad movies have been made from scripts that fulfilled the basic requirements of having a main character of heroic proportions who launched himself on a quest for love or something which was a matter of life and death — because the devil is in the details. Once the (admirable) main character has launched himself on his (worthwhile) quest, what keeps the audience plugged into the film and transported into the action is suspense. And suspense is created when the hero comes up against obstacles that prevent him from attaining his objective. When the hero encounters an obstacle, the audience find themselves going back and forth between *hoping* that the hero can overcome the obstacle and *fearing* that he cannot. This vacillation between hope and fear creates suspense. To create great suspense, the audience must alternately fear with great dread that the hero will fail, or perhaps even be killed, and then hope passionately, with an intensity bordering on elation, that he will succeed. The more intensely the audience hopes, the more intensely they fear, the greater the suspense will be. The more powerful the suspense, the more complete the hold of the transportational effect on the audience. Suspense is what sucks them into the story and makes them forget about themselves. Suspense is ultimately what makes all great films great. This is true not just of action films, but love stories and art films as well. No matter if they are watching *Romeo and Juliet* or *Casablanca* or *Chasing Amy*, the audience is constantly being driven back and forth between passionately hoping that the boy will get the girl and not merely fearing, but dreading, that he will not. No matter if it is *The Rules of the Game* or *Citizen Kane* or *The Piano*, throughout the film the audience vacillates between elation and despair as, one moment, it seems as if the main character will attain his noble objective and fulfill his humanity, and then, at the next moment, it seems certain that he will fail, in which case, he might as well be dead.

Suspense is where most scripts fall down — because in order for the transportational effect to keep its hold on the audience, the film has to become *increasingly* more suspenseful. One pivotal moment has to be followed by another of greater consequence. If not, the audience's interest will flag. To do this the scriptwriter must constantly top himself. Each obstacle the hero encounters has to be increasingly daunting. And if he fails to overcome that obstacle, the consequences have to become increasingly more disastrous. Otherwise, even though the hero may be confronting great obstacles and performing heroic acts to overcome them, the audience, in the back of their minds, is going to start to think, "Okay, that's pretty cool. But what else can you show me?"

And I am not just referring to Gen-X and Gen-Y audiences who, because they have grown up on video games and MTV, demand that their thrills be spiked right into the vein and amped to the max. Any audience of any age can become jaded very quickly. This is simply a function of the laws of perception and human nature. The more frequently we repeat an experience, the less impact it has on us. If you go down the same street every day, eventually the buildings on the street become the visual equivalent of white noise. They are there, but habit has conditioned your brain to the fact of their existence, so you don't notice them. In the same fashion, if the stakes do not go up throughout the middle of a film, the audience starts to become habituated to the level of suspense and, accordingly, the all-important transportational effect starts to weaken.

Rare is the moviegoer who has not sat through more films that suffer from this weakness than he would like to recall. It is so common, screenwriters have coined a term to describe it: **second-act sag**. A film with second-act sag invariably starts out well. It has a hero we care about and some sort of **hook** that captures our interest. (Very few films get made without a good hook because the hook is what the studios rely on to sell the picture.) But about halfway through the film, our interest starts to wane because, even though the hero is getting closer to his objective, in doing so, he seems to be going over old ground. We start to tune out.

One of the most important duties of the first time director during the preproduction period is to read and reread his script to make sure that throughout the second act the stakes continually go up. If they do not, then his film will suffer from second act sag, and all of the Herculean labors he performs during the actual production of the film will be for naught. To make sure that the script of his breakthrough film does not suffer from second act sag, the first time director must hold each scene up to this acid test: He must ask himself if in each scene, as the hero approaches his objective, (1) do the obstacles become more daunting, and (2) does the hero have more and more to lose if he fails?

One of the most significant factors contributing to the success of the film *Crimson Tide* was the consummate skill with which the writer, Michael Schiffer, continually jacked up the stakes and made the obstacles more formidable as the film progressed. At the outset of the movie, the main character, Commander Hunter (Denzel Washington), wants only to have a successful cruise on the nuclear sub, *SS Arizona*, so that he will get promoted to captain and be rewarded with a nuclear submarine of his own to command. His fate is in the hands of the commanding officer of the *Arizona*, Captain Ramsey (Gene Hackman). As the sub sets out on a dangerous mission, Ramsey flat out tells Hunter that all the wannabe captain has to do is make him happy and then Hunter will be virtually guaranteed of being promoted and getting his own sub. This moment comes about 15 minutes into the film. From this point on, disaster strikes about every 15 or 20 minutes. Things get worse and worse for Hunter. He seems to be driven further and further from his objective, while the forces arrayed against him become more and more awesome. Ramsey instantly distrusts Hunter and casts him in an adversarial role, humiliating him in front of the crew. (So much for Hunter's hope of getting his own sub on the strength of Ramsey's recommendation.) Next, they are attacked by a Russian sub. The *Arizona* is severely damaged and starts to sink. Now on top of his personal battle with his mistrustful, bull-headed captain, Hunter has to battle the Russians in order to save his own skin and the lives of all his crew. Hunter (granted, with Ramsey's help) saves the sub. But then the *Arizona* gets a message to launch their nukes at the Russians. Right after the first message, it gets a second launch message, but, by accident, the second message is cut off. So, the exact intent of the second message is unclear. Ramsey says they have to launch, because orders are orders, and, in nuclear war, first strike is everything. Hunter disagrees, arguing that the second message might have been a message *not* to launch, and with World War III and the fate of mankind in the balance they cannot proceed until they are certain of the contents of the incomplete message. They get into a violent argument. In order to prevent the captain from launching, Hunter stages a mutiny and takes over command of the ship. But the charismatic Ramsey, to whom all the officers onboard remain loyal, quickly stages a counter-mutiny and retakes control of the boat. Now, Hunter has to force Ramsey and all of his fellow officers to forsake the time-honored Navy rules governing chain of command and listen to him instead of the captain. If they do not, all of humanity goes up in a mushroom cloud. It's no longer Hunter against the captain, or Hunter against the captain and the Russians. It is now Hunter against the captain, the Russians, and almost the entire crew — with the future of all mankind on the line.

That's the kind of escalation of stakes and obstacles you need to keep your audience transported into the action of the film. The first time director is advised to make certain that the script of his breakthrough film embodies an equally dramatic escalation. If it does not, he must go to work with the writer to make sure that it does. If the writer will not, or cannot, assist him, he should do the rewrite himself. Otherwise, all of his subsequent labors as a director are for naught. If the script does not pass this acid test, the film made from the script will never hold the audience as it could or should.

Again, these standards are met by great films of all genres, not just films that deal in overt forms of suspense. At the beginning of *Romeo and Juliet*, Romeo and Juliet enjoy the love and support of their separate, powerful families. All that's at stake is their intense, adolescent infatuation. By the end of the second act, they have sacrificed the love of their families, they are alone in the world, and their lives are on the line for their love. In the beginning of *Breathless*, the film that launched Jean-Luc Godard's career, all that the hero, played by Jean-Paul Belmondo, has to lose is his tenuous and light-heated attachment to a pretty American tourist, played by Jean Seberg. By the end of the second act, his infatuation has grown into love and he ends up sacrificing his life in the pursuit of that love. If you were to chart on a graph the escalation of stakes and obstacles in each Frank Capra film, from *It Happened One Night* through *It's a Wonderful Life*, they would all follow an almost identical, ever mounting, hyperbolic curve. The same could be said of every hit children's film, from *The Wizard of Oz* through *Finding Nemo*. The examples are endless. The simple fact remains: A director cannot make a commercially successful movie in which the stakes and obstacles do not continually increase. The first time director must do everything in his power to make sure that the script of his breakthrough movie comes up to this standard.

Attaining Perfection in Casting

You have got to come close to perfection in casting if you are going to make a great film. How do you achieve perfection? Never settle. You must keep on casting with the same single-minded maniacal determination with which Captain Ahab sought Moby Dick, right up until you kill the casting director or the casting director kills you. Whether you are doing it yourself, or you have a top-tier casting director aided by a battalion of associates, assistants, and secretaries, you have to keep working the phones and keep the door open until the actor who is *perfect* for the part walks in. You may never find the perfect actor. But if you adopt this attitude, if you remain convinced that as good as the best choice you have already discovered may be, you can always do better, you will be rewarded.

Adopting such an uncompromising attitude is difficult. You are certain to take a lot of flack for being unreasonable and impossible. Obviously, if by holding to such astronomical standards you start to seriously jeopardize your relationship with your producer or the money people, then you are going to have to back down. But only back down far enough or long enough to re-ingratiate yourself with the key players. If they have a clue about filmmaking, they will be on your side all the way. Before they come down on you for holding the casting director to an impossibly high standard, they should be ready to fire the casting director or to let the casting director quit. They should understand that all you are trying to do is everything in your power to enable *them* to achieve *their own* ends.

The guiding principle of being tireless and uncompromising in casting is valid in all films, from the most humble student productions to the most exalted, megabudget studio films. How much money you can pay your actors determines what pond you can fish in, but no matter the pond, you still must cast your net again and again, as widely as possible, in order to land the biggest fish. In the case of *Back to the Future*, Zemeckis made the mistake of casting Eric Stoltz because the studio insisted that he meet a certain deadline for the start of production. They made him pack up his net and go home before he was ready. Sure, they had met their deadline for the start of principal photography, but they had not found one of the essential components for their film: the perfect Marty McFly. The studio would have saved a lot of money if they had not rushed Zemeckis into production.

I have seen this same scenario repeated hundreds of times while I have overseen the production of student films as a professor. Most of my student directors must go into hock just to scrape together the cash to pay for film, processing, and telecine. Paid actors are beyond their grasp. So they are fishing in a different, but not necessarily smaller, pond than Zemeckis or Spielberg. In almost any American city there are thousands of amateur thespians who will work for nothing more than a copy of the finished product with which to build their portfolios. No matter the situation, from out of those thousands, you can find the handful you need to make up your perfect cast, provided that you throw your net wide enough and often enough.

I tell my student directors to tape their casting auditions and, when they are done casting, to make me a tape of their picks. Then, no matter what, I tell them they can do better. Those that have the determination and the vision to do as I advise are always rewarded. They look longer and harder, and they always find a better cast. The longer they look, the harder they look, the better the cast gets. The very best films are always those that, besides having a great script, go through a long, exhaustive casting process.

As a first time director casting his breakthrough film, you are going to be casting in a more exalted pond than the pond of my student directors, and a less sacred pond than the one in which Zemeckis was casting for *Back to the Future*. Which pond that is will be determined by your casting budget. But the key to success in all ponds is the same: You must never compromise. The laws of statistics dictate that the more people you read for a part, the more likely you are to cast an actor who will win an Oscar for his performance. Hopefully your producer has the good sense to see the logic in that maxim. If he doesn't, you've got bigger problems than casting.

How Do You Define Perfection?
Casting Your Leads

It is not easy to define perfection. But I think it would be unconscionable for me to tell you to find it without giving you some idea of how to identify it. There are as many different kinds of perfection as there are roles. For the sake of simplification, I advise homing in on two qualities that an actor can exhibit: likeability and richness. Generally speaking, your protagonist and leading roles are likeable in the extreme and not so rich, whereas your supporting parts are very rich, but frequently not so thoroughly likeable. The reason is obvious. The more likeable the protagonist, the more completely and intensely the audience will be able to identify with him. The more intensely the audience identifies with the main character, the more fully they can enter the action of the film (provided that the script is also great).

So what exactly is likeability? How do you identify it? The easiest way to clarify this complex question is to simply look at our greatest actors in some of their greatest roles. Likeability is what makes the audience identify with and care about Dustin Hoffman as Enrico "Ratso" Rizzo in *Midnight Cowboy*, even though Ratso is angry, ugly, filthy, ignorant, and manipulative. Likeability is what makes the audience identify with and care about Robert De Niro as Jake LaMotta in *Raging Bull*, even though LaMotta borders on paranoid schizophrenia. Likeability is what makes Marlon Brando lovable, heroic, and so beneficent as to be almost godlike as Don Corleone in *The Godfather*, even though Don Corleone is the kind of guy who, if you cross him, is going to cut your favorite horse's head off and put it in your bed. Likeability is what makes the audience watching *American Beauty* root for Kevin Spacey as Lester Burnham, even though he is driven to destroy his connection to the American dream and commit an act of pedophilia in the process.

Because they are complex characters and embody both positive and negative characteristics, Ratso Rizzo, Jake LaMotta, Don Corleone, and Lester Burnham are not only likeable, but rich. They are almost all, at different times, mean and kind, weak and strong, ugly and beautiful, righteous and debased. Since they embody both positive and negative attributes, they are not going to please all of the people all of the time. Some segments of some audiences will not be able to identify with them, in *spite of* their likeability. But each of these leading actors is blessed with a powerful inherent humanity that will touch almost all members of all audiences and lead them to forgive these characters for their failings.

When the main character of a film is as rich as those mentioned above, it puts an extra burden on the likeability of the actor who must portray that character. If the likeability quotient is not high enough, the film will not draw wide audiences. If it is a big budget film, it will fail. This is why the studios prefer to make movies that feature main characters that are not so complex. It is easier for all members of all audiences to identify with such characters. The films they are featured in are more palatable, and so, more likely profitable. In *Titanic*, the main character, Jack Dawson (Leonardo DiCaprio) proves himself to be in all ways wonderful. His only shortcoming is that he is poor. In *Batman*, Bruce Wayne (as portrayed by Michael Keaton, Val Kilmer, or George Clooney) is incredibly brave, smart, and idealistic; his only shortcoming is that he feels a little burdened having to save the world on a regular basis. In *The Graduate*, Benjamin Braddock, the role played by Dustin Hoffman, is a sweet, idealistic young man who is trying very hard to be true to himself. His only problem is that he is naïve and too easily led astray.

The first time director on his breakthrough project must do everything in his power to make sure that his protagonist and the actors in his leading roles are blessed with as much likeability as possible — the more, the better. Admittedly, by claiming that a director can successfully cast his film by homing in on likeability and richness in his actors, I have oversimplified the process to make my point. Still, likeability is absolutely crucial in your protagonist. Without it, your movie will never succeed.

Casting the Supporting Roles

In casting the supporting roles for his film, the first time director should home in on richness of character. The audience should be intrigued by and interested in the characters playing in support of the leads. They do not have to find them likeable, because they do not have to identify with them. Richness of character enables an actor to be mercurial. If he brings this mercurial quality to the role he is playing, the audience will never be able to anticipate his next move. They will remain fascinated with him; every time he appears on screen will be a treat. If you look down the list of the actors who have won the Oscar for best supporting role, you will find that they all are quintessentially mercurial and rich in character. James Coburn in *Affliction*, Cuba Gooding Jr. in *Jerry Maguire*, Kevin Spacey in *The Usual Suspects*, Martin Landau in *Ed Wood*, Tommy Lee Jones in *The Fugitive*, Gene Hackman in *Unforgiven*, Jack Palance in *City Slickers*, Joe Pesci in *GoodFellas* — all of these actors relied on their inherent richness of character because the roles demanded that they convincingly embody both positive and negative human attributes. In *Jerry Maguire*, Cuba Gooding is believably flawed. As Jerry tells him, he lacks heart and commitment. He is too focused on money and success. But, at the same time, he is a fighter and a loyal friend. Martin Landau in *Ed Wood* is self-destructive, self-indulgent, facile, and nasty, but he is professional and dignified, as well as a warm, if inconstant, friend to Ed Wood. Gene Hackman in *Unforgiven* and Joe Pesci in *GoodFellas* are both vicious and homicidal, but in addition to being a believable killer, Hackman manages to come off somehow dignified, and Pesci, when his role demanded it, seems believably childlike and light-hearted. Kevin Spacey's role in *The Usual Suspects* literally turns on his ability to seem harmless and yet latently lethal.

Generally speaking, with supporting actors, a first time director should focus on their range of emotion. The greater their range of emotion, the richer their character. The richer their character, the more unexpected their behavior. This complexity will drive up the audience's interest level in them and thereby intensify the all-important transportational effect of the film on its viewers. Rich supporting characters enhance the audience's overall viewing pleasure and put the first time director that much closer to his objective of making a film which will launch his career.

Content and the Producer – Sometimes They Come from Different Planets

Content is everything for the first time director. His first professional gig will not become his breakthrough gig, it will not propel him into the top tier of working directors if — when it comes to content — his film is not flawless. Unfortunately, the first time director rarely has complete control over the content of his film. Inevitably, until a director has a track record of having either directed several moderately successful films or one thoroughly successful film, he will have to share control over the content of his film with those who are putting up the money for his breakthrough gig: the producer, the studio, the backers, or some sort of combination of the three. Therefore, to some extent, the first time director's fate is not in his own hands.

As talented and capable as he may be, the first time director cannot make a breakthrough film unless his producer and the other parties he has to defer to have good judgment in script and casting. The director may know exactly how to rewrite the script so that it goes to a higher level and becomes incredibly compelling and suspenseful from beginning to end, but if the producer doesn't like those script changes, the chances are they will never get made, and the film will never become a breakthrough film. The director may have discovered the next Kevin Spacey and want to cast him in the lead for his film. But if the producer doesn't have the insight to realize that someone who looks like Kevin Spacey can be just as compelling and likeable as someone who looks like Tom Cruise; if the producer refuses to hire the next Kevin Spacey and insists instead on hiring an actor who is as handsome as Tom Cruise, but cannot act as well and lacks the humanity of the actor that the director has discovered — then the first time director's film will not become his breakthrough film.

The first time director has no choice but to defer to his producer and the financial backers of the film because he cannot fire them. However, they will not hesitate to fire him, if he pushes them too far when they disagree over script and casting. Content is everything, but the content of the film — good, bad, or indifferent — will be meaningless if the director succeeds in getting himself replaced. It has happened many, many times to many talented, even brilliant, first time directors.

This is all too understandable. After all, script and casting *are* everything. A first time director, no matter how brilliant, can make only a mediocre movie if he is saddled with a mediocre script and a weak cast. If the movie is mediocre, he will be held responsible and will be deemed mediocre, no matter how brilliant he actually is. He may be tempted to direct the film because he is impatient to launch his directing career or because he needs the paycheck. But he would be well advised not to give in to these short-term concerns and to wait until he is given a script and a cast that will do justice to his talent. Otherwise, his talent may go forever unnoticed and unappreciated.

One big reason why so many bad movies are made, year in and year out, is because producers in general and low budget producers in particular do not really know what it takes to make a good movie. As studio executives are so fond of reminding those of us who think of ourselves as artists, it is called show *business* or the film *business*, not show art or the film art. The skills and talents needed to raise the money to make and sell films are very different from the skills and the talents required to actually turn out the product.

Most of the low budget producers whom I have met or worked with were brilliant salesmen. They could all sell ice to the Eskimos. But they understood the product that they sold in the same way that a shoe salesman understands shoes. They knew the trends. If that year, square toes were in, they knew that. "You want square toes? We got the best square toes in the world!" That was their line. They could use it to raise the money to make and sell the product. But when it came to understanding the process by which the product that they sold was made, they were about as clueless as a shoe salesman when it comes to making shoes. This is why during the years when I was directing low budget films there was one *Fatal Attraction* and at least a thousand knock-offs. It took one producer who actually knows good content when he sees it to establish the trend: Michael Douglas. He read the script and had the guts and the brains to get the script made into a film, because it was a great script, not because erotic thrillers were "in" that year.

What the first time director has to try to figure out is whether he is working with a real producer, like Michael Douglas, or a shoe salesman. This is a very hard call to make, especially during the early stages of preproduction. At this stage, the first time director has known the producer for all of a couple of weeks… a month at the most. It is hard to get a solid fix on anyone's true capabilities that fast. And then, since the producer is a human being, he is going to be a jumble of contradictions.

I explained earlier how the script for *Crystal Heart* was fatally flawed, and how I did serious damage to my relationship with Pedro trying to get him to understand that it was pointless to shoot a love story in which the audience never gets to see exactly how the boy and the girl fall in love. I also knew that another project I directed, *Never Too Young to Die*, about the son of James Bond which was going to be made on a $3 million budget — when real Bond films were running about $40 or $50 million a pop — would never fly and just look like a cheap rip-off. Its only chance was if it acknowledged what it was, made fun of itself, and came off campier than the campiest moment in any Bond film. I could not admit any of this to the producer, Matt. It was clear that Matt adored the script (almost as much as he loved himself) and had absolutely no intention of making *Never Too Young to Die* any campier than any Bond film. This was because Matt was completely clueless when it came to anticipating how an audience would react to his film. Like most low budget producers, he underestimated the audience and assumed that they would not see his movie for what it was. When I told him, a week or two into preproduction, that as much as I *loved and adored* the script I still thought it could be improved, and suggested that I take a pass at it, he looked at me a little suspiciously and told me, "Come in on Saturday and we'll do it together." Then, he held up his pen and informed me imperiously, "Any changes in the script are going to have come through this pen."

That should have been my signal to bail out on *Never Too Young to Die*. But I came in that Saturday and the Saturday after that and the Saturday after that, thinking if I persisted, I could bring Matt around to seeing it my way. And, in fact, I brought him around some. In the version of *Never Too Young to Die* that went before the cameras, the villain, very ably played by Gene Simmons, was a hermaphrodite. He dressed in drag, did a live stage show, and like a sort of anthropomorphized killer frog, stuck his monster tongue down the throat of any female who came within range. So I got Matt to camp up a few scenes, but with camp, half measures are not effective. *The Rocky Picture Horror Show* does not flicker in and out of camp. It goes all the way. Matt, like an overgrown 10-year-old, was in love with most of the Bond genre clichés. He insisted that many of them be played straight. At many moments, the final film takes itself completely seriously, which prevents it from sailing into the realm of the absurd, where it properly belongs.

It would be unwise to try to dictate any hard and fast rules on when the first time director should hold his nose and jump and go ahead and make his first film with a shoe-salesman-cum-producer, even though the film is inherently flawed, and when he should bail out and quit the project. Every case will be different, depending on the producer and the scope of the crucial changes with regard to content that he is forbidding the director to make. I would advise every first time director who is at loggerheads with his producer over script changes or casting decisions to have a very sober conversation with himself about whether his ultimate goals as a director are going to be met by directing a film that is inherently flawed.

How to Be Almost Producer-Proof: Write the Script

Because I am not a great writer, I had to launch my directing career as a hired gun — a director for hire, as opposed to a writer-director who generally shops a script he has written along with himself as the director of the proposed project. When it comes to low budget breakthrough filmmaking, the hired gun is always at a certain disadvantage. My experience was a testament to this. Since I was a hired gun, my producers first acquired the script and then hired me. Therefore, I was dependent on the taste and judgment of my shoe-salesman-cum-knock-off-artist low budget producers. If you are a writer-director, several other scenarios are open to you by which you, the producer, and the script can come together. They are all vastly superior to those one must face as a hired gun.

Please do not delude yourself into thinking that you are a writer-director rather than a hired gun, and that you can further your directing career by directing from your own material, unless everyone you show your scripts to tells you that you are

when your friends give you feedback on your scripts, and it is
some positive, some negative — hear them! They're your friends.
they are bending over backwards to be kind. If the best they can do is to give
you a mixed review, forget it. You aren't a writer-director. Not yet. You are not
going to be doing yourself any favors trying to break through directing from a
script that you have written.

Putting it simply, you are wasting your time unless you *know* that you are at least
as good as the following writer-directors and their breakthrough scripts: Woody
Allen/*What's Up, Tiger Lily?*, Francis Coppola/*The Godfather*, Brian
DePalma/*Sisters*, Martin Scorsese/*Mean Streets*, Oliver Stone/*Platoon*, Bob
Zemeckis/*Back to the Future*, James Cameron/*Terminator*, Spike Lee/*She's Gotta
Have It*, Jim Jarmusch/*Stranger Than Paradise*, John Sayles/*The Return of the
Secaucus Seven*, Gregory Nava/*El Norte*, Joel Schumacher/*The Incredible Shrinking
Woman*, Michael Mann/*Thief*, Christopher Columbus/*Heartbreak Hotel*,
Cameron Crowe/*Say Anything*, John Hughes/*Sixteen Candles*, Joel Coen/*Blood
Simple*, Kevin Reynolds/*Fandango*, Quentin Tarantino/*Reservoir Dogs*, Kevin
Smith/*Clerks*, John Singleton/*Boyz in the Hood*, Neil LaBute/*In the Company of
Men*, Paul Anderson/*Boogie Nights*, Alexander Payne/*Citizen Ruth*, Wes
Anderson/*Bottle Rocket*, Kimberly Pierce/*The Boy Next Door*.

The advantage of shopping yourself as a director with a script under your arm is
that if it attracts the attention of a producer and he tells you he wants to make it
into a movie, then your worries are over. Because, assuming that your script is
breakthrough material, then your producer is not a shoe salesman but the real
thing. To single out your script from the many that cross his desk, he has to be a
producer with brains, guts, and taste. If this is the case, he will actually help you
make all the hard choices that you will have to make in the course of rendering
your script into a finished film.

Two other scenarios for success: Number one, he is a shoe salesman who wants to
make your script because you have included enough mainstream elements that
even a shoe salesman can spot it as a saleable product. Or, number two, the quality of the script has attracted other bankable elements, like a known star, so that
the shoe salesman can rest assured that the film made from the script will make
money on the star's name alone. Amazingly, sometimes film art and the film business just, by chance, overlap in this ironic fashion. If this is the case, your worries
are *almost* over. Your knock-off-artist-producer has unwittingly handed you a
great script to direct from: your own. You won't have to endure the maddening
ordeal which every hired gun has to face when he gets hired by a shoe-salesman
producer — to talk or trick the producer into doing a rewrite so you can make a

movie that is truly worth the effort. You've dodged that bullet. Now, all you have to do is find a good, if not a great, cast and then pray that the producer actually manages to come up with the bucks needed to get the script shot. In any case, you are way ahead of the game.

At one point my career brushed up against Quentin Tarantino's in a way that led me to believe that the people who ran the company that put up the money to make Tarantino's breakthrough film, *Reservoir Dogs*, were really just shoe salesmen who were funding the film — not so much because they were able to perceive that a great movie could be made from Tarantino's script, but rather because they could see that there were enough bankable elements attached to the script so that, no matter what, they would make money on the project. This same producing team, I will call them Sheila and Simon, had volunteered to put up $1.5 million to produce a film from a script called *Car Crazy* that I had co-authored for Universal Studios, but which Universal had decided not to green light and had put into **turnaround**. This meant that any company could produce the script, provided they compensated Universal for the fees that they had paid to me and my writing partner — a mere pittance, since my writing partner and I were unknowns and had written the script for Writer's Guild scale. Sheila and Simon said their company, Sheman Productions, was interested in doing this, so my partner and I met with them. At the meeting they told us how much they loved the script to *Car Crazy*, which was the story of how a small-town, all-American teenage boy comes of age and gets the respect he hungers for by building the fastest hot rod in town — sort of *Karate Kid* meets *American Graffiti*. They told us they loved it so much *they would give us $1.5 million to make it*! Furthermore, they had so much faith in me as a director *they would let me direct*! All we had to do was get Keanu Reeves, Christian Slater, or River Phoenix to agree to star in it. Little mind that, at that time, Reeves, Slater, and Phoenix all had at least a $2 million asking price for their services on any picture. As to how we would pay the star and have any money left over to make the picture, neither Sheila nor Simon had any advice. That was our problem.

Later on, at a party, Sheila told me, in so many words, that they had made the same generous offer to Tarantino, provided he could get Harvey Keitel to work in his movie. This is why I tend to doubt that Sheila and Simon had any understanding of the artistic merits of *Reservoir Dogs*. Their commitment to that film, like their commitment to *Car Crazy*, was based on simple math. Sheman Productions made its money selling to foreign distributors. Sheila and Simon knew they could easily make $1.5 million on the foreign sales of *any film* starring Harvey Keitel, Keanu Reeves, Christian Slater, or River Phoenix — provided it had a story that made sense and enough sex, violence, or action to satisfy the tastes of foreign viewers. This is how Sheila and Simon discovered Quentin Tarantino.

If anyone deserves to claim that they gave Tarantino his break, it has got to be Keitel. He obviously read the script, saw the artistic merit in it, and then, as he is wont to do for deserving little groundbreaking films, got it made by simply agreeing to defer his paycheck or work for scale.

The story of *Reservoir Dogs* shows that a writer-director has an advantage over a hired gun when it comes to making sure that when he goes to launch his career, he'll be working from a script that can do the job — even when a shoe salesman is producing it. Bottom line, the writer-director comes with the script, so the producer is removed from the process of selecting the script. This makes it more likely that the film will be an artistic success. You might even end up having the sort of dream relationship with your producer that a fellow director once described to me this way: "A good producer gets the money, gets the script, and *gets out of the way*!"

How to Be Producer-Proof: Write the Script and Raise the Money

In some cases, the secret weapon of the script gives the writer-director the advantage of being able to make his breakthrough film by completely dispensing with *any* producer to whom he has to answer. Many a writer-director of note has launched his career by being able to scrape together enough money to make his breakthrough film on the strength of the script alone. When this is the case, the writer-director, in effect, acts as his own producer. The money comes from those who back the project, either because of the artistic merit of the script or because they are friends or relatives. If this is the case, the writer-director, when it comes to all creative decisions, has only himself to answer to. Generally, the producer on this sort of project functions as a line producer who tells the writer-director how much money he does or doesn't have to spend. But exactly how he spends it is pretty much the director's own decision. A partial list of the writer-directors of note who fall into this group, and the projects they authored to launch their careers would consist of: Martin Scorsese/*Mean Streets*, Spike Lee/*She's Gotta Have It*, Jim Jarmusch/*Stranger Than Paradise*, John Sayles/*The Return of the Secaucus Seven*, Gregory Nava/*El Norte*, Joel Coen/*Blood Simple*, Kevin Smith/*Clerks*, and Neil LaBute/*In the Company of Men*.

So what if you are just a hired gun director? Do you have a chance? Yes, but less of a chance. If you and your producer have irreconcilable differences over the script, there is a very real chance that the movie you make with that producer will not launch your career. Even worse, it may end it. Everything else — given a super abundance of talent, ingenuity, charm, and persistence — can be overcome. But, if it ain't on the page, it ain't on the stage. That's a timeworn cliché because it happens to be so true. There are two other sayings that apply here. They are not as well known, but they are equally valid. The first is "You only get a couple of chits in this business, so you have got to make every one of them count." The second is an original Bob Zemeckis aphorism: "You don't work your way up in this business. You are discovered and go straight to the top." To which he added, "It's a club. They invite you into the club, and once you're in, you're in for good, unless you really screw up." The first time director will have only one chance in his entire life to make his first feature film. He should make that one chance count. If he hits a home run his first time at bat, like Spielberg, Cameron, Tarantino, or Michael Cimino, then he is in the club for life — unless he screws up royally, like Cimino did.

The list of first time directors whose first films bombed and were never heard from again is very, very long. There are no well-known names to bandy about here to prove my point, because these individuals disappeared beneath the waves without a trace. Lance Young, a very successful, highly respected, hip studio executive at Paramount in the early '90s under Gary Luchese always wanted to direct. He got his chance and made a film from a script he wrote called *Bliss*. On many levels it was an excellent film, but it was not a hit. Lance left the business for a couple of years and is now a studio executive at DreamWorks. Because of that initial defeat, Lance is probably going to have to wait much longer than he would like before he gets a second chance to launch his directing career.

Zemeckis' first two films, *I Wanna Hold Your Hand* and *Used Cars*, were both big disappointments at the box office in their initial release. After he made those films, Bob got a lot of consolation from a lot of powerful people, like Spielberg, Lucas, John Milius, Lew Wasserman, and Frank Price (at the time, the studio boss at Columbia). They all lined up to tell him not to worry, that he had made two excellent films, and that he was undeniably an excellent director. But none of them offered him any real jobs. Bob's directing career was very much on hold for almost five years. When he finally got his next break it did not come courtesy of his powerful friends, and it was not on a studio picture. It was to direct a movie for an independent production company in Vera Cruz, Mexico. It was an action-adventure comedy that was to be shot on a shoestring $7 million budget. The film was *Romancing the Stone*, and the rest, as we all know, is history. Bob was very fortunate that Michael Douglas, the film's producer, had enough vision and film-making savvy to look at Bob's first two films and recognize that, despite the fact that they had not made money, they had been made by a incredibly talented director — who would happily travel to the steaming jungles of Mexico and work his ass off for peanuts in order to get his directing career out of the deep freeze.

Bob was extremely fortunate. That other crucial element that every first time director needs on his side if he is going to breakthrough into the club — luck

— had played right into his hands. All wannabe directors reading this book should not count on being so lucky. They should not tempt fate. If your producer faces you across the desk, as Pedro did with me, puts his beefy, ham hock of a hand on the script as if it were the Bible, and tells you "Dees eez dee script! We shoot dees!" you had best think twice about continuing with the project. If to your mind the script is very much in need of a rewrite, it might just be time to say, "Sayonara, Pedro!"

Remember that the script is not the sole component of the content of a film. The cast also figures as a part of the raw clay that the director has to shape. You cannot make a great film without a great cast but you can probably make a very good one. *Sisters, The Return of the Secaucus Seven, She's Gotta Have It, Stranger than Paradise, Blood Simple, Salvador, I Wanna Hold Your Hand, El Norte, Say Anything, Clerks, Boyz in the Hood, Hard Eight, Swingers, Bottle Rocket, In the Company of Men*, and even Spielberg's *Sugarland Express*, were all made from great scripts. They all became breakthrough films for their first time directors. But, with the exception of Goldie Hawn in *Sugarland* and John Cusack in *Say Anything*, most of the casts of these films have not been heard from since. On the other hand, you could argue that *Mean Streets* would not have been Scorsese's breakthrough film without Harvey Keitel and Robert DeNiro; *Terminator* would not have been the launching pad for Cameron's spectacular career without Schwarzenegger; and *Reservoir Dogs* would not have put Tarantino in the club for life without Keitel. So don't destroy your relationship with your producer over casting decisions. Argue forcefully for your choices right up the point where you feel you might do permanent damage to whatever good will exists between you and your producer, and then back off.

As always, there are exceptions to this rule. It is hard to imagine Woody Allen breaking through as a director without Woody Allen to star in his films. A film that is character driven and hinges on one central character, as Allen's early films do, could be fatally handicapped if the right actor is not cast in the pivotal role. So, in certain rare instances, it is conceivable that a first time director would be well advised to walk off such a film if the producer keeps him from casting the right actor in the pivotal role.

As for making a film with only a competent cast, you will have to be a talented director of actors. You had best understand Method acting. If you don't, you've got to be smart enough and instinctive enough to come up with instructions for your actors that will enable them to take their performances to a higher level. You will have to know just what to say to get them unstuck when they get stuck, to make their mediocre moments good, and their good moments great. But it can be done. I'll show you how in Chapters 6 and 7.

CHAPTER 2 | SUMMARY POINTS

■ On his breakthrough gig, the first time director should be ready to move heaven and earth to assure that the content of his film is of the highest caliber — the content being the script and the cast. If the script is solid, then you're protected, even if the cast is only competent.

■ Before they undertake their big breakthrough gig, all first time directors should have spent a reasonable amount of time trying to understand and incorporate the wisdom of one of the great screenwriting gurus.

■ The first time director must understand and take to heart the fundamental truth that, if the audience is transported into the drama of the film, they will sit there happily for the entire two hours with their eyes riveted on the screen, even if the look of the film is decidedly low-tech.

■ The audience must know who the main character of the film is and what that character wants — and they must want him to get it. If the audience does not care a great deal, then either the hero is not sufficiently heroic or his quest is not truly a worthy quest.

■ The defining quality of a true hero is self-sacrifice and selflessness. It is best if, early on in the film, the hero performs a selfless act.

■ A good rule of thumb to make sure that the audience will very much want the main character to achieve his objective is to simply require that the objective is either one of two things: love, or something the hero must be willing to give up his life to get.

■ Once the (admirable) main character has launched himself on his (worthwhile) quest, then what keeps the audience transported into the action is suspense. The film has to become increasingly more suspenseful. The stakes must continually go up as the hero nears his objective.

■ To make sure that the script of his breakthrough film does not suffer from second-act sag, the first time director must ask himself if in each scene, as the hero approaches his objective, (1) do the obstacles become more daunting, and (2) does the hero have more and more to lose if he fails?

■ You have got to come close to perfection in casting if you are going to make a great film. The rule of thumb on how to achieve this is to never settle.

■ Don't destroy your relationship with your producer over casting decisions. Argue forcefully for your choices right up the point where you feel you might do permanent damage to whatever good will exists between you and your producer, and then back off.

■ In the day-late-dollar-short world of low budget filmmaking, there are many producers who are shockingly lacking in the ability to discern a good script from a mediocre one. Furthermore, most low budget producers cannot distinguish a truly likeable and compelling actor from one who is merely attractive and competent.

■ I would advise every first time director who is at loggerheads with his producer over script changes or casting decisions to have a very sober conversation with himself about whether his ultimate goals as a director are going to be met by directing a film that is inherently flawed.

■ Many a writer-director of note has launched his career by being able to scrape together enough money to make his breakthrough film on the strength of the script alone. When this is the case, the writer-director, in effect, acts as his own producer.

■ Do not delude yourself into thinking that you are a writer-director rather than a hired gun, and that you can further your directing career by directing from your own material — unless everyone you show your scripts to tells you that you are a great writer.

PART TWO:
VISUAL DESIGN

CHAPTER 3 | CAMERA BLOCKING

Why Move Your Camera?

The results are in. It's now final. Sidney Lumet has started to move his camera. Therefore, the revolution which Spielberg started in the early '70s is complete. Before Spielberg, a director had a choice. Whenever possible, he could move his camera and use lenses to force perspective, like Orson Welles, or he could do it occasionally, like Capra, or rarely, if at all, like Lumet.

By the mid-'70s Spielberg's phenomenal success had all but wiped out the choice. Spielberg had set the visual standard for the business. Every director was hip to the trend — the more your movies looked like Spielberg's, the more work you were going to get. For those of us who started careers in Spielberg's wake, the pressure to ape the master was intense. As time went on, the pressure became even more intense. In the early '80s along came MTV, which pushed camera movement and forced perspective to its logical conclusion and beyond by ushering in the hyperactive, shaky camera of Joe Pytka. In Pytka's breakthrough commercials the camera jumped, jittered, zoomed in and out, and hunted around as if it had a mind of its own. That brought about the Snoopy Camera of *NYPD Blue* and *Homicide*, which not only had a mind of its own, but seemed high on speed or something so energizing, it *never* stopped moving. And yet, through it all, the great Sidney Lumet held firm. Static wide shot, over the shoulder's, close-up, close-up, extreme close-up if necessary; that's how he shot his films. And they were fantastic. *Serpico*, *Dog Day Afternoon*, *Prince of the City*, and *The Verdict* succeeded so completely on every other level, they did not have to look like Spielberg's.

Through the '80s and '90s, the toys for moving the camera got better and better. The steadicam, the sky cam, the luma crane, the shot maker enabled Spielberg and all those who were shooting in his style to make the camera perform like Tinker Bell. Directors who had always moved their camera, moved it more wildly and more often. Why not? With the new technology, they could add still greater intensity to the visual aspect of their films. Scorsese moved his camera so much in *The Color of Money* a friend of mine quipped, "The cameraman should have gotten paid by the yard." And yet, Lumet would not budge. Static wide shot, over the shoulder's, close-up, close-up.

Hereafter, for the sake of convenience, I am going to refer to the style in which all major studio movies are shot today — with a consistently moving camera and regular use of forced perspective lenses — as the **Spielbergian style**. This is not to say that he invented this style. Hitchcock and especially Welles pioneered it. Kubrick and a handful of others used it to good end in the two decades before Spielberg burst on the scene. But the success of Spielberg's films established this style as the industry standard.

Those of us who shot in the Spielbergian style would declare: "You have to move your camera whenever possible to be taken seriously as a director!" And every time, we would have it thrown back in our face that the great Lumet never moved his camera. Of course, there were other notable holdouts: Rob Reiner and (generally speaking) Woody Allen. But none as notable or as longstanding as Lumet.

And now the mighty Lumet has fallen. So, without further discussion, let me state that to make it as a director in today's film business, whenever possible, you *must* move your camera, and force your perspective (a technique to be addressed in Chapter 5). You can elect not to, but it will cost you. You will seem old-fashioned and un-hip, and more importantly, your films will lack the visual intensity of those who shoot in that style. Since building a career as a director is next to impossible, it's simply self-destructive and dangerous to not shoot in what has come to be the universally accepted style of the moment. You may feel that you are to contemporary film what van Gogh was to late 19th-century painting. To that I say, you better be ready to throw your life away for your art, as van Gogh did, and you best be sure your talent is as monumental as his was.

When Do You Move Your Camera?

When I advise moving the camera whenever possible, I do not simply mean whenever there is space to do so — whenever it is physically possible. What I am addressing is the question of when your film is best served by a moving camera — when it is most appropriate. Believe it or not, many good directors have not quite figured exactly when this moment occurs. After I had worked for 20 years in the business, I still did not have a hard and fast rule which I could apply to help me to determine exactly what factors constituted an opportunity to move my camera. Then Bob Zemeckis visited one of my directing classes and laid it out for my students *and* me.

The principle behind what I call **Bob's Rule** is that the story is the most important component of a film, and so everything else in the film — be it acting, art direction, music, lighting, sound, editing, or camera movement — should serve the story. You should move the camera whenever possible to add visual energy to the film, but only in a manner which enhances the story or at least does not detract from it. Stated simply, all good camera movement is invisible.

Even those directors with the most energetic camera styles — the guys who ought to pay their cameraman by the yard — would be hard pressed to refute the underlying truth of this principle. Very few people would pay $10 or more to sit in a theater for two hours and watch all the cool camera moves in *GoodFellas, Natural Born Killers, Pearl Harbor,* or *Face Off* cut together in a non-narrative fashion. As mentioned earlier, they go to be transported in space and time into the lives of the major characters of those films.

If at some point in mid-film, the line of the story becomes unclear or stops and the audience finds itself watching a cool camera move — no matter how cool that camera move — the audience's overall enjoyment of the film will suffer because the spell has been broken. For that moment, they are not a Mafia don or a Jedi warrior or even a junkie trying to stay clean, like the hero of *Trainspotting.* They are just themselves with bills to pay, a car that's double-parked, and a date who might be acting like a jerk. So a good objective for any first time director would be to move his camera as much as possible to look as hip and MTV-wise as he can, right up to the point where the audience would actually take notice and say, "Look at that cool camera move." In other words, this is why camera movement is essential, but should always be invisible. When it becomes visible or noticeable, camera movement detracts from the story.

Unfortunately, some good working directors go too far in their effort to satisfy today's audiences' taste. They get so caught up in their desire to energize and MTVize the visual aspect of their films, they start moving their camera in an arbitrary way, irrespective of story. Martin Scorsese, Brian DePalma, Oliver Stone, Sam Raimi, Michael Bay, John Woo, and a handful of others fall into this group. Because, on the whole, these directors do splendid work, and because they tend to be more cutting-edge than other established directors, many young or first time directors are tempted to copy them. Do so with caution. These directors make good films but their films suffer whenever they overlook the central truth of Bob's Rule. Even the members of Generation X demand a great story to lose themselves in. *Pulp Fiction, Clerks, Reality Bites, Trainspotting, Dark City, Go!,* although cutting-edge, have great stories. Scorsese, Stone, and DePalma may not realize it, but as much as the public likes their films, it would like them more if they could just avoid the temptation of occasionally losing the audience at the expense of making a cool camera move.

Externally and Internally Generated Camera Moves

For camera movement to be invisible, it has to be externally or internally generated by whatever is on the screen — preferably the person or thing which, at that point in the film, is driving the story. An **externally generated camera move** is simply a tracking or panning shot. Something in the frame moves; the camera tracks or pans with it to keep it in frame. The externally generated moves are by far the most common. Everything, from shots of jet aircraft filmed from other aircraft — air to air shots — like those in *Top Gun*, which can go on for hundreds of miles, down to a simple panning or tracking shot which follows a character as he gets up from his desk and crosses to the window, can be lumped together in this group. It's easy to understand why these moves never call attention to themselves and never detract from the story. The camera is moving quite literally to keep up with the story. If the camera did not move, the person or thing which is driving the story would slip offscreen.

Probably 95% of all camera moves in theatrical features are externally generated. And since, in the post-Spielbergian era, moving the camera has become *de rigueur*, externally generated camera moves probably make up more than half of all shots used in feature films. At first glance, that may seem like a high percentage. Why is it that whatever is driving the story always seems to be about to move off camera, making it necessary for the camera to move in order to keep that something framed up on screen? The answer to this contains one of the keys to successful camera blocking.

The camera has to keep moving to keep up with whatever is on screen, because, ever since Spielberg started doing it all the time, directors now almost always start a scene with the camera framed up tighter on the principal object in the scene than was the custom in the pre-Spielbergian days. After framing it up tight, they then have that principal object take off moving. Since the camera is virtually on top of the principal object, it has to make a countermove to keep that object in frame.

If the principal object is the huge boulder which has been booby-trapped to catch up with and crush Indiana Jones after he lifts the idol off of its pedestal in the opening sequence of *Raiders of the Lost Ark*, then Spielberg puts the camera fairly close to boulder, and when the boulder takes off, the camera has to back up fast to keep the boulder in frame. (The camera does not move as fast as the boulder; the boulder gains steadily on the camera. Herein lies much of the excitement in the scene, for this shot is Indiana's point of view, and as the boulder looms larger in the frame, it seems as if it is going to run over him.) Meanwhile, Indiana has taken off running as fast as he can to get away from the boulder. Spielberg has him framed up in a medium close shot before he starts running, so when he takes off, the camera has to take off with him, otherwise the shot will fall apart because he will be too far away from camera and disproportionately small in the frame. By placing the camera close to the principal object and then moving that object, Spielberg has given his camera an externally generated, story-based reason to move. It satisfies Bob's Rule that the camera should move whenever possible, but the move should serve the story and so become invisible.

In the pre-Spielbergian era, directors used a wide master shot to capture the movement of the principal object in the scene. They backed the camera way off, and framed it up wide enough so that the shot would contain, to use the above example from *Raiders*, the entire beginning, middle, and end of the boulder's journey. This way they did not have to move the camera in order to film the whole length of the boulder's course. It could be done in one static wide shot. They would also do tighter shots of the boulder when it started and finished rolling. Then they cut three static shots together to cover the boulder's movement. By keeping the camera at a distance from the moving objects, they eliminated the need for a moving camera.

Conversely, the key to moving your camera in the post-Spielbergian era is to begin a scene framed fairly tight on the central object in the scene, have that object take off moving, and force the camera to counter in different directions in a series of externally generated moves. The camera could be pushed back like the boulder, pulled along like Indiana, or in the same way, pushed screen left or screen right, up or down, and all possible combinations of the above. The central object pushing the camera could be as big as the boulder or as small as the feather that floats through the credits of *Forrest Gump*. This strategy is the one which all directors who move their camera according to Bob's Rules use to block not only action scenes, like the scene from *Raiders*, but also dialogue scenes between actors. In a dialogue scene, the actors walk and talk at various times in the scene, forcing the camera to counter in various directions to keep them properly framed.

By following this strategy which required that the camera move at the beginning of almost all scenes, Spielberg added an ingredient to moviemaking which became virtually indispensable: **eye candy** — basically the same stuff which makes it fun to look through a kaleidoscope. When the camera moves to keep the central object, which is also moving, in the center of the frame, any other object in the scene which passes through the frame blurs or strobes slightly. The more pronounced the strobbing or the blurring, the more energized the frame, the more eye candy. Eye candy, along with the comic book look brought about by using lenses to force perspective, are Spielberg's two major contributions to the visual side of filmmaking. With these two contributions, he changed forever the way that films looked and made it necessary for all but the most secure directors who came along in his wake to imitate his visual style.

The externally generated camera move is the most common way of generating eye candy in the Spielbergian style while also sticking to Bob's Rule. But there are other ways of doing it; probably the next most common is the **internally generated camera move.** To say a camera move is internally generated is to say that the camera is moving to keep up with whatever is being seen or felt by someone or something on screen. These are essentially point of view (POV) shots. They move to show us what the character who is driving the story is seeing or feeling. This explains why internally generated shots never detract from the story. They are much less commonly used than externally generated camera moves, but are equally varied.

The most common and easy to understand internally generated camera movement is a moving POV shot. A good example of a moving POV shot can be found in the thriller Bob Zemeckis made as an homage to Alfred Hitchcock: *What Lies Beneath.* Early on in the film, the female lead, Claire (Michelle Pfeiffer), comes up the stairs in her large (haunted) house and sees steam coming out of the crack under the door to her bathroom. She walks up to the door and pushes it open. After that, Zemeckis alternates between tight shots on Claire's face, which reveal her searching eyes, and moving POV shots which dolly forward into the bathroom as she walks into the room and approaches the tub against the far wall (Figures 3.1 through 3.6). Unlike an externally generated camera move, the moving POV shot pushes in on the tub, but there is no person or thing in the frame which the camera is moving with in order to keep that object in frame. All we see is a shot which moves closer and closer to the tub, which happens to be mysteriously filled to the brim with steaming water. This movement is central to the story because it is what Claire sees as she walks into the bathroom and approaches the tub. Claire did not fill the tub, nor did her husband Norman, who is asleep in the adjacent bedroom. So the audience is asking itself along with Claire, "Who filled the tub?" When she gets to the tub, Claire gets her answer. In the water, along with her own reflection, Claire sees a reflection of the ghost of the young blonde girl who is haunting her house.

Just as a **physical POV shot** is always invisible because it shows us what a character in the story sees, what I call an **emotional POV shot** is invisible because it shows us what a character in the story is feeling. Probably the most common emotional POV shot is when the camera pushes in from a medium close-up to a tight close-up on a character as he catches sight of someone or something off camera, or thinks of something or someone. What he sees, either with his eyes or with his mind's eyes, generates a surge of emotion inside him. That emotion could be surprise or joy or fear or wonder or recognition or whatever, but in all cases it is fast and intense. In this case, you could say the camera was tracking with the character's heart as it "rises in his throat." I call this little fast push-in an "oh-my-god!" shot.

Figure 3.1

Figure 3.2

Figure 3.3

Figure 3.4

Figure 3.5

Figure 3.6

Another typical example of a camera movement which is internally generated — an emotional POV — is when the camera, on a crane, sweeps up in the air and away from a character who has just, in the course of the film, found himself to be alone in the world. The camera's movement makes him smaller and smaller in the frame and so can be said to be expressive of his internal emotions — his feelings of insignificance, weakness, and vulnerability.

The internally generated camera moves above are expressive of simple, common emotions. This explains why so many directors frequently use them. But internally generated camera moves are as various and complex as the emotions that generate them. Some of them are strange, one-of-a-kind moves. In the film *Shine*, director Scott Hicks uses such moves to show the audience what the main character, David Helfgott, is feeling as he suffers a nervous breakdown while playing Rachmaninoff's Concerto No. 3 in concert. This shot — it is actually a series of moving close-ups on David (Figures 3.7, 3.8, and 3.9.) — could be thought of as the antithesis of an externally generated camera move because, while the object in the frame, David, never moves, the camera never stops moving. David remains seated at the piano playing the concerto throughout. He rocks back and forth or sways from side to side as he plays, but otherwise never moves. As the piano piece rises in intensity, all the tight shots on David become more kinetic. Like a drunken bumblebee, the camera bobs and weaves around his head as he starts to have his breakdown.

No doubt, as Scott Hicks intended, anyone watching this scene closely in a darkened theater quickly begins to experience vertigo. What the audience sees gives them an inkling of what the main character is feeling: disorientation, nausea, distress. Yet even though the camera is gyrating wildly, its movement is virtually unnoticeable, because it draws the audience even deeper into the story by both showing them what is taking place on an emotional level and also enabling them, as much as possible, to feel what the main character is feeling.

This is virtuoso camera blocking according to Bob's Rule. At this particular moment, you might say the camera is acting up a storm. The gyrations around the actor's head are as wild and crazy as the wildest and craziest moves to be seen on MTV or an episode of *Homicide* or *The Shield*. And yet they are virtually invisible because they exist primarily as an expression of what is happening in the story at that moment and only incidentally as cool camera moves. They never stand out as something to be noticed in themselves but blend in with all the threads which Hicks is weaving together — sound, editing, lighting — to create the whole cloth of his story about this troubled genius.

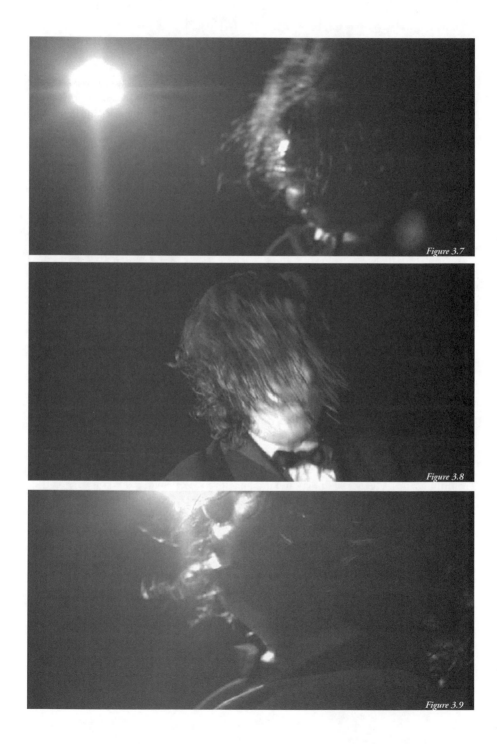

Figure 3.7

Figure 3.8

Figure 3.9

Moving Establishing Shots

Occasionally, at the very beginning of a scene, a director may make a camera move that does not track with an object moving in the frame, and so cannot be said to be externally generated, nor does it move to show us what someone in the scene is seeing or feeling, and so it can not be said to be internally generated. But these moves, which I call **moving establishing shots,** are only there to serve the story and so do not break Bob's Rule. They serve the story in the same way as a classic establishing shot, but they move. A **classic establishing shot** is a high, wide ¾ angle shot of the place where the ensuing scene is to occur. The high, wide ¾ angle shot is the best way to establish a three-dimensional object because it shows us the front, the side, and the top of that object, along with whatever sits on the same plane of the object and surrounds it. One of the most famous establishing shots in film history — Hitchcock's shot of the *Psycho* house with Norman Bates silhouetted in the window — is actually a low, wide ¾ angle shot. Hitchcock put the house up on the hill and the camera below it because the house looks more imposing and ominous when seen from a low angle looking up. Generally the camera is placed up high in order to show the audience the top of the place and the surrounding grounds where the ensuing scene is about to unfold. In this way, the high, wide angle gives a more complete idea of the physical make-up of the location.

This is what establishing shots are for. The camera is backed off far enough and placed at an angle that will most effectively set the stage for the drama that is about to take place. Rather than do this with a static shot, like the shot of the *Psycho* house, directors in the post-Spielbergian era have devised a way of setting the stage, but doing it with a moving camera — all the better to generate eye candy with. There are basically two ways to do this. Either the camera starts out on an extreme close-up of some small but significant object in the scene — a framed photograph, two wine glasses clinking, something being typed out on a computer screen — and then pulls back along a circuitous or straight path, revealing the other significant objects in the scene one by one as it retreats. Or it does just the opposite, starting out wide, for example on a high shot of the whole huge expanse of a Las Vegas casino, and then descending and tightening past various players and objects (which generally prove key to the following scene) before arriving at the principal player seated at a poker table, and then finally pushing in on an extreme close-up which shows that he's holding a straight flush.

Neither of these moves is externally or internally generated. The camera seems to have a mind of its own, but it does not call attention to itself. The audience remains transported into the fantasy world of the story, because the camera is primarily moving in or out to show us that which we need to know in order to understand what happens next. We are accustomed as viewers to being introduced to scenes in films in this way — through an establishing shot. So if the camera starts to move to give us some more specific information about the setting, we do not see the movement. We accept it for what it is: a story device that is just as transparent as other pieces of film language, such as an edit or a dissolve. Such moving establishing shots fall well within the bounds of Bob's Rule. Like externally and internally generated moving shots, they provide the first time director with yet another opportunity to whip up eye candy to satisfy the tastes of the post-Spielbergian, MTV-weaned audience.

Those Who Break Bob's Rule and Why They Do It

About halfway through *Chasing Amy*, there is a scene between Amy (Joey Lauren Adams) and Holden (Ben Affleck), during which they have a back and forth conversation while sitting in the front bucket seats of a car driving down the road. Each actor is framed individually in a single shot, a close-up, but there are no edits. When Amy speaks, the camera is pointed at her (Figure 3.10). As soon as she finishes her line, the camera pans over to Holden (Figure 3.11), just in time to catch his line (Figure 3.12). When he finishes, the camera swings back to catch Amy's next line. Even though the pan to get from one actor to the other is as short and as brief as a camera move can be, it is much more noticeable than the wild gyrations of the camera in the scene from *Shine* described earlier. This is because it is neither externally nor internally generated. Both actors remain seated throughout the scene. The camera cannot make an externally generated move because there is nothing moving in the frame to track with. Neither actor is experiencing any great surge of emotion. They are just exchanging information. So, this little pan cannot be said to be internally generated.

As one watches the scene, one is struck by the camera's uncanny ability to always leave one actor just as he finishes speaking and manage to get to the other actor just before he starts. The camera seems to have a mind of its own. Its movements are not being driven by the story, but rather by someone in the back seat operating the camera — namely, the cameraman.

As soon as the audience becomes aware that a technician behind a camera is controlling what they are seeing, then, on some plane between a conscious and unconscious level, they perceive that what they are watching is not real, but a simulation of reality. When this happens, the transportational properties of the film are diminished or even destroyed. I would imagine that most of the people who enjoy *Chasing Amy* derive much of that enjoyment from fantasizing that they are one of

Figure 3.10

Figure 3.11

Figure 3.12

the smart, funny, sexy main characters in the film, in the throes of entering into a romance much more risky, hip, and quirky than any romance they have experienced or ever will experience. I doubt that most adults can watch that camera move and at the same time submit to that fantasy. If they become aware that a cameraman and a director dictated what they are seeing, then they realize that they are sitting in a darkened theater watching actors on a screen saying lines. If that's the case, they cannot be imagining they are Holden or Amy.

I suspect that writer-director Kevin Smith thought that panning the camera back and forth in this way added something to the film by providing it with a little extra eye candy, or perhaps he decided to shoot the scene this way so as to say to the audience, "See, they are having a verbal ping pong match, so the camera is panning back and forth as if it were following a ping pong ball." But, in my opinion, neither the eye candy nor the artistic/esthetic conceit adds to the film as much as it takes away by destroying the transportational properties. Because these camera movements are not either externally or internally generated by something on the screen, they call attention to themselves. This momentarily stops the story cold and diminishes the film's overall impact.

Smith might have also been borrowing from the camera style used on successful television shows like *Homicide*. I refer to this style as the Snoopy Cam because it is derived from the Shaky Cam style started by commercial director Joe Pytka. The Shaky Cam bounces around constantly as if it were always looking for the most important point on the screen. The Snoopy Cam generally is more focused or intelligent than the Shaky Cam because it always points right at what it wants to look at, as if it had a mind of its own. It often seems to be the POV of some easily distracted, invisible, mute member of the cast who is in the middle of every scene. So, in the above described clip from *Chasing Amy*, the camera swings from Amy to Holden as if it were the point of view of a third person in the car. The *Homicide* camera generally behaves just this way. It rarely follows Bob's Rule for camera movement, so it is constantly calling attention to itself and constantly distracting the viewer from an uninterrupted, seamless appreciation of the story.

I have used this style while directing rock videos, television shows, and corporate profiles for companies like Time Warner (to show at their annual shareholders meeting). The Snoopy Cam worked for these projects because, as is the case with *Homicide*, *The Shield*, and for that matter, TV commercials and rock videos in general, the style of the piece was as important, if not more important, than its content. Because the Snoopy Cam, like the POV of a big dog, is constantly wagging its head around, it generates an endless supply of eye candy. It also constantly breaks the flow of the story and calls attention to itself. It is a very "in-your-face" style. This works for TV shows and rock videos and commercials, because in all these formats it is of paramount importance to stand out by seeming to be the most cutting-edge.

The makers of *NYPD Blue*, *Homicide*, and *The Shield* no doubt decided to use the Snoopy Cam style in an effort to convince the viewing public that, even though they were another knock off of all the cop shows that have been on the air since the original *Dragnet*, they were more up-to-date than the competition. This hipness has to be immediately apparent — something that the audience can instantaneously perceive while surfing the channels or eating popcorn or changing diapers or all the other things that people do while watching TV. After all, as Pauline Kael aptly observed, TV is more a piece of furniture than a medium. The in-your-face quality of the Snoopy Cam style, by dint of the fact that it is constantly interrupting the flow of the story and calling attention to itself, effectively serves this demand for style over substance.

In all fairness to the makers of *Homicide*, *The Shield*, and most other primetime shows that use the Snoopy Cam, it must be noted that their stories and their characters are very strong. If they were not, these shows could not maintain their popularity. Ironically, because the Snoopy Cam is constantly moving, after viewing an episode of *Homicide* or *NYPD Blue* for five minutes, you start to take the moving camera for granted and tune it out. This helps the story come through. But still, something in the narrative is inevitably lost. And evidently, as important as story is to the makers of these programs, it is not of the same paramount importance as it is to a filmmaker like Bob Zemeckis. When they opted for the Snoopy Cam style, these producers and directors must have made an informed decision that, given the special attention-grabbing demands of television, it was a good idea to sacrifice story in the interest of strengthening style.

The Snoopy Cam seems to work on TV. Its wildly gyrating camera moves would be disorienting and nauseating if seen on a movie theatre screen, but on a 20-inch TV set they merely call attention to themselves. Such attention-grabbing cheap shots do not belong in a theatrical feature, especially one made by Martin Scorsese, Brian DePalma, Oliver Stone, or Sam Raimi. As I mentioned before, these immortals and a few other directors of their stature occasionally get carried away trying to get their audience to gawk at some bravado camera movement, and make the mistake of breaking the thread of their story. When they do so, they provide a less than exemplary role model for the first time director. For the safety of those starting their careers as directors, I would like to identify one such stylistic faux pas of the masters, and make it clear why, at these moments, they should not be emulated — unlike their vast body of work.

Figure 3.13

Figure 3.14

Figure 3.15

In the middle of *The Untouchables*, we find ourselves in the street outside the boarding house where the character played by Sean Connery lives (Figure 3.13). As a man in a trenchcoat walks down the sidewalk, a completely unlit figure jumps up on a box outside the second floor window of the house (Figure 3.14). There is a cut, and then the camera is looking in through a window at Connery, inside the boarding house. The camera then, for no apparent reason, flies in through the bathroom window (Figure 3.15) just as Connery passes by the open doorway to the bathroom (Figure 3.16). Without cutting, the camera then races up and down the main hallway of Connery's apartment, seemingly looking for him (Figures 3.17 and 3.18). It then spots Connery in a room at the end of the hall (Figure 3.19) and glides down the hall toward him as the score becomes increasingly ominous. This long steadicam shot does not, to my mind, succeed as an internally generated POV shot of some unknown, possible assailant who is stalking Connery in his apartment, because DePalma has never carefully set up this POV. If we are seeing Connery through the eyes of someone else in the story, we need to have been shown who that someone is. The conventional way of doing this is in a two-shot in which we see both Connery and the man who is going to be following him — at the moment this man falls in behind Connery. This is the way it was almost always done by DePalma's idol, Alfred Hitchcock. This way, when we cut to the POV shot tailing Connery, we immediately realize that we are seeing through the eyes of the character who is tailing him. When the setup shot is included, the movement in the POV becomes invisible. We pay scant attention to it, because we understand why it is there. With the setup shot, the moving POV shot conforms to Bob's Rule because it is internally generated.

But DePalma, who knows better, seems to do a deliberately bad job of giving us the setup shot. The result is that the film lapses into confusion. As the shot eats up a great deal of screen time negotiating this cinematic slalom course, the audience is forced to ask themselves, "Who's following Connery? There was a guy lurking around in the shadows outside Connery's boarding house, but is that the guy? If that's the guy, why didn't I ever see him (in the same frame) start to follow Connery? And if that's the guy, who is he? I never saw him before (which is to say, earlier in the film, introduced as a character in a way that is part of our film language)." Since the shot was not effectively set up as the POV of someone in the film, the audience's confusion as to who's following Connery inevitably will lead many of them to the logical answer: the only person following Connery is the cameraman, or to be more specific, the cameraman using a steadicam. Because this mystery POV goes on for fully 60 seconds — during which the camera gracefully glides around corners, negotiates narrow hallways, and floats through windows — it fairly begs the audience to say to themselves, "What a cool camera move!" It's almost as if DePalma had decided to do a demo of the steadicam and all the cool eye candy it can churn out, right in the middle of his film.

Figure 3.16

Figure 3.17

Figure 3.18

By interrupting his film with this attention-grabbing steadicam commercial, DePalma all but dispels his audience's perception of the fantasy that he had so artfully drawn them into up to that point — namely, that they are Elliott Ness locked in a battle to the death with Al Capone in Chicago during the Roaring '20s. This transportational effect is what they paid their money for, and DePalma has had the good sense to deliver it everywhere else in the film. This is why the film was a hit. Accordingly, the aspiring director is urged to copy almost everything else that DePalma did in *The Untouchables*, but avoid this mystery POV shot.

It could be assumed that DePalma actually wanted the audience to be aware that someone was following Connery, but be confused as to who that someone was because, at this point in the story, a Mafia hit man has just started following Connery; by not showing us just who that hit man is, DePalma was probably hoping to instill in the audience the same sort of agitated curiosity which Connery has to be feeling as soon as he senses that he is being stalked. But my gut tells me that before the audience arrives at this rather cerebral, pseudo-structuralist conceit, they spend a lot of time literally in the dark, wondering what the hell is going on. I have heard it said that confusion is the enemy of drama, and, in this instance, I strongly agree. This mystery POV shot takes a great deal more away from DePalma's film in clarity and drama than it might add by giving the audience a momentary glimpse into Connery's feelings.

However, I suspect that DePalma's real, larger purpose in breaking Bob's Rule was that he, along with Scorsese, Stone, and Raimi, all occasionally need to prove that they can deliver the very same "pumped-up, adrenalized movie experience that's often less literal, less naturalistic, and more impressionistic," which producer Scott Rudin has described as the hallmark of a new wave of directors. The implication of Rudin's quote and the thrust of the article in which it appeared, was that, as of the late '90s, this "new wave of directors" led by John Woo, Michael Bay, Simon West, Danny Boyle, and Gary Grey was on the verge of usurping DePalma, Scorsese, Stone, and Raimi as the hot young directors in town.

DePalma, Scorsese, Stone, and Raimi — even though they know better — occasionally break Bob's Rule in order to deliver what I call a stylistic cheap shot because the guys who hand out the directing jobs in Hollywood have such short memories. The constant pressure to be identified as a flavor-of-the-month director who possesses that intangible something, that *je ne sais quoi* which the studio executives don't quite understand and so can't resist, is what forces good directors, like DePalma, to occasionally abandon the good storytelling techniques which are the true source of the success of their films, to stop the story cold and force the

Figure 3.19

audience to pay attention while they do a shot which veritably screams: "THIS IS KINETIC, THIS IS ENERGIZED, THIS IS OVERHEATED, THIS IS HIP! I'M DIRECTING HERE!"

In every film he directed up to *A Simple Plan*, Sam Raimi almost always had his camera flying around wildly. Since he made that film in 1998, he is much more restrained with his camera movement. In visual style, his more recent work is much closer to a classic Alfred Hitchcock film than a classic Sam Raimi film. I would argue that this is because Raimi has come to realize that storytelling is paramount to good filmmaking and that all the wild camera moves of his earlier films distracted from the story.

If you want to prove that you can make your camera fly like the best of those directors who ought to be paying their cameramen by the yard, you can do so to your heart's content, within the budgetary constraints of your film, and never break Bob's Rule. As I stated earlier, the wild gyrations which director Scott Hicks uses to show us David Helfgott's emotional POV just prior to his nervous breakdown are as wild and crazy as the wildest and craziest moves to be seen on MTV or any episode of *Homicide*. If you want to prove to Scott Rudin and the other kingmakers that you are a master of the overheated style of moviemaking which they identify with bankable directors, then do it with this sort of shot. Use camera movement that is internally generated and shows what the main character is feeling, thereby enriching the story.

Bear in mind, you don't have to limit yourself to internally generated shots if you want your camera to fly around like Tinker Bell and wow the powers that be. Like everything else in Quentin Tarantino's bag of tricks, the Steadicam shot which he uses to show us John Travolta trailing Uma Thurman through "Jack Rabbit Slims" restaurant in *Pulp Fiction* veritably screams of hipness (Figures 3.20 and 3.21). Here Tarantino uses the Steadicam to do a shot that ranks right up there with the best of Busby Berkeley for length and complexity. It probably covers close to 100 yards and features dozens of actors and extras. The camera gyrates around constantly, whipping up a glut of eye candy, more than an MTV junkie could ever hope for and as much, if not more, than in DePalma's mystery POV shot.

And yet it is all externally or internally generated. The Steadicam essentially tracks with Travolta as he makes a very circuitous tour of the restaurant on his way to his table. It behaves much like a handheld news camera "covering" Travolta's entrance. For the most part, it stays in a ³/₄ back angle following him through the restaurant (Figure 3.22) so that when one of the waiters or waitresses, who are all dead ringer look-alikes of '50s icons, cruises by and turns his head, we can see his slightly tripped-out reaction (Figure 3.23). At one point the camera glides off his look onto the Ricky Nelson look-alike on stage (Figure 3.24), thereby showing us what Travolta sees, momentarily becoming a moving shot that is internally generated. But he reappears in the shot (Figure 3.25), at which point it again becomes externally generated because it is following his movement.

This is camera blocking at its best. With every pan, glide, and gyration, it enhances the story. It is cutting-edge style in the service of substance. With it, Tarantino both burnishes his image as a master of the overheated moviemaking style of the '90s *and* sustains the momentum of his narrative. If a new director in his first film could pull off a couple of gyrating emotional POV shots like the ones from *Shine* and a couple of long cruising shots like Travolta's entrance to Jack Rabbit Slims in *Pulp Fiction*, he would certainly establish that he — like Scott Hicks or Quentin Tarantino — was as much a master of that style. More importantly, he would be following the central tenet of Bob's Rule. He would be moving his camera in the most effective way possible: to heighten story.

Now That You Know the Rules, It Gets *Really* Complicated

Bob's Rule says to move the camera whenever possible, and that means *at every opportunity*, provided the movement is internally or externally generated and so does not detract from the story. But knowing *when* (and when not) to move your camera is the easy part. The hard part of directing according to Bob's Rule is knowing exactly *how* to best design all those camera moves needed to meet the requirement that a good director moves the camera whenever possible. The rules are simple. I have kept them that way to make them easy to understand and to

Figure 3.20

Figure 3.21

Figure 3.22

remember. The hard part is applying these simple rules to the myriad of possible applications in every scene in a film.

Take for example a scene that takes place in a simple living room set — a three-sided box under a proscenium arch, with exit doors stage left and right, a sofa center stage, and two arm chairs at either end. Put the camera on a jib arm and mount it on a dolly looking in at the arch from the open side — where the audience would sit. Have two actors walk in talking and sit down, followed by a third actor who enters and addresses them while remaining standing, after which they all exit together. If the camera, according to Bob's Rule, can move to track with the motion of any of the actors as they walk in or out of the room, then you have two chances to move the camera when they come in and one chance to move it when they leave. That makes the choices of how to design your moving shot seem pretty simple.

But the camera could start out up high and come down to an ant's POV, or start low and swing up, or start tight and pull back wide. All told there are probably at least 20 or 30 moves the camera could possibly make. The actors could come in side by side, or in single file, or wander in seconds apart. There are five different places where they could sit. This means there are 25 different seating configurations. The third actor, who comes in alone and remains standing, could probably stand in 20 or 30 different places. The "story" requires that he be somewhere in the room where he can talk with the first two actors. That means that there are least 500 different configurations of the three actors on their final marks. Then all three of them leave together, and they have a choice of two doors to leave by, so there are 54 different possible configurations of how they leave the room.

When it comes to designing moving shots, when you consider all the different places the actors could go (all the **actor blocking**) and all the different places the camera could go (all the **camera blocking**) the number of choices a director has to make in laying out his moving shot is astronomical. This is the challenge of what classically is referred to as mis en scene and what I prefer to call camera blocking. Both are labels for that which a director does to design the look of his film. **Mis en scene**, to my understanding, includes all the work that the director must do with the art director to design everything that the camera sees in his film. I prefer to specifically refer to camera blocking because camera blocking does not in any way involve the director's work with the art director, and is only about the way that the camera moves and how that contributes to the look of the film. The decisions that a director must make to successfully block his camera are difficult because of the numerous ways the camera can be blocked in any scene. To successfully block his camera, a director must solve a very complicated three-dimensional trigonometry problem.

Figure 3.23

Figure 3.24

Figure 3.25

In truth, the example above is quite simple and streamlined. The more actors in the scene, the bigger the set, the more places for them to go, the greater the number of options. Think of all the options in a police squad room — all those people in one room scurrying around like ants! This is why camera gymnastics have become a hallmark of all the cop shows. *Hill Street Blues* started it, and *NYPD Blue* and *Homicide* continued the proud tradition. The directors on these shows were obviously encouraged, if not required, to jump on the squad room scenes and move the camera as much as possible to jack up the visual interest level to the max.

And we haven't even considered lens selection. Lenses affect the look of a moving shot every bit as much as actor blocking and camera blocking, and so they add exponentially to the number of choices facing a director preparing to move his camera. What do all big-name directors do with their director's viewfinder (that little black lens you see hanging around their neck in all their press photos)? Select lenses, provided they actually know how to force perspective with lenses and are not wearing the thing to try to look cool.

We will get into lens selection in Chapter 5. Right now I want to give you a road map to negotiate through all the choices when you sit at the location where a certain scene is to be shot — with your script open to that scene — and start to lay out your shots. Where do you start? How do you see the forest from the trees? My suggestion: Come up with a good moving master. Everything else will fall into place. That's what the next chapter is all about.

CHAPTER 3 | SUMMARY POINTS

- The principle behind Bob's Rule is that the story is the most important component of a film, and so everything else in the film — be it acting, art direction, music, lighting, sound, editing, or camera movement — should serve the story.

- You should move the camera whenever possible to add visual energy to the film, but only in a manner which enhances the story or at least does not detract from it. Stated simply, all good camera movement is invisible.

- For camera movement to be invisible, it has to be externally or internally generated by whatever is on the screen — preferably the person or thing which, at that point in the film, is driving the story.

- An externally generated camera move is simply a tracking or panning shot. Something in the frame moves; the camera tracks or pans with it to keep it in frame.

- To say a camera move is internally generated is to say that the camera is moving to keep up with whatever is being seen or felt by someone or something on screen.

- A physical POV shot is always invisible because it shows us what a character in the story sees; an emotional POV shot is invisible because it shows us what a character in the story is feeling.

- Moving establishing shots are only there to serve the story and so do not break Bob's Rule. They serve the story in the same way as a classic establishing shot, but they move in basically two ways. Either the camera starts out at the very beginning of a scene on an extreme close-up of some small but significant object in the scene and then pulls back, revealing other significant objects as it retreats; or it does just the opposite, starting out wide and then coming in tight on the person or thing that is propelling the drama.

- The decisions that a director must make to successfully block his camera are difficult because of the numerous ways the camera can be blocked in any scene.

CHAPTER 4 | THE GOOD MOVING MASTER

The Four Tasks of a Good Moving Master

In theory, the best moving master does four "tasks" and does them equally well:

1. It shows the audience everything it needs to see (in the scene).
2. It concentrates the audience's attention on the center of the drama.
3. It generates eye candy.
4. It picks up some coverage.

That's it. Now, you know everything you need to know about shooting a good moving master. The bad news is that when it comes to applying those four simple principles to the very specific and unique requirements of each scene in a film, it becomes devilishly tricky. I'm going to break down Task 1 first, but after that I am going to go out of order, jumping next to Task 4, then Task 3, and finally Task 2.

Task 1 – Shows the audience everything it needs to see in the scene.

By definition, **a master** must reveal the plane of battle on which the ensuing action will take place — along with all the men, materiel, and geographical features which will play a significant role in that action. It has to show the audience where everything of importance in the scene is in relation to everything else. To continue the battle metaphor: If you were going to film Pickett's fateful charge at the battle of Gettysburg, according to my logic, in the first shot you would need to see the Union forces in blue on one side of the frame, behind the stone wall of Cemetery Ridge. Then on the other side of the frame you would reveal the Confederate forces in gray, emerging from the woods in which they had taken cover, both before and after the charge. In between the two forces would be the expanse of the wheat field that the Confederates would try repeatedly, heroically, and ultimately unsuccessfully to cross (Figure 4.1).

Figure 4.1

The master sets the geography of the scene. So if the Union is camera left, and the Confederates are camera right, then a cautious director would take care in all the coverage which he shoots for this master to make sure that the Union soldiers continue to fire their rifles at the right side of the frame and the Confederate soldiers continue to charge at and fire their rifles at the left side of the screen. This way, even though in the coverage the audience sees only Union soldiers in blue in one shot and Confederate soldiers in gray in the next shot, they can still put the whole thing together logically in their heads and understand that the opposing sides are shooting at each other. The master implants an image in the viewer's mind as to where the players in the scene are in relation to each other. It sets the rules. The director has to play by those rules until he establishes a new set of rules by going to another master, a mini-master, or a neutral angle. This big-picture example of Pickett's Charge clearly illustrates how a master physically sets the geography for a scene.

Most masters start wide and go tight, although some start tight and go wide. The hypothetical master of Pickett's Charge goes from the general to the specific. A master that starts tight and goes wide that has been seen by almost all avid movie-goers on the planet was the first shot of Captain John Miller played by Tom Hanks in Spielberg's *Saving Private Ryan*. It's the master Spielberg shot to establish Miller and his platoon in a landing craft ready to hit Omaha Beach on D-Day. It starts on a tight close-up of Miller's fear-palsied hands bringing his canteen to his lips and then pulls back to reveal, one by one, every other equally terrified soldier in the boat.

In the hypothetical master of Pickett's Charge, the key physical objects that the audience has to see to understand and follow the story are the two heroes in the very middle of the Confederate line as it charges insanely across the wheat field towards the Union army. This is the dramatic setup for what happens next in the story: one of the heroes is shot and killed. In the master from *Saving Private Ryan*, the key physical objects that tell the story are: Tom Hanks' shaking hands; the captain's bars on his helmet; the platoon of puking, praying, tobacco-chewing soldiers in front of him; and the landing craft pitching about in the ocean. Seeing these objects, the audience understands that Tom Hanks is the captain of a platoon of terrified GIs trapped in a landing craft about to hit the beach. These are examples of masters that show the audience everything that it needs to see to understand and follow the story.

An example of a master that shows the audience everything it needs to see to believe the story (as well as to understand and follow the story) is the master that Bob Zemeckis designed to tell part of the story of *What Lies Beneath*. The gist of

Figure 4.20

what transpires in this scene is as follows: Claire (Michele Pfeiffer) mistakenly accuses her neighbor, Warren Feur (James Remar), of murdering his wife. Claire makes this accusation by tracking Feur down to a theater where he has just attended a performance. She confronts him in the lobby of the theater, which is packed with theatergoers exiting after the performance, and righteously denounces him in a loud voice as a "murdering son-of-bitch," turning heads and causing the exiting theatergoers to freeze in their tracks. At that moment, Feur's wife comes sailing out of the ladies restroom, and, gliding up to his side, asks him, "Honey, is everything all right?" This makes it seem to everyone present that everything is far from all right in Claire's head. This is the **plot point** that has to be put across in the scene. At the sight of a hale and hearty Mary Feur, Claire blanches and gags and seems truly on the verge of mental collapse.

What the master must show the audience so that they can truly believe this scene is the little icon of a figure wearing a dress, the universal symbol of a ladies restroom, on the door of the room that Mary Feur exits, just after Claire denounces Warren Feur as a murdering son-of-a-bitch. Zemeckis made sure that it was evident in the shot right behind Mary's head (Figure 4.20). This icon is the logical lynchpin of the scene. It makes it completely believable that Mary Feur could be in no way present in the scene one instant, and appear the next. Any other solution would have made the scene unbelievable, since such a convenient momentary disappearance demands a logical explanation. If Zemeckis had not been careful to show the audience that icon, and Mary had just come out of any door or around a corner, it would have seemed too easy and too convenient a way to advance the plot. In the vernacular of my students, it would have seemed "cheesy." So the director must put that ladies restroom icon in his master in order for the audience to understand and believe what transpires in the scene — namely, that a sane woman (and of course the point of the movie is that Claire is the most sane person in the story) loudly insists that a husband murdered his wife, only to have the wife appear seconds later.

To sum up, Task 1 requires that the director design his moving master so that it shows the audience everything that it needs to see to understand and believe the scene. Everything that the master has to show to the audience includes all the physical objects in the scene that the audience needs to see to understand where everything is in relation to everything else, as well as all those physical objects that play an important role in the unfolding of the drama, such as the icon on the ladies restroom door.

Task 4 – Picks up some coverage

Anyone who has studied camera blocking or watched the dailies of a professional dramatic film is already aware that almost all working professional directors work Tasks 1, 2, and 3 into every moving master that they shoot. Task 4 is not systematically used by all working professional directors. But it can be an invaluable tool for all first time directors, who (unless they are already established movie stars of the caliber of Tom Hanks or Kevin Costner) will be working on a project that is budgetarily compromised. It doesn't matter if you are breaking in as director on a $10 million studio film or a $10,000 rock video; you will not have enough time and money to do what you are expected to do. Whoever has hired you will expect you to make a product that matches the competition using a fraction of the money they use. If you are gifted, you could probably make a competitive product, provided nothing goes wrong. Unfortunately, Murphy's Law is a given. Things will inevitably go wrong. The airtight budget you have been strapped with in all likelihood will not provide you with the necessary time and money to compensate for these setbacks. You must make every effort to get ahead of schedule and under budget so that when Murphy's Law strikes, instead of being sunk in red ink you stay afloat.

If you include Task 4 — picks up some coverage in your masters — you can stay ahead of Murphy's Law and improve your chances of succeeding. This truth can be proven mathematically. Every setup takes time. Exactly how much time depends on the speed of your cinematographer and the aesthetic standards he is trying to match. Nestor Almondros, the late great Spanish cinematographer, preferred natural light, and so the directors with whom he worked, along with the entire shooting company, would have to wait — sometimes hours — until that big arc light in the sky was just where Nestor wanted it to be. On the other hand, the average setup in *The Blair Witch Project* or a typical rock video takes much less time.

For the sake of simplicity, let's confine this discussion to the kind of film that is typically thought of by aspiring directors as a breakthrough film: a 35mm theatrical feature. If you are shooting in 35mm and attempting to come to the level of most theatrical features, it takes at least a half hour to do even a simple static close-up. By the time you have moved the tripod, leveled the head, checked the focus, adjusted a couple of small lights or reflectors, tweaked the hair and the make-up, slated the shot, and got a print take, at least 30 minutes have rolled by. If any unforeseen difficulty is encountered in the process, it could take 45 minutes.

If you are doing a low budget feature, you probably will shoot at least three scenes a day, if not more. So if you incorporate Task 4 and pick up some coverage in each of the three masters you shoot for those three scenes, you will have to shoot at least three fewer setups to complete the day's work. This means that by including Task 4 in your masters, you will save yourself from $1^1/_2$ to $2^1/_4$ hours of work each day. These hours will add up, so when Murphy's Law strikes, as it inevitably will, you will be ahead of the game. Instead of falling behind and going over budget and suffering all of the ensuing consequences from having your nervous shoe-salesman-cum-producer constantly telling you that "what you do eez shiet" or having the bonding company or the studio threatening to remove you and hire a real director — instead of those headaches, all of the higher-ups will leave you at peace and let you do your best work.

Even if you consider yourself to be an uncompromising artist who refuses to cut corners, or if you are shooting your first film for Disney and you happen to be Michael Eisner's illegitimate son (so you have all the time and money you could dream of), you should still put Task 4 to work for you. Because picking up some coverage in each of your masters will put you ahead and give you the time to shoot additional, arty coverage. Additional setups give you more options in editing and enable you to upgrade the quality of the finished product.

How does a master become coverage? As an example, let me go back to the master of Pickett's Charge at Gettysburg. In that master, because it incorporates Task 1 and accordingly shows the audience everything they need to see to understand the scene, the opening of the shot would most likely be comprised of the Union forces in blue on the left side of the frame, the Confederate forces in gray on the right side of the frame, and the wheat fields in between.

In reality, it would be a bitch to get that shot. The camera would have to be hundreds of feet in the air. If you had an unlimited budget, you would generate the shot using CGI animation. For the sake of discussion, I am going to continue to describe and refer to a master that starts with such an impossible shot. This battle scene can be envisioned in the abstract and so, in order to illustrate my points about moving masters, I will continue to refer to this hypothetically.

At the start of this master, the camera would have to begin impossibly high up in the air shooting down on the field of battle in a classic ³/₄ high, wide establishing shot (Figure 4.1 – page 79). I would put the camera up over the Confederate forces and angle it camera left, so the shot actually favors the Union forces and looks more or less down on the top of the Confederate forces as they emerge from the cover of the wood, camera right, and start marching camera left across the field. The camera would then drop down and dolly left with the movement of the Confederate forces. It would have to simultaneously pan right about 45 degrees off the Union forces and pause framed up on the line of the Confederate forces. In this way, the master of the entire battlefield would become a piece of coverage: a tighter establishing shot on the Confederate forces as they start across the field (Figure 4.2 – page 85). Now, simultaneously, while dollying back as the Confederate troops march towards the camera, I would crab camera left and slow the retreat of the dolly. This would tighten the shot until it became a ³/₄ high, wide-angle on a battalion of Confederate soldiers in the front line with an officer on horseback in the right side of frame (Figure 4.3). This would be the third piece of coverage picked up in this one moving master. The officer would then give the command to charge and the platoon would storm forward toward the left side of the frame. The crane would continue to retreat in front of the line of soldiers, but at such a rate that the frame tightened on two Confederates (Figure 4.6 – page 87). The master has now become a two-shot. Logic dictates that the two actors featured in the two-shot would be two of the lead actors. As they charge toward the camera, and a little bit right to left, the actor who is camera right is shot and he falls (Figure 4.7). The actor who is camera left spins around and drops to his knees to tend to his fallen comrade. The camera drops with him so that it is shooting over his right shoulder on the wounded man (Figure 4.8 – page 89). This gives you yet another piece of coverage, as the master has now become an over-the-shoulder shot. The soldier who is wounded could tell his buddy to leave him to die. The buddy could exit frame left and the camera could push into a single as the wounded man dies (Figure 4.9).

Later in this chapter, I refer to another scene from *What Lies Beneath* to illustrate how Zemeckis shoots a good moving master. In designing the master for this scene, Zemeckis went out of his way to put Task 4 to work for him, so far out of his way that he completely eliminated the need for any additional coverage. He shot the entire scene in one shot. The master became all the coverage needed. Bob finds that the elegance and flow of this shooting style lends itself to certain films. Other big name directors, who have the time and the money to shoot their movies in whatever visual style they like, often end up leaning on Task 4 in shooting their

Figure 4.2

Figure 4.3

Figure 4.4

masters so that the need for additional coverage is eliminated. This elite cadre of directors includes Brian DePalma, Martin Scorsese, James Cameron, Michael Bay, and John Woo.

And so there is all the more reason for a first time director on his breakthrough feature to put Task 4 to work! In addition to all of the fore-mentioned practical reasons, using Task 4 also adds aesthetic elegance to the look of his film. If he can master Task 4, the first time director can make his breakthrough directing gig resemble the work of the directors now setting the standard in Hollywood.

Task 3 – Generates eye candy

Again, to be clear, eye candy is what you see when you look through a kaleido-scope, i.e., shifting patterns of light and color. Most commonly in film you get this kaleidoscopic effect when you move the camera past static objects. You also get it when objects in the frame of the camera are themselves moving, provided their movement does not duplicate the movement of the camera. Before editing on film was replaced by digital editing, you could always tell your camera move-ment was generating eye candy if, when you held the film to the light, you saw lots of blurry frames. Since a film camera shoots 24 static images every second (unless it is being over-cranked for slow motion or under-cranked for fast motion), almost all moving objects captured in the frame will have blurred edges. The more blurry frames, the more eye candy. Many rock videos are comprised exclusively of shots in which the camera is flying around or the band is jumping around, or both. If they are shot on film, these videos are wall-to-wall blurry frames.

How much eye candy do you want to generate in each master? If you want to get a reputation as a hot young director, I would say — provided you follow the rules I laid out in the last chapter and your camera moves never detract from the story — have at it! The more eye candy, the better. My guess is that the reason Michael Bay and John Woo started moving their camera in every shot was to outdo the master, to out-Spielberg Spielberg. If you want to make sure that you are per-ceived as a fresh, cutting-edge director, emulate Bay and Woo as much as you can without violating your own individual aesthetic preferences. Nurture everything in your shooting style that is unique, while pumping as much eye candy as you can into each frame in order to come up to or exceed today's professional standards.

In the hypothetical master of Pickett's Charge, there is eye candy in just about every frame. To get from the establishing shot of the entire battle field (Figure 4.1 – page 79) to the shot which features the entire line of the Confederate forces

Figure 4.5

Figure 4.6

Figure 4.7

as they start across the field (Figure 4.2), the camera will have to pan right, drop down precipitously, and then back up rapidly ahead of the advancing line of Confederate soldiers. The fast drop out of the sky will produce the most eye candy. Every static object the camera sees during this drop will blur slightly.

To get from the shot of the line of the Confederate forces to the shot of 50 Confederate soldiers and one officer on horseback (Figure 4.2 to Figure 4.4), the camera will travel right to left along the front line of soldiers and continue to back up as fast as the soldiers advance. The right to left movement of camera relative to the line of soldiers will produce some blurry frames and some eye candy. Since the line of soldiers is advancing while the camera backs up in front of them, these two almost identical movements tend to cancel each other out and produce few blurry frames and little eye candy.

In the two-shot (Figure 4.6), the two featured soldiers will be running forward as fast as they can. As they run, they will be lurching from side to side in the frame and their legs will be moving up and down. All of these movements are counter to the movement of the camera and so will register as blurry frames and generate eye candy. When the soldier on the right is hit and falls backwards away from the camera, this movement will register as blurry frames. When the camera stops its retreat, pushes forward, and then drops down as the soldier on the left kneels over his fallen buddy, the camera will be moving in the opposite direction of the other Confederate soldiers, who will continue to charge forward past the camera, generating a fair amount of eye candy on edges of the frame (Figure 4.8).

In the previous chapter I noted that, generally speaking, the way a post-Spielbergian director goes about designing his shots so that they logically require the maximum amount of camera movement is to frame up a tight single on the principle object in the scene — such as the boulder that almost rolls over Indiana Jones — and then have that object take off moving. The camera has to take off moving in the same direction and at the same speed as that moving object or it will slip out of frame. It is worth noting that most eye candy is generated not from the featured object in the center of the frame, which generally is moving in the same direction as the camera, but by the static objects on the edges of the frame that the featured object moves past or in front of.

In the master of Pickett's Charge, the advancing line of Confederate soldiers is literally driving the story in the beginning of the shot. When the wide shot tightens into a two-shot, it is the two Confederate soldiers who are the lead actors. They are driving the story and the camera is moving in the same direction as they move and at the same pace, so, in fact, their movement does not generate most of the eye

Figure 4.8

Figure 4.9

candy. The eye candy comes from the comparatively inconsequential static objects that the moving camera passes in the course of keeping up with the principal objects. Therefore, to generate eye candy, the first time director on his break-through film must work to design his moving masters so that the person or thing that is driving the story passes in front of objects that generate the most eye candy.

Objects that generate the most eye candy are objects that — because of their shape, color, or brightness —seem to be moving or actually are moving in a different direction than the camera. So if the camera is moving vertically, anything that is obviously horizontal will generate the most eye candy. If you were doing a shot of Superman flying up the face of a tall building with lots of horizontal window mullions, each mullion that crossed the frame would strobe across the lens and appear to be moving downward. In every frame, each mullion would be blurred at the edges. This is where you get your eye candy.

If the camera is moving horizontally, anything that is obviously vertical will generate the most eye candy. If you were shooting Tom Sawyer walking proudly in front of the picket fence he just painted, the vertical slats of the fence will generate the eye candy. The horizontal movement of the lens will make the white vertical bars of the fence slats strobe across the lens and actually appear to be moving in the opposite direction of the camera. Each slat of the fence would be blurred on the edges in every frame. This is where you would get your eye candy.

As noted above, most of the eye candy in the master of Pickett's Charge would be generated by the movement of the camera past static objects in the frame. The fast drop on the crane at the beginning of the shot would generate the most eye candy, especially if you positioned the camera so that it dropped vertically across the horizontal branches of a tall tree (Figure 4.2). The source of the eye candy in the subsequent right to left movement of the camera along the front line of advancing Confederate soldiers will come primarily from the horizontal movement of the camera across the vertical figure of each soldier. To add eye candy to this part of the shot, the director can arrange with his art director to make sure that a significant number of the soldiers that the camera passes in front of carry tall vertical banners and battle flags (Figures 4.3, 4.4, and 4.5).

To sum up, when the aspiring director lays out the moving masters of his breakthrough feature, he should focus intently on the static objects that his moving camera passes in front of. This is the key to generating the maximum amount of eye candy.

Moving masters do not move continuously. At the end of the master of Pickett's Charge, the camera goes into a static over-the-shoulder shot on the fallen hero (Figure 4.8). When a moving master stops moving, then most of the eye candy switches over and is generated by those objects in the frame that are still moving. The eye candy comes from the ranks of Confederate soldiers that continue the charge, rushing past the fallen hero and his buddy (Figure 4.8). Their outlines will be blurred in each of the 24 frames that go through the camera each second. Once the camera stops, those objects that are most prominent in the frame because of their size, color, and brightness, and which are moving most dynamically, generate the most eye candy.

The first time director on his breakthrough film should design his moving masters so that even when the camera stops moving, the frame is filled with eye candy. He can do this by framing the static moments of his moving master so that they take place in the midst of objects at the location that are constantly in motion. A cliché example that comes to mind would be to frame a close-up of a couple kissing in a waterfall. Or he can work with his department heads to bring objects to the location to fill his static frames, such as the extras playing Confederate soldiers who charge past the static camera framed up on the over-the-shoulder shot of the fallen hero (Figure 4.8).

Task 2 – Concentrates the audience's attention on the center of the drama

As I said in the previous chapter, in the post-Spielbergian era, directors systematically provide themselves with a reason to move their camera by starting the scene framed up tight on the principal object in the scene, and then having that principal object take off moving. This requires the camera to perform a counter-move to keep the principle object in frame. If the camera doesn't move, the shot will fall apart because what is carrying the story at that point in the film will literally slip out of frame. In all scenes that involve dialogue, which is to say all scenes except action sequences, the principle object in the scene — that which is driving the story forward — is the person who is talking.

The best way for a moving master to concentrate the audience's attention on the center of the drama is to keep both eyes of the actor who is talking in frame. The eyes are the focal point of the drama of the scene. We all know this instinctively. If one actor is talking and the others are not, we look specifically at that actor's eyes. The only exception to this would be if the silent reaction of an actor who was not talking were more important and more compelling at that particular moment in the film. This happens very rarely — so rarely, that for the sake of simplicity, I will overlook it and pronounce that the actor who is talking is always carrying the scene. If the first time director follows this rule on his breakthrough feature, he will probably never go wrong. On his second feature, he will have learned enough to become sensitive to the very rare exceptions to the rule, and can respond to them on his own without the aid of this book.

This provides the first time director with an easy-to-follow rule in order to make sure that all his moving masters actually accomplish Task 2 (concentrates the audience's attention on the center of the drama). To do this he must keep both eyes of the actor who is talking in frame. Both eyes is ideal, but this can only happen in a moving master if the two or more actors in the scene are talking while walking side by side down a hallway or down a road, facing the camera and not each other. This is unusual. When we talk to one another we generally face each other. So, if the camera is framed up on both eyes of Actor A, it will be on the back of the actor he is talking to: Actor B. As soon as Actor B starts talking, in response to what Actor A has said to him, the master will suddenly be no good, or "fall apart" because Actor B will be driving the scene and the audience will not be able to see his eyes. As a result, the post-Spielbergian director while shooting a good moving master must have his actors and his camera perform a complicated minuet whereby they keep maneuvering around in relation to one another so that, as much as possible, the actor who is talking is facing the camera.

After 20 years of directing, I still find it a daunting challenge to go to the location where I am scheduled to shoot a four or five page dialogue scene involving two or three or more actors, sit down with my script open to the first page of the scene, and try to work out in my mind's eye exactly where all the actors will walk and talk and pause and walk and talk some more, and how the camera will move in response to their movement so as to not only keep them in frame, but also stay framed up as much as possible on both eyes of the actor who is talking. It's a three-dimensional trigonometry problem made even more difficult by the fact that there are a multitude of possible answers, but the first time director has to determine which is the most elegant solution — the one which Spielberg or Scorsese or Campion would have come up with. That's what he has been hired to do, and if he wants to land his all-important second feature, that's the answer he is going to have to hit upon.

Only when a first time director actually tries to make his breakthrough film look like a Spielberg film does he discover how much forethought and preparation go into coming up with all the good moving masters that give a film that profession-al look. It's like fine Swiss watch. Even a child can tell time. But as to exactly how all the fine parts in the watch actually work in conjunction with each other to move the hands so that the watch accurately tells time — you have to be a mechanical genius or highly trained watchmaker to understand that.

How Zemeckis Shoots a Good Moving Master
Following the Dictates of the Four Tasks

When Zemeckis was shooting *What Lies Beneath*, I got a chance to visit the set one night with six of my directing students. I was gratified to discover that Bob was moving his camera just as I teach my students to move theirs, following all of the rules that I advocate in this book, *but even more so!* More so, in that he has become even more daring with his camera movement — validating my theory that the post-Spielbergian director must move his camera whenever possible — yet follow-ing his own rule that the movement must always be in support of the story and therefore invisible.

By twisting the 1st AD's arm, I managed to get my students positioned like flies on a wall, right up next to the path of the moving camera as Zemeckis laid out the master of the scene when Claire (Michele Pfeiffer) mistakenly accuses Warren Feur (James Remar) of murdering his wife. In laying out this master, Zemeckis scrupulously followed Bob's Rule and packed his master with Tasks 1, 2, 3, and 4.

To give the reader a more concrete understanding of both the theory and practice of shooting a good moving master, I will describe how Zemeckis went about his directorial duties that evening.

The shot starts framed up on Claire as she comes running into the lobby of the huge auditorium, weaving her way through a sea of extras portraying the theatergoers who are exiting the building. Her husband, Norman (Harrison Ford), is hot on her heels, and the camera is in front of the two of them, being driven backwards by her forward movement (Figure 4.10). Therefore, Zemeckis has made sure that his camera movement is externally generated. The camera has to move to keep up with the person who is driving the story at that moment: Claire. She will not speak until she gets to where Feur is standing, but when she does speak the audience will be able to see both of her eyes. So Zemeckis has taken care to put Task 2 (concentrates the audience's attention on the center of the drama) to work in this master. Zemeckis has also designed the shot to make sure that the audience sees everything that they need to see to understand or believe the scene. So he has made sure that his master is strong on Task 1 (shows the audience everything it needs to see in the scene).

Some of the work of Task 1 has already been done by the shot that precedes this master. Zemeckis staged a portion of the drama leading up to this confrontation between Claire and Feur outside the theater. Norman chases Claire down just outside the theater and stops her before she can go in. It just so happens that from where they are standing, they can see into the lobby through a wall of large glass picture windows. Norman, as he does throughout the bulk of the movie, tries to convince Claire that she is not acting rationally, but as he is doing so, she catches sight of Feur through the windows as he crosses the lobby. The shot immediately preceding the master is Claire's POV of Feur as he crosses the lobby (Figure 4.11). By cutting immediately from this shot to Claire, now inside the theater and racing across the lobby with Norman behind her, Zemeckis is employing the visual shorthand that he knows the MTV-weaned audience of today can easily read. The audience cannot see Feur in the shot at the very beginning of Zemeckis' moving master. They can only see Claire striding quickly left to right across the lobby with Norman a few strides behind her. But because the audience has seen Feur through Claire's POV in the shot immediately preceding this master, they know that Claire is headed straight for Feur and that he is somewhere just out of frame, camera right. The reason the audience cannot see Feur at the beginning of the master is because,

Figure 4.10

Figure 4.11

Figure 4.12

in keeping with the Spielbergian style, Zemeckis wants to move his camera whenever possible, and to necessitate this he has started the scene framed up tight on the principal object in the scene — Claire — and then had that principal object take off moving. Most directors before Spielberg would have put the camera on the other side of the lobby from Claire and framed it up with Feur in the foreground and Claire in the background, crossing the lobby towards him. But the way Zemeckis starts this master, the camera has to back up just as fast as Claire moves forward in order to keep her in the middle of the frame. As soon as it starts moving, it starts generating eye candy and in so doing fulfills the requirements of Task 3 (generates eye candy). In this Zemeckis master, as is usually the case, most of the eye candy is generated when the moving camera passes static objects or objects that are moving in a direction other than that of the camera. As Claire rushes in and the camera backs up in front of her, it goes by a number of extras who are standing still or filing slowly out of the theater in the opposite direction. These extras will have blurry edges and so generate some eye candy (Figure 4.10.) To jack up the eye candy level a bit higher, Zemeckis had one extra cross between Claire and the camera. To do this, the extra had to be practically running out of the theater. His cross generates the most eye candy in these opening seconds of the master (Figure 4.12.)

In understanding how a good moving master goes about fulfilling the disparate demands of the four separate Tasks, I find it useful to picture the performance of the master being registered on four bar-graph LEDs, such as one often sees on a VU meter used to register how a piece of music is modulating across different frequencies of sound. The best master is the one that keeps all four LEDs as close as possible to peaking from the beginning to the end of the shot. On this imaginary performance meter, Zemeckis' master at this point in the shot (Figure 4.10) would be registering about 80% on the graph for Task 1 (shows the audience everything it needs to see). The LEDs on the two bar graphs for Task 2 (concentrates the audience's attention on the center of the drama) and Task 3 (generates eye candy) would be very close to peaking out.

The graph for Task 4 (picks up some coverage) would have yet to appear, indicating that at this point, there was nothing the master could possibly do to fulfill the requirements of this Task. There has been no exchange of dialogue, no back-and-forth conversation. People generally face each other when exchanging dialogue. This is what usually necessitates coverage. If one actor is facing north and the other south, the camera cannot keep whipping back and forth from north to south. The only good way to do this is in cuts, and with cuts comes the need for coverage.

What the first time director wants to do on his breakthrough project is keep all four LEDs up as high as he can throughout the entire shot. But only on the rarest of occasions will all four be close to peaking; generally all four LEDs will be sliding up and down between 50% and 80% as the director balances the competing needs of four disparate sets of requirements against each other. The goal is to avoid being too slavishly attentive to the needs of any one Task. That will inevitably throw the balance off.

With that said, it should be noted that in shooting this master, Zemeckis was somewhat slavishly attentive to the needs of one particular Task. But, being anything but a first time director, he had no need to obey the dictates of this book. His budget on *What Lies Beneath* allowed him the freedom to do anything he wanted. And in this movie Zemeckis aspired to give the film a very fluid, stylized look by shooting as much as he could in **oners** — masters that covered everything that the audience needed to see in each scene in one, single, continuous shot that required no cutaways. Oners get it all. They eliminate the need for any coverage, so there are no edits. This gives the finished film a very fluid, elegant look.

To do oners, the director has to be a slave to Task 4 (picks up some coverage). As soon as the need for coverage arises, which generally takes place when there is a back and forth conversation — a moment of confrontation — the camera movement somehow defeats the need to cut to a different angle. In the above scene, this moment comes when Claire confronts Feur, who is just off stage camera right (Figure 4.13):

CLAIRE

You!... You think you're pretty
smart, don't you?

She then goes on to accuse him of murdering his wife. As soon as the words are out of her mouth, Feur's wife emerges from the ladies room and asks him, "Is everything alright?" At this, Feur gives Claire a very concerned look and asks, "Are you alright?" Claire of course is anything but alright. She is mortified and shaken. Ordinarily this sort of back and forth exchange would be achieved in two separate angles. In *What Lies Beneath*, Zemeckis defeats this need for coverage by getting the camera to swing around in a dramatic clockwise arc from the two-shot of Claire and Norman (Figure 4.13) onto the opposing three-shot favoring Feur and his wife (Figure 4.14), and then swing back onto a variation on the two-shot of Claire and Norman (Figure 4.23) in time to catch the look on Claire's face when she sees that Feur's wife is alive and in perfect health.

Figure 4.13

Figure 4.14

Figure 4.23

So if the camera is facing north (Figure 4.13), then it ends up swinging from north to south and back to north again. In so doing, this particular master from *What Lies Beneath* (like most oners) picks up a ton of eye candy and gets the whole scene in one shot. This means that the LED meter described above would register 100% for both Task 3 (generates eye candy) and Task 4 (picks up some coverage). In this respect, it deserves to be emulated by first time directors — because first time directors should try to shoot masters that kill as many birds as possible with one stone. In this master, the only way that Zemeckis can shoot it in one is by flying his camera back and forth from north to south and back to north. To have the master perform to the maximum when it comes to Task 4, he has to pull out all the stops satisfying Task 3.

A first time director on his breakthrough project is advised to not go as far as Zemeckis did in *What Lies Beneath* by attempting to shoot all of a scene using only one shot. That is too ambitious and too expensive.

I already pointed out that from the top of scene down to this point Zemeckis was hitting about 80% at Task 1 (shows the audience everything it needs to see). This also is just as I prescribe, because it is most important to satisfy the demands of Task 1 at the beginning of a scene when the audience needs to get the lay of the land. So where does that leave Task 2 (concentrates the audience's attention on the center of the drama)? The beauty of it is that the way Zemeckis blocked the actors in this scene, the center of the drama moves on its own accord from north to south and back to north again — from Claire and Norman to Feur and his wife and back to Claire and Norman. So, in fact, the actual process by which Zemeckis fulfills Task 2 enables him to do a brilliant job at Tasks 3 and 4. He makes it look like it all just fell into place, but it takes the skill of a great director to make it feel that natural. Most of that skill comes by blocking the actors so that the center of the drama shifts from actor to actor in a way that allows the camera to keep up without whipping around violently or breaking the rules governing externally and internally generated camera movement — either of which would call attention to the camera movement and detract from the story.

I call this skill Task 2 Mastery. The first time director must acquire this skill in order to become proficient at shooting good moving masters. The shifts in the center of the drama move the camera, and those camera movements in turn are the means by which the master satisfies the demands of all the Four Tasks. Therefore Task 2 Mastery is the key to shooting good moving masters.

In almost all instances, Task 2 Mastery is achieved through actor blocking (in addition to camera blocking) because the way the actors walk and talk determines how the center of the drama shifts. The only exception comes when there is a moving establishing shot at the beginning of a scene. In this case, actor blocking does not drive the center of the drama. The center of drama just takes off moving on its own at the top of a scene to establish the geography of the spot where the scene is about to take place. The camera movement remains invisible because the audience has come to accept this form of visual shorthand.

The first time director attains Task 2 Mastery, like Zemeckis, through skillful blocking of his actors. Ironically, the director determines how he will block his actors after he has decided what he wants his camera to see. Directors whose area of expertise is performance, along with most actors, might say that I have got it backwards. They would contend that the drama of the scene is the top priority and it should determine how the actors are blocked and what the camera sees. But the reality of directing in post-Spielbergian Hollywood is that the visual make-up of a scene is frequently just as important, if not more important, than the dramatic content. In films today, the story is told visually as well as theatrically. In any case, before he sets to work on coming up with a good moving master for a scene, the director must go to the location, read the entire scene while standing where he is going to shoot it, and set his priorities in terms of the Four Tasks.

When Zemeckis went to the auditorium where he was going to shoot the scene from *What Lies Beneath* (and I know he went there before the day of shooting, because that is a rule he taught me and he lives by it), he read the scene through, looked at the lobby, and decided that this was a scene he could shoot in a oner. So satisfying the needs of Task 4 (picks up some coverage) became paramount.

On the other hand, if it were a different script and a different location, the director might decide that the needs of Task 2 (keeps the audience focused on the center of the drama) were the top priority. This would be the case if the scene contained a pivotal dramatic moment in the plot — for example, the scene in *American Beauty* when Angela, the cheerleader, and Lester, the main character, are about to make love and she tells him that she is a virgin. In such a scene, it would be crucial to see both actors' eyes in every shot — and the closer the better. The needs of all the other Tasks, most of which require a lot of camera movement, would be minimal.

I shot a good master for a scene in the opening of *Night Vision*, one of the low budget features I directed, in which the needs of Task 1 (shows the audience everything they need to see to understand the scene) were my top priority. This was because it was the first time the audience would get to see the apartment inhabited by the main character, played by Fred Williamson. One crucial aspect of the character Fred was playing was that he was a recovering alcoholic who lived in a single room in a homeless shelter. Much of what this character was about was portrayed through the visual aspect of this room. Accordingly, in the moving master for the first scene that took place in this room, I made sure that at the very opening of the scene the camera saw almost all four walls.

If the director makes Task 1 his top priority, as in the above example, he almost always pulls out all the stops satisfying that Task at the very beginning of the scene. After that, Task 1 can compete with the other Tasks on an equal footing. It is worth noting that, even if Task 1 is not the director's top priority in a scene, he still must favor that Task at the beginning of the scene as much as he can. The master of Pickett's Charge described earlier will not make much sense unless, before you see the Confederate army charge, you see the Union army facing them on the other side of the wheat field. Inevitably, the director favors Task 1 at the beginning of a scene, but in some instances more so than usual.

Sometimes a director decides that he is just going to pull out all the stops and cram as much eye candy as he possibly can into his moving master. Usually this is because the scene takes place in a location that lends itself to getting eye candy, such as a casino, an amusement park, a rock concert, a nightclub, a rave, or a city street lined with neon lights. Also, if the scene is only going to be about eye candy, then one would assume it was light on content (both dramatic and visual) — that the story was not going to be advanced significantly either through dramatic moments, as in the example from *American Beauty*, or through visual storytelling, as in the example from *Night Vision*.

In any case, the first decision a director must make before he can start to lay out his moving master is which one of the Four Tasks he is going to favor — and to what extent he is going to favor it. After the director has decided in what manner he is going to strike a balance between the Four Tasks, he then turns his attention solely to Task 2. As I explained above, in every case except a moving establishing shot, the camera is going to move to follow the shifting center of the drama. So in the scene from *What Lies Beneath*, after he determined that he was going to favor Task 4 and shoot a oner, Zemeckis then used Task 2 Mastery to motivate the camera from north to south and back to north again.

If the camera is facing north (Figure 4.13 – page 97), then it is facing southeast more than south (Figure 4.14). Instead of a complete 180, it has made about a 135-degree pivot. It could not make this pivot in one quick pan. That would look like a whip pan and call attention to itself. The camera has to come around by degrees. In the opening exchange between Claire and Feur, the drama is all about

Claire and her mounting passion that leads her, in a loud voice in the middle of a crowd, to accuse Feur of murdering his wife.

> CLAIRE
> You!... You think you're pretty smart, don't you? You think you got away with it. But I know you killed her, you murdering son-of-a-bitch!

> FEUR
> (not understanding)
> Who?

> CLAIRE
> Don't give me that shit! Your wife!

Claire's mounting passion provides Zemeckis with a good excuse to start the camera on its pivot from north to southeast. He can push the camera in on her and Norman, and start it around to the east (Figure 4.16). The move will not be visible because the audience will read it as an expression of Claire's mounting anger. This push-in is internally generated — it emphasizes that anger.

If the camera was facing north (Figure 4.13), then in Figure 4.16 it has come around almost 45 degrees to the east (Figure 4.17). This master started out as a head on two-shot on Claire and Norman; it has become a ¾ side angle on them (Figure 4.16). Norman now brings the camera around to about 90 degrees to the east, almost at right angles to where it was (Figure 4.13), by taking a big step to camera right (Figure 4.18 – page 103) in order to deliver his line sotto voce to Feur.

> NORMAN
> I'm sorry. She's very upset.

The camera has to move in a clockwise arc from northeast in order to keep Norman in frame. So the move seems completely externally generated, natural, and invisible to the audience. This clockwise 90-degree pivot from north to east picks up Mrs. Feur on the extreme right edge of the frame (Figure 4.18). She is exiting the ladies room, which is visible behind her (Figure 4.20), and rushing up to the side of her husband moving left to right. The lobby has fallen completely silent. Everyone is staring at Claire and Warren Feur. This explains Mary Feur's hurried movement, the concern on her face and in her voice as she glides up to his side and simply asks:

> MRS. FEUR
> Honey?

Figure 4.16

Figure 4.17

The camera follows her movement to camera right, picks up Feur on the right side of frame, and ends up in the three-shot favoring Feur and his wife (Figure 4.14 – page 97). In so doing, the camera completes its clockwise rotation through about 135 degrees from north to the southeast (Figure 4.21). Since the camera was following Mrs. Feur from the ladies room to her husband's side, its movement can be said to be externally generated and accordingly calls no attention to itself.

Figure 4.18

Figure 4.19

Figure 4.20

In this way, Zemeckis uses Task 2 Mastery to move the center of the drama so the camera has to move to keep up with it. The frame swings around from the two-shot on Claire and Norman to the two-shot on Feur and his wife, all the while remaining invisible. At this point, Zemeckis is halfway towards completing his attempt to shoot the scene in one shot and so completely fulfill the needs of Task 4 (picks up some coverage). Of course by keeping the camera moving to get the entire scene in one shot, he is also doing a brilliant job of satisfying the needs of Task 3 (generates eye candy). And since the camera is moving to keep the center of the drama in frame, he is doing a very good job of satisfying Task 2 (keeps the audience focused on the center of the drama). As to how he is doing at satisfying Task 1, I will leave a more detailed discussion of that for later; suffice it to say that on the basis of Tasks 2, 3, and 4, this is an excellent master. It has kept three of the four LED bar graphs almost peaking. On this basis alone it is a very good master.

Figure 4.21

Where specifically does Zemeckis use Task 2 Mastery to nail this master? Zemeckis had to make sure that Norman took up a position to camera right of Claire after chasing her into the lobby (Figure 4.13). If he had landed camera left of her, he would not have been in position to carry the drama from camera left to camera right: from north to southeast. Zemeckis also had to stage the drama so that Claire continues to raise her voice and is almost shouting when she tells Feur, "Don't give me that shit! Your wife!" This makes the crowd fall silent and stare at the two couples. So the audience understands why Norman has to lower his voice and take a big step from camera left to camera right towards the Feurs (Figure 4.18): so that he can deliver his explanation/apology sotto voce. As I recall, Harrison Ford (Norman) did not have a scripted line at this point in the scene. Zemeckis concocted this line: "I'm sorry. She's very upset." on the spot and gave it to Ford, just so Ford would become the center of the drama. This way, by having Norman take a big step toward the Feurs to deliver his line in a low voice, Zemeckis came up with the crucial link he needed to get his camera to pivot from north through 135 degrees to southeast. Finally, Zemeckis also had to take care to stage the entire confrontation in front of the ladies restroom. The positioning of the couples in relation to the restroom door from which Mrs. Feur emerges (Figure 4.20) makes it necessary for the camera to keep moving left to right to follow Mrs. Feur as she rushes up to Feur's side (Figure 13). In so doing, it completes its clockwise pivot from north to southeast — all the while invisibly following the shifting center of the drama. This is Task 2 Mastery at its best.

So in Figure 4.14, Zemeckis is halfway home in his drive to shoot the scene in one. He has swung his camera from north to southeast but he still has to get it back to north. Accomplishing this was comparatively easy. After Feur's wife joins Feur (Figure 4.14), he turns to Claire and with righteous spite announces: "I did not murder my wife!" Then Zemeckis has Feur lean forward towards Claire, who is off stage camera left, lower his voice and ask her, "Are you alright?" As Feur leans forward, the camera pivots from southeast back to east (Figure 4.22) and as it does

Figure 4.22

so, Norman comes to dominate the center of the frame. Norman then takes a big step camera left. The camera continues to pivot to keep him in frame. This counterclockwise pivot causes Claire to reappear in the left side of the frame (Figure 4.15). The camera has now swung from southeast back to northeast. As Norman steps toward Claire, he whispers to her, "Alright, Honey." In this way the center of drama is shifted from Feur to Norman and then back to Claire. The initial part of this camera move is clearly externally generated by Feur's leaning forward to camera left and Norman's subsequent step to camera left. But what keeps the camera pivoting more to camera left is an internally generated move meant to reveal that Claire is clearly not alright, but profoundly shaken to see Feur's wife alive and well. The camera moves into a 3/4 frontal shot on her face, drawn there by the mounting intensity of her trauma. At the same time, Norman moves from his mark at camera right behind Claire to stand camera left of her (Figure 4.23) so as to show her the way out, whispering as he moves something inaudible in her ear, like "Come on, let's go." Norman's right to left move makes the last portion of the camera's pivot externally as well as internally generated. The camera is again pointing north (Figure 4.23), and Zemeckis has achieved his objective, shooting the entire scene in one shot (Figure 4.24).

To do this, he relied on his Task 2 Mastery. He took care to block his actors so that by walking and talking they caused the center of the drama to shift in such a way that by following these shifts, the camera was able to pick up all necessary coverage.

The camera never stopped moving and he got the scene all in one. So on my LED bar graph, the columns representing Task 3 (generates eye candy) and Task 4 (picks up some coverage) would have been pinned up against the top at 100% throughout the entire scene. But the same could not be said for the LED bar graphs representing Task 1 (shows the audience everything it needs to see) and Task 2 (keeps the audience focused on the center of the drama). They would have been sliding up and down between 50% and 80%. There is nothing wrong with this. This is an excellent master.

When it comes to shooting good moving masters, it's just like everything else in life: You have to give something up to get something. Up until this point in my discussion of this Zemeckis master, I have focused on how Zemeckis went about fulfilling his priorities. That is because that's the key to laying out a moving master. You come to it with certain priorities in mind. You have analyzed the scene and decided that the particular needs of the scene could best be met if the master worked hardest to fulfill one or more of the Four Tasks. Furthermore, the emphasis can shift throughout the scene. One or more of the Tasks can be favored at the beginning, middle, or end. For example, in the master I shot for the scene in *Night Vision*, my game plan was to point the camera into every corner of the room.

Figure 4.23

Figure 4.24

I decided to push Task 1 (shows the audience everything that they need to see). But, in fact, I pushed it so hard from the top of the scene, by about one-third of the way through, the audience had seen the whole room. After that, Task 1 became less of a priority.

After deciding which of the Four Tasks he is going to favor and in which part or parts of the scene, the director comes up with a rough notion of how the master will unfold. He then goes about seeing if he can get his actors to walk and talk in such a way that will make sense for the scene, while at the same time driving the

camera around in such a fashion so that it satisfies his preconceived visual priorities. As he does this, he is going to hit some rough spots. He is going to realize
that in order to meet his preconceived priorities, he is going to end up doing a less
than brilliant job of fulfilling one of the Four Tasks. But he is going to learn to
accept that, and to make some well-calculated compromises in order to achieve his
overriding objective.

Zemeckis makes a significant trade-off in his master, which enables him to accomplish his overriding objective of shooting the master in one continuous shot, but
which simultaneously compromises his ability to fulfill the requirements of one of
the other Four Tasks — in this case, Task 2 (keeps the audience focused on the
center of the drama). Taken as a whole, this scene is fundamentally a confrontation between Claire and Feur. The essence of the drama portrayed in the scene
occurs when Claire loudly accuses Feur, in public, of murdering his wife. He
emphatically and righteously denies her accusation. The height of drama comes
in Claire's line, "Don't give me that shit. Your wife!" and in Feur's line, "I did not
murder my wife!" To deliver the full emotional impact of Claire's accusation to
the audience, Zemeckis should have had the camera framed up as close as possible
to her face in a slightly off center, full frontal close-up. This way the audience
would see both of her eyes. To deliver the full emotional impact of Feur's denial,
he should have framed up the same shot of Feur.

In both cases he failed to do this. Claire delivers her line in a $3/4$ frontal two-shot
that is more profile than $3/4$ (Figure 4.16 – page 102) and Feur is almost in profile
(Figure 4.14 – page 97) when he comes out with his line. Using my formula
that states the more eyes the better, when it comes to fulfilling the requirements
of Task 2 and focusing the audience on the center of the drama, Zemeckis only
shows the audience $1^{1}/_{2}$ of Michelle Pfeiffer's eyes and only one of James Remar's
eyes. In both cases he should have shown the audience two eyes.

Zemeckis was fully aware of this. In his next film, *Cast Away*, he minimized camera movement throughout the middle of the film when the character portrayed by
Tom Hanks is marooned on a desert island. You get to see both of Tom Hanks'
eyes at every emotional peak that occurs during this long middle section. But he
was working with a different visual game plan when he shot *Cast Away*. For *What
Lies Beneath*, his overriding objective was to shoot each scene in one continuous
shot. To accomplish this, he had to fudge a bit when it came to delivering the
drama to the audience. The reason he shot both Pfeiffer and Remar in a profile
at the height of their passion was because that way the camera had less distance to
travel from Pfeiffer to Remar in order to tie them into the same shot. And since his
objective was to link all the shots into one long continuous master, this literally put
him closer to his objective.

This is the key to shooting a good moving master. You have to approach this very important job ready to compromise. If you try to come up with a camera blocking plan that completely fulfills the demands of all of the Four Tasks equally well, you will end up almost paralyzed by the difficulty of the task, and, most likely, spend more time than you can afford preparing your camera blocking. You cannot keep all four LEDs pinned at 100%. The lesson to be learned for first time directors is that, like Zemeckis, you must start out understanding what your priorities are for the scene. This will give you an organizing principle that will guide your making all of the little trade-offs like the ones Zemeckis made. But you should limit the number of Tasks you prioritize. It's best to stick to one or two.

That is where the masters for your breakthrough film will differ from Zemeckis' master from *What Lies Beneath*. You could ask your slightly green crew to shoot a oner for one or two scenes in the entire film. Asking them to shoot oners for almost every scene, like Zemeckis did, would probably put you over budget and behind schedule.

The spirit of compromise will enable you to make all your decisions quickly and correctly when you are at the location by yourself preparing your moving masters. If you are really smart and have a knack for this kind of three-dimensional trigonometry, you might finish all your homework and get a good night's sleep. If you can do that, you're better at the Four Tasks than I am. In all my years of directing, I have never been able to do this crucial part of the director's work quickly enough to drive home and get a good night's sleep. But, to quote the immortal words emblazoned on my favorite rock video unit manager's T-shirt: "Sleep is for beginners."

CHAPTER 4 | SUMMARY POINTS

- The best moving master does four "Tasks" equally well:

  - Task 1 shows the audience everything it needs to see (in the scene).
  - Task 2 concentrates the audience's attention on the center of the drama.
  - Task 3 generates eye candy.
  - Task 4 picks up some coverage.

- By definition, a master must reveal the plane of battle on which the ensuing action will take place — along with all the men, material, and geographical features which will play a significant role in that action. The master implants an image in the viewer's mind as to where the players in the scene are in relation to each other.

- Task 1 requires that the director design his moving master so that it shows the audience everything that it needs to see to understand and believe the scene.

- If he can master Task 4, the first time director can make his breakthrough directing gig resemble the work of the directors now setting the standard in Hollywood.

- When the aspiring director lays out the moving masters of his breakthrough feature, he should focus intently on the static objects that his moving camera passes in front of. This is the key to Task 3, generating the maximum amount of eye candy.

- In all scenes that involve dialogue, which is to say all scenes except action sequences, the principal object in the scene — that which is driving the story forward — is the person who is talking.

- A director attains Task 2 Mastery when he can block his actors so that the center of the drama shifts from actor to actor in a way that allows the camera to keep up with it without whipping around violently or breaking the rules governing externally and internally generated camera movement.

- The shifts in the center of the drama move the camera, and those camera movements in turn are the means by which the master satisfies the demands of all the Four Tasks. Therefore, Task 2 Mastery is the key to shooting good moving masters.

■ Before he devises a good moving master for a scene, the director must go to the location, read the entire scene while standing where he is going to shoot it, and set his priorities in terms of the Four Tasks.

■ If the director makes Task 1 his top priority, he almost always pulls out all the stops satisfying Task 1 at the very beginning of the scene.

■ After the director has decided in what manner he is going to strike a balance between the Four Tasks, he then turns his attention solely to Task 2. In every case except a moving establishing shot, the camera is going to move to follow the shifting center of the drama.

■ If you try to come up with a camera-blocking plan that completely fulfills the demands of all of the Four Tasks equally well, you will end up almost paralyzed by the difficulty of the task. Learn to compromise.

CHAPTER 5 | LENS SELECTION –
WHY FORCE PERSPECTIVE?

If you are going to make it as a director of mainstream theatrical features, you have to force perspective. Why? For the same reason that you have to move your camera — because every director of note has been doing it since Spielberg burst on the scene in the early '70s using forced perspective as part of his signature style. Orson Welles was the first mainstream Hollywood director to practice "lensemanship" as we know it today — although, to my knowledge, one of the first Hollywood movies which made regular use of forced perspective to heighten its story was Disney's animated feature, *Snow White and the Seven Dwarfs*, made in 1938. Other directors, like Stanley Kubrick, made regular use of forced perspective before Spielberg started directing. But since the mid-'70s, when Spielberg's style became the money style, it has become de rigueur for all mainstream Hollywood directors to force perspective.

Like camera movement, forced perspective should only be used to heighten the story. Using lenses in a manner that calls attention to itself, making the audience aware of the camerawork and taking them out of the story, is ultimately counter-productive. It weakens the overall impact of the film for all the same reasons moving the camera in a self-serving manner does. The best rule of thumb on the set of your first feature is to force perspective whenever possible, so your films come up to the visual standard set by Spielberg. But, like Spielberg, Zemeckis, and others, make sure that such cinematographic enhancements always serve the story, and so remain invisible.

Lens Selection As a Joint Responsibility
between Director and Cinematographer

You should understand the basics of lens selection in order to control the look of your movie. If you always leave the decision for which lens to use up to your DP, your movie will not look the same way on screen as it does in your head. The lens you use for a shot, along with the camera position/movement and composition, determine the look of the shot. You have to understand and control all three in order to control the look of your movie. But relax. Of the three, lens selection is by far the easiest to master, and once mastered, it can yield impressive results. A little understanding goes a long way toward the goal of putting a distinctive personal stamp on the visual aspect of your film.

Most of the professional DPs I have worked with put up some form of resistance to my coaching them on lens selection. Some are polite or light-hearted about it and some are downright ornery. The message is always the same, whether it's given, jokingly, in the spirit of co-operation, or meant to have the same effect as the brittle crack of a rattlesnake's rattle. What all these cameramen are saying is "You're out of your territory, Mr. Director, so watch your step!" Take your DP's resistance in stride. Understand that you are sort of treading on his turf. One step further and you would be questioning his selection of the f-stop.

The DP has to work with the director on the camera blocking because camera blocking is dependent on actor blocking. But he doesn't need you to pick the lens and set the f-stop. He would just as soon do this on his own. That way the look of the film is solely an expression of his artistry. When you start to meddle in lens selection, you are working on the DP's canvas, but you must do this because the look of the film can help or hinder the telling of the story, and the story is your responsibility. In this crux lies the irony of the director/cinematographer relationship. It's his canvas. He does the painting, but you tell him what to paint, and, in the end, you are held responsible for how the painting comes out.

Another factor in the equation that determines the chemistry of the director/cinematographer relationship is industry clout. If you are a first time director and you have been intentionally teamed with a renowned cinematographer with a track record as long as the Nile, then you may consult with him on lens selection, but in the end, it would be politically savvy for you to defer.

Similarly, the pecking order on the set of every episodic TV series that I have worked on as a director places the DP above the director. Only the show runner, the executive producer, the star, and (sometimes) the line producer can make him back down. The DP is usually hand picked by the star. The "look" of the show is his personal creation. All of the crew are his boys. He has been supporting them financially, carrying them from job to job, sometimes for 20 or 30 years. The DP is there every day, episode after episode, season after season, whereas the directors come and go, rotating on and off the show. Sometimes as many as six or seven different directors will be hired in the course of a 20 plus episode season. Compared to the DP, the director is just an interloper — a queen for a day.

This was never more clearly illustrated to me than when I heard Benny Colman, a DP who I worked with on *The Fall Guy*, describe the time he had been obliged, in the course of a debate over lenses, to take the great Spielberg down a notch or two. Benny was an old, old timer. He had started in the business working on Tom Mix westerns. In those days, the lenses used in American films were mostly made by Kodak and were measured in inches. Even though widespread use of American-made lenses died out after World War II, Benny still called all the lenses we used on *The Fall Guy* by their equivalent length in inches — just to remind everyone on the set that he had more than half a century of experience under his belt.

Benny was more than 80 years old, but he still fancied himself a dandy. He wore patent leather shoes that matched his pastel, double-knit leisure suits, and doused his thinning hair with so much Grecian Formula, it turned purple when backlit by a strong arc light. Any attractive actress who did not joyously submit to being kissed and hugged and politely felt-up a half a dozen times a day by Benny, and did not respond to his avuncular sexual banter by matching it thrust for thrust, ran the risk of finding herself looking shockingly plain in her close-ups.

Benny had been the DP on *Marcus Welby, M.D.* According to him, during his tenure, Spielberg, who started his directing career doing episodic TV at Universal, was hired to do a special one-hour episode of *Welby*. Prior to the shooting, Spielberg submitted a list of all the specialized camera equipment that he felt he would need to shoot the episode he envisioned.

"I took one look at that list and started crossing shit off!" Benny boasted gleefully one day when I was directing an episode of *Fall Guy*. "I mean, that smart-ass kid had every trick lens in the F&B Ceco catalogue on that list... a 9.5, a retro focus 10, a 300, a 600, and on top of that, a hot-head, a Steadicam, a Titan crane! You name it, he had it! And I crossed 'em all off. I mean, hell! If you can't shoot it with a one-inch, a two-inch, or a three-inch, it ain't a *Welby*!"

In the Tom Mix days, a one-inch was used for all establishing shots. The two-inch was used for all two-shots and the three-inch for all close-ups. By forcing the great Spielberg to shoot his *Welby* episode with these or similarly elemental lenses, Benny had deprived Spielberg of the instruments which he used to give his movies a different, more dynamic look, and ultimately, to transform the visual aspect of all mainstream films. But when it came to *Marcus Welby*, it was Benny, who had learned his tricks shooting Tom Mix movies, who knew better.

There is an interesting footnote to this story. According to another old hand in the editorial department at Universal, Spielberg's *Welby* still had a more dynamic visual aspect than all other *Welbys*. In the end, the young film god in the making, although he was probably not even 20, had bent the crusty old lord of the manor to his will. My guess is that Spielberg was able to get Benny to shoot it the Spielbergian way, because he stood up to the old curmudgeon and knew so much about lenses, he probably won Benny's grudging respect and co-operation.

The lesson in this little bit of Hollywood lore is that when you get your break-through gig directing, whether it is an episodic TV show like *Marcus Welby, M.D.*, a low budget indie feature, or a studio movie, if you are going to make sure that the finished product represents your best work, then, like Spielberg, you have to have a good command of lens selection.

Remember, filmmaking is a collaborative medium. Put your DP's knowledge and experience to work for you. Listen to his suggestions, and don't nitpick. If he's acting ornery, don't ride him too hard. I generally leave the lens selection up to the DP on all shots except those that call out for a forced perspective or some other very specific look. I want the DP to take ownership of the film. He will do a better job if he feels like it's *his* canvas. So let him do the painting. But know your lenses so you can talk to him and guide him while he paints. This way the picture will come out looking the way you envisioned it. If your DP is gifted, it may come out looking better than you envisioned. In either case, it represents your best work.

The Basics of Perspective

Lens selection is easy because, to the extent to which you need to master it in order to succeed as a director, you only have to fully understand two visual concepts: how "normal perspective" is altered by 1) a telephoto or "long" lens and 2) a wide-angle lens. Normal perspective doesn't take much work to understand. **Normal perspective** is how objects in the foreground look in relation to objects in the background through the naked eye. If you were looking at three cows in a pasture, even though they are all the same size, the one closest to you, in the foreground, is going to look the largest. The one farthest away from you, in the background, is going to look the smallest (Figure 5.5). The one in the middle, or in the middleground, is going to look smaller than the one in the foreground and larger than the one in the background. This is how normal perspective alters the way things look the further away from you they are. Size and distance are

Figure 5.5

diminished as they recede into the background. If you're shooting on 16mm film, the 25mm lens would give you this perspective. In 35mm film, the 50mm lens produces a normal perspective.

Lenses for 16 cameras give you the same look as lenses for 35 cameras that are twice their length. For the sake of simplicity, and because the vast majority of feature films are shot on 35mm film, from this point forward I am only going to refer to 35 lens lengths. If you want to translate this into lenses for 16 cameras, simply divide by two.

Unless some unusual aspect of the story demands it, the longest lens you would ever have occasion to use on the set of your breakthrough directing gig is a 300mm, and the widest lens is a 9.5mm. A 300mm gives you an ultra-telephoto look. This is the look of that common shot of the horse and rider galloping right at the lens across the desert, in which you see the heat wavering up off the desert floor, and the horse and rider ride and ride but never seem to get any closer; they always remain off in the distance, hanging, suspended in the middle of the frame. The 9.5 gives you a "fisheye" look: what you see through the peephole of a door. Okay, that's it. Now you know everything you need to know about lenses. Almost.

The 300 and the 9.5 are the two extremes. Every other lens does what they do, except less so. If you fully understand what the extremes do, you can easily extrapolate what all the other lenses do. For example, anything shot with a 150mm lens will give you a telephoto look that is half as extreme as a 300. A 100mm produces a medium telephoto or medium long shot. A 75mm is slightly long. A 50mm, as we said, is normal. On the wide-angle end of the spectrum, a 20mm lens gives you a standard wide shot, a 30mm a medium wide shot, and a 40mm a shot more normal than wide. *Now* you know everything about lenses that you need to know. Well, not quite.

Does all this seem like a lot of numbers and abstractions? Why don't I go into more detail and explain just what a 30mm medium wide shot looks like in comparison to a 20mm, standard wide shot? I could, but I would be forcing you to read pages and pages of numbers and abstractions. There is a much better way to learn your lenses: Get hold of a 16mm camera or a digital camera and do all the camerawork on a bunch of films for yourself or your friends. If you hate cameras and don't want to make a fool of yourself trying to play cinematographer, then, at least, get hold of a 35 single lens reflex camera with a 12mm to 125mm zoom lens and shoot a half dozen rolls of film with it, using as many different lens settings as possible. Even the worst technophobe shouldn't be afraid to do this, because if you use a camera with an automatic exposure feature, it takes very little technical expertise to focus the lens. What you shoot may not be in a league with Ansel Adams' work, but most of your pictures will come out, so you won't be flushing

away the developing costs. If you don't want to pay developing costs, you can perform the same experiment using a digital camera that will take a zoom lens. Then
download your images onto your computer. Cull out the misfires and ponder the
keepers. Or if you can get your hands on a mini-DV cam, go out and shoot an
hour's worth of tape. Use the extreme wide angle and telephoto settings half of
the time, and all of the settings in between the other half.

If you do any of the above and study the results, you will give yourself a lesson in
lens selection which is more complete, easier to grasp, and will stay in your brain
longer than anything I could write in this book. Why? For the same reason that
cavemen started drawing on walls: because a picture is worth a thousand words.
By studying the look of what you shot with the long lens and seeing how it differs from normal perspective, and then looking at what you shot with the wide
angle and figuring out just how it differs from normal perspective, you will give
yourself a powerful empirical lesson in how lenses change the perspective and
alter the look of a shot.

If you have no experience with still or motion photography, I would advise doing
the above before you even read further. In any case, if this is your first attempt to
follow in the footsteps of Spielberg, Kubrick, Zemeckis, et al. by mastering lens-
manship, then as soon as you have finished reading this chapter, you must go out
and play around with telephoto and wide lenses. This is the only way to guarantee that you remember the principles of lens selection long enough to use them
when you get your breakthrough directing shot. If you don't pick up on this tip,
then you are bound to forget most of what you read here.

Extreme Telephoto and Extreme Wide-Angle
versus Normal Perspective

Figure 5.1 shows you the normal perspective of a 50mm lens. The girl in the foreground, who is three feet tall (from the waist up), appears shorter than the truck
in the middleground, which is 12 feet tall. The truck appears shorter than the
smokestacks in the background, which are 100 feet tall.

Figure 5.2 shows you the perspective of an extreme wide-angle lens. The girl looks
taller than the truck and the truck looks taller than the smokestacks. This is
because, when seen through an extreme wide-angle lens, foreground objects look
bigger than they do to the naked eye and background objects look smaller.

The wide-angle lens also forces the perspective so that all distances between the
objects in the frame are expanded. The smokestacks in the background look

Figure 5.1

Figure 5.2

Figure 5.3

smaller and further away from the viewer than they would to the naked eye, and the girl looks larger and closer.

Figure 5.3 shows you the perspective of the extreme telephoto lens. The truck has grown in relation to the girl, as have the smokestacks. They all look to be about the same height. Extreme telephoto lenses make both middleground and background objects look larger than they do to the naked eye. Extreme long lens shots radically compress the distance between objects in the frame. The middleground and the background both seem to be squashed together and forced into the foreground.

To get the wide-angle forced perspective look (Figure 5.2) or the telephoto forced perspective look (Figure 5.3), the camera has to be moved in relation to the objects in the frame. To the naked eye, or when seen through a lens with a normal perspective, the girl seems smaller than the truck. To distort the size of the foreground object — the girl — to make it seem larger than the truck or the smokestacks, the camera must be moved closer to it.

Similarly, when using an extreme telephoto lens, the camera must be moved further away from the subject of the shot in order to keep foreground, middleground, and background all in the same frame.

It is important to remember that the camera has to be placed extremely close to the foreground object in order to get a forced perspective wide-angle shot, and a good distance away from the foreground, middleground, and background objects in order to achieve a forced perspective telephoto look. Don't go ahead and draw a storyboard of the shot, or put it down on your shot list, without asking yourself if you can actually position the camera extremely close to or extremely far away from the subject of the shot.

A wide-angle forced perspective shot (Figure 5.2), would be almost impossible to get if the foreground object was a sea otter instead of a girl (and the middleground and background were a boat and an island instead of a truck and some smokestacks). You would need waterproof camera housing and a cameraman in scuba gear to get the shot, and the chances are those items aren't in the budget.

Similarly, if you were shooting on a sound stage you could not compress the girl, the truck, and the smokestacks into the same shot (Figure 5.3), unless you could open the doors to the stage and move the camera a block or two down the street. If there were no doors on the stage, this shot would be impossible to get. Neophyte directors who want to give their films the Spielbergian look often forget to check the exact physical parameters of the location which they will be shooting in, to make sure that the camera can be placed extremely close to or extremely far away from the objects in the shot.

Lenses – Field of Vision
and Depth of Field

In addition to forcing perspective, wide-angle and telephoto lenses alter the look of a shot in two other noticeable and important ways: by affecting the field of vision and the depth of field. That means the lens you use can make what you see through the camera either very restricted and narrow as if you were looking through a tunnel, or very wide and all encompassing, which is the way we see the world through our own eyes. The lens can also keep everything in the frame in sharp focus, or restrict the focus to one narrow plane in the foreground, middleground, or background. Before an aspiring director can become adept at lens selection, he must also understand these two other ways lenses change the look of shot.

An extreme telephoto lens compresses what the camera sees from one side of the frame to the other. It seems to narrow the frame. That's why you can only see about a 20-meter wide section at the back of the parking lot in which these photos were taken (Figure 5.3).

By contrast, the wide-angle lens widens what the camera sees from one side of the fame to the other. Looking through a lens with normal perspective (Figure 5.1), you would be able to see about a 50-meter section of the parking lot running from one edge of the frame to the other. Looking through an extreme wide-angle lens (Figure 5.2), you can see a section almost 100 meters wide through the middle of the parking lot.

With an extreme wide-angle lens, the focus is deep. Usually it encompasses everything in the frame. The image of the girl and the truck are hard-edged and sharp (Figure 5.2). The smokestacks are a little blurry, but this is because this photo was made immediately next to the ocean and there was a lot of moisture in the air. If shot in the desert with this lens, all three objects would be in sharp focus. With a normal lens (Figure 5.1), the foreground is slightly out of focus, whereas the middleground and the background are in focus. With an extreme telephoto lens, the focal plane is squashed and narrow. Figure 5.3 does not give you a good idea of the limitations of the focal plane in most long lens shots, because it was shot in bright daylight with a special split diopter filter, so that the girl, the truck, and the smokestacks would all be in focus. Without the diopter filter and in lower light levels (Figure 5.3a), only one of the three objects — the girl — could be held in sharp focus, while the truck and the smokestacks are a little soft. This is usually the case when using an extremely long lens. You usually have to decide if you want the foreground, the middleground, or the background to be sharp and hard-edged, because ordinarily you can only get one of the three in sharp focus.

Figure 5.3a

General Applications of Different Lenses

The different lenses lend themselves to different dramatic applications. Wide-angle lenses "see more." Their depth of field and their field of vision are greater, which means when you use a wide-angle almost everything in the frame is in focus, and the frame is expanded on the right and left, top and bottom. These properties make the wide-angle the logical choice for an **establishing shot** — the shot that shows the audience everything it needs to know about the place where the scene that follows is going to unfold. When you want to see it all and it's big — whether it is an outdoor location, the exterior of a building, or the interior of a room — and it has a couple or a couple of thousand people in it, then a wide lens, which is to say a 9.5mm up to a 20mm, is the lens of choice.

Telephoto lenses "see less." Their depth of field and their field of vision are limited, which means that when you use a telephoto lens it's as if you were looking through a tunnel. The frame is narrowed on the sides as well as on the top and the bottom. Unless the objects in the frame are very far away from the camera, you can usually only fit one or two of them in the frame. And if those objects are in focus, they will probably be the only objects in the frame in clear focus. Whatever is behind them, as well as whatever is between them and the camera, will be out of focus.

Because telephoto lenses see less, they lend themselves to close-ups and other tight shots of just one or two things. The shot can be tight on something big or small — a car driving down the road, a boat at sea, a runner on a track, a couple on a park bench, a mother hugging her baby, a beautiful girl's face, a hummingbird and a flower, a drop of dew on a leaf. The bigger it is, the further away from the camera it must be, because the lens has such a narrow field of vision. You cannot fit an entire car or boat in a telephoto lens, front and back or bow and stern in the frame, if you are too close to it.

Telephoto lenses are ideal for close-ups and tight shots, not only because it is difficult to fit much more than one object in the frame, but also because the focal properties of these lenses make it unlikely that anything else in the frame, apart from that object, will be in focus. So the lens itself *focuses* all attention on that single object. As explained above, the telephoto has a shallow depth of field. So if the single object in the shot is a car, a girl's face, or a hummingbird, and the lens is focused in on the car, the girl, or the hummingbird, then that object will be the only thing in the shot in sharp focus, no matter whether the object is in the foreground, the middleground, or the background. Everything else will be a little soft or completely fuzzy. The subject of the frame seems to be picked out by the lens. These properties of the longer lenses — those lenses 100mm in length and longer — make them the lens of choice when you want all of the audience's attention focused on just one thing in the frame.

The rule of thumb which states that differences in depth of field and field of vision make wide-angle lenses best for establishing shots and telephoto lenses the lens of choice for tight shots, holds true when it comes to the other most important characteristic of lenses: perspective.

As I stated above, ultrawide-angle lenses distort the image so it ends up looking like what you see through a peephole in a door. Everything seems bowed and bulbous, as if the image was plastered to half a sphere about the size of a soccer ball and then held up to your face. With the camera at eye level, a 12-foot high pillar, two feet wide, right in the middle of the frame, would seem to be just inches wide at the top and the base, but fat, bloated, and about five feet wide in the middle. This is the "fisheye" distortion of an ultrawide, 9.5mm lens.

All lenses on the wide side of the spectrum up to 30mm distort perspective in the same way. These lenses do not flatter the human face or figure. A close-up of a beautiful woman's face with a fisheye lens would make her look like a German sheperd. Her nose would be huge; her ears would be tiny and would appear to be about a foot behind her eyes. That is the extreme example, but all wide lenses have a hint of this same distortion and so should be avoided for close-ups of people, in particular, and anything else that would not be flattered by being made to look more rounded.

On the other hand, the **compressed perspective** of a telephoto lens — the way that it seems to marry the foreground, middleground, and background so all focal planes seem to be on top of each other — actually makes objects in the camera look thinner than they do to the naked eye. Telephoto lenses diminish depth and therefore bulk. Because of this effect, these lenses lend themselves to close-ups and tight shots of the human face and body and anything else except something which might look better if it were plumper or bulkier — like a tomato, a tank, or a wrestler.

The **expanded, rounded perspective** of the wider lenses lends itself to that which is geographical and architectural. Big, wide-open exterior spaces — vistas, if you will — are made to look more like vistas by the rounded distortion of the ultrawide lenses. The fisheye distortion bends the horizon and curves the lines of perspective, but most people actually find this look pleasing — perhaps because it suggests the curve of the earth. The fisheye look has become a sort of visual shorthand that says "big."

Buildings and interior spaces — courtyards, rooms, etc. — take on added depth when shot with a wide lens. A 50mm lens with its "normal" perspective lends no distortion to interior spaces, but this can actually make such spaces appear slightly cramped and smaller than they are in reality. The wider lenses, with their more rounded perspective, seem to open interiors up and make them more livable and attractive. An ultrawide lens gives a noticeable curve to all the architectural lines of a room or building. But this fisheye distortion is interesting and actually calls attention to that which is pleasing in the configuration of the lines in the space.

Some may disagree with all the above. These are purely aesthetic judgments, and so strictly a matter of taste. But almost all of the DPs whom I have worked with would tell you that wide lenses are best for wide, establishing shots and telephoto lenses are better for tight shots and close-ups. And the chances are they would back this up by citing the reasons given above.

Most of the shots that fall in between establishing shots and close-ups are medium shots that are best shot with 35mm to 65mm lenses. These shots and these lenses don't make much of a statement one way or the other. For this reason, I don't pre-occupy myself with them. If I am going to try to enhance the look of my film by using a specific lens, I focus my energies on those lenses that have the greatest impact: the wide and ultrawide, the telephoto and extreme telephoto. When you get your breakthrough gig, I would advise you to do the same. You can count yourself as lucky if you find the time and energy to even do that.

Forced Perspective Made Easy

Okay, you still don't quite get it. You hated geometry in high school. You're an artist not an engineer, and besides, all these numbers and words used to describe how things look just put you sleep. Well, I have come up with a formula which gives you an easy way to remember just how telephoto and wide-angle lenses change the way things look on film. I cooked this up because, even though I liked trigonometry and played cinematographer for my friends in film school, sometimes I get a little muddle-headed on the set. Such brain-lock is understandable, given the level of stress on the sort of day-late-dollar-short production that takes a chance on a first time director.

So here's the little cheat sheet that I carry around in my brain: coolie hat, mega-phone, fluorescent tube. That's it. The most important ways that lenses distort perspective is encapsulated in the physical properties of those three objects. Just picture those three things in your head or see Figure 5.4, if you're having trouble. The coolie hat is very wide at the brim and tapers down to point. It is a perfect cone. The megaphone is like the ones still used by cheerleaders at college and high school football games. It also is cone shaped, but the cone is open at the top — where the cheerleader puts his mouth. At the wide end, where the sound comes out, it is narrower than the wide brim of the coolie hat. The megaphone is longer

Figure 5.4

than the coolie hat, so if you put them side by side on the ground, the megaphone would stand much taller. Now the fluorescent tube pictured in the drawing has to be a long one — say, eight feet. It would have to be the kind used in factories and offices. So it is longer or taller than the megaphone, and much longer or taller than the coolie hat. Unlike the coolie hat and the megaphone, the tube is tubular and not cone-shaped. From one end to the other, it is about as wide across as the mouth of the megaphone.

Just for the sake of argument, let's say all three — coolie hat, megaphone, and fluorescent tube — have the same volume. In other words, if you filled them with air or water or any other stuff (sand or bee-bees), they would hold the same amount.

Now let's go back to the three cows in the pasture — the ones we used at the beginning of this chapter to explain normal perspective. Even though all three cows are the same size, they seem to get smaller the further away they are from you. This is how the naked eye, or a lens with a normal perspective, would alter their appearance. These cows would fit into the megaphone (Figure 5.5 – page 116). Well, not really, but if they were the "stuff" that was going into your shot, and you were using a 50mm or a normal perspective lens, then the cow in the foreground would be the largest, the cow in the middleground the second largest, and the cow in the background the smallest. They are diminished in size by the normal perspective lens in the same proportions as the megaphone.

If you were to shoot the three cows with an ultrawide-angle lens, you would first move the camera very close to the closest cow, and then the lens would diminish the cows in size in the same way that the coolie hat diminishes in size from the brim to the point (Figure 5.6). This is how the cows would fit into the frame of a shot using the wide-angle lens. The closest cow would be by far the biggest — much bigger in proportion to the other two cows compared to how it looks through a lens with a normal perspective —whereas the cow furthest away in the point of the coolie hat would be tiny compared to the way it looks "normally."

If you were to shoot the three cows with an extreme telephoto lens (you would do it from a camera position much further away from the cows than the position used to recreate a normal perspective), then the cows would seem to fit into the fluorescent tube (Figure 5.7) since all three would seem to be about the same size. This is because, as was explained, background *and* middleground objects seem larger in relation to what is in the foreground of an extreme telephoto shot.

So there it is. Coolie hat, megaphone, fluorescent tube — lens selection for dummies. But the most elegant thing about this simplification of the properties of wide-angle and telephoto lenses is that it holds true for the way in which these lenses alter spatial relationships, distances, and therefore movement in the frame.

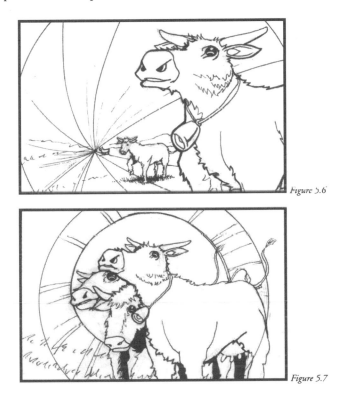

Figure 5.6

Figure 5.7

Film is movement. The effect of lenses on movement in the frame is the most important part of the role they can play in shaping the look of your film. If a shot is not static — if there is movement in a shot — when selecting the right lens for that shot, you have to give the greatest weight to how that lens will affect the look of the movement. This is because, if you are watching a film, your eye focuses on and follows whatever is moving in the frame. You may be looking at the whole frame, but what your brain really sees is that which is moving.

How Lenses Affect Movement

I have saved explaining how lenses affect movement in the frame until now, because my coolie hat-megaphone-fluorescent tube rule makes this important visual tool easy to understand and remember. Let's go back to the three cows stuffed into the megaphone (Figure 5.5.) This is how they would look to the naked eye or through a lens with a normal perspective. If a hawk were to fly into the frame, fly by the cow in the background, and then fly up to the cow in the foreground, its movement would seem normal — the same way it does to the naked eye (Figure 5.8).

Now if the hawk were to make the same maneuver in the coolie hat, its movement would be accelerated by the lens. The hawk is actually covering the same distance at the same pace, in the same amount of time. But, because of the distortion of the extreme wide-angle, as the hawk travels from the background to the foreground, it will go from being very tiny to being very large (Figure 5.9). As it passes through the foreground and out of frame by the camera, it will seem to explode in size and then vanish.

The ability of the wide-angle lenses to exaggerate motion from background to foreground is one of their most useful and vivid properties. This makes the wide-angle a lens of choice when shooting action sequences. Remember that the coolie hat is shorter than the megaphone. Therefore, movement from the tip of the coolie hat to the open end is going to seem much more rapid than movement from the narrow end of the megaphone to the wide end.

If the hawk were to make the same maneuver in the fluorescent tube, its movement would be slowed down by the extreme telephoto lens. Because of the distortion of an extreme telephoto lens, the three cows in the fluorescent tube seem to be about the same size (Figure 5.7). So as the hawk flies from the cow in the background to the cow in the foreground (Figure 5.10), it will not seem to grow much in size. Again, it is covering the same distance at the same pace, but because its image in the frame grows imperceptibly, it doesn't seem to make much progress. Its motion in the frame is slowed. Even though its wings are flapping, it seems to hang in the same spot.

Figure 5.7

Figure 5.8

Figure 5.9

Figure 5.10

This is how the extreme telephoto shot produces the classic shot mentioned earlier: the rider coming at the camera across the desert as the heat wavers up through the frame. The rider rides and rides but he doesn't seem to get anywhere — because the telephoto lens diminishes progress, and so seems to slow motion. This is why the fluorescent tube is much longer than the megaphone. Movement from one end of the fluorescent tube to the other is going to seem to take longer and be slower than normal — normal being the appearance of movement from the narrow end of the megaphone to the wide end.

Remember, even though distance between the foreground and the background has been diminished by the telephoto lens, it seems to take longer to get from one end of the fluorescent tube to the other because movement has also been *diminished* and, as a result, progress has seemingly slowed down. So the hawk flying from the cow in the background to the cow in the foreground (Figure 5.10) seems to be in the same place, but when viewed from an angle perpendicular to the camera (Figure 5.11) — a side view, if you will — it is actually making progress.

Similarly, the hawk moving from the background cow to the foreground cow in the coolie hat (Figure 5.9) is covering the same distance as the hawk in the megaphone or the fluorescent tube. The side view (Figure 5.11) is a representation of its movement not only in the fluorescent tube, but also in the coolie hat and the megaphone. But the hawk will seem to cover ground much more rapidly in the coolie hat because of the way the wide-angle lens distorts its size and the size of everything around it. It will explode in size in the lens as it moves into the foreground, because, when seen through an extreme wide-angle lens, foreground objects are made enormous and background objects tiny. This distortion of size actually seems to *expand* distances in the wide-angle, even though paradoxically, those expanded distances can seemingly be crossed more rapidly. The coolie hat represents the extreme wide-angle, because it is short and can be seemingly crossed rapidly, but any cow in the tip of the coolie hat will be tiny in comparison to the cow at the base, and so seem to be much further away.

Figure 5.11

If these seemingly contradictory properties of the extreme lenses have got you a little dazed and confused, a surefire remedy is at hand. Pick up that mini-DV camera and go out and replicate the examples of the cows and the hawk. The easiest way to do this is to tape a friend of yours riding a bicycle toward the camera down the sidewalk next to a row of cars parked at the curb. The parked cars will stand in for the cows and the bike for the hawk. Have your friend ride towards you once and shoot him with the zoom lens at the widest setting. Make sure that he rides the bike right up to where you are with the camera and comes as close as possible to hitting the lens without actually doing so. This is necessary because the property of the wide-angle lens that enables it to make motion in the frame seem more rapid *increases* the closer the moving object gets to the lens. If you do it right, the bike should go from looking very tiny in the lens to very large as it passes by the lens. In this way it would represent the rapid movement of the hawk from background to foreground in the coolie hat or when seen through a wide-angle lens.

Next, zoom the lens in to its most telephoto setting. If your camera has a doubler feature to make the lens setting twice as telephoto, then engage the doubler feature. Have your friend sit on the bike exactly where you were stationed with the camera when you taped him using the wide-angle setting. Walk away from him down the sidewalk until when you look through the camera back at him seated on the bike he fills the frame from top to bottom. This is your second camera position. Have your friend on the bike note where he is on the sidewalk and tell him that is his end mark. Then have him go back to where he started the first time and ride the bike down the sidewalk towards you until he hits his end mark. (Because of the narrow depth of field of a telephoto lens, your friend may be out of focus at the beginning or the end of his ride.) This should approximate the prolonged, seemingly slower movement of the hawk in the fluorescent tube or when seen through a telephoto lens.

Last, repeat the experiment a third time. You should do the taping halfway between the first camera position and the second camera position. Your friend on the bike should start where he has always started and stop on the same final mark. Tape him with the zoom on the camera set halfway in between fully zoomed out and fully zoomed in. This should represent the movement of the hawk in the megaphone or when seen through a lens that approximates normal perspective.

A picture is worth a thousand words, and once you have something of yourself invested in those pictures, the way they have been altered by the extreme lenses will start to have meaning for you. Look over the results of your friend riding his bicycle towards the camera taped at the widest lens setting, the most telephoto, and the one in between, and apply the logic of the three cows in the coolie hat, fluorescent tube, and megaphone. In the end you should have a very effective tool for remembering how the properties of wide-angle and telephoto lenses affect movement in the frame. Yes, film is indeed movement. By altering the way movement appears in the frame, lenses offer a director yet another way to shape the medium of film to meet his artistic ends. So start now and learn your lenses if you want to become a filmmaker in the fullest sense.

CHAPTER 5 | SUMMARY POINTS

■ The best rule of thumb on the set of your first feature is to force perspective whenever possible, so your films come up to the visual standard set by Spielberg. But, like Spielberg, Zemeckis, and others, make sure that such cinematographic enhancements always serve the story, and so remain invisible.

■ You should understand the basics of lens selection in order to control the look of your movie.

■ Leave the lens selection up to the DP on all shots except those that call out for a forced perspective or some other very specific look. Have the DP take ownership of the film. He will do a better job if he feels like it's *his* canvas. But know your lenses so you can talk to him and guide him while he paints. This way the picture will come out looking the way you envisioned it.

■ Lens selection is easy because, to the extent to which you need to master it in order to succeed as a director, you only have to fully understand two visual concepts: how "normal perspective" is altered by 1) a telephoto or "long" lens and 2) a wide-angle lens.

■ Unless some unusual aspect of the story demands it, the longest lens you would ever have occasion to use is a 300mm, and the widest lens is a 9.5mm. A 300mm gives you an ultra-telephoto look. The 9.5 gives you a fisheye look. The 300 and the 9.5 are the two extremes. Every other lens does what they do, except less so. If you fully understand what the extremes do, you can easily extrapolate what all the other lenses do.

■ When seen through an extreme wide-angle lens, foreground objects look bigger than they do to the naked eye and background objects look smaller. The wide-angle lens also forces the perspective so that all distances between the objects in the frame are expanded. In addition, the field of vision is widened so the camera sees more from one side of the frame to the other. With an extreme wide-angle lens, the focus is deep. Usually it encompasses everything in the frame. Wide-angle lenses "see more."

■ Extreme telephoto lenses make both middleground and background objects look larger than they do to the naked eye. Extreme long-lens shots radically compress the distance between objects in the frame. The middleground and the background both seem to be squashed together and forced into the foreground. In addition, the long lens compresses the field of vision so the camera sees less from one side of the frame to the other. The focal plane is shallow, so only one part of the frame — background, middleground, or fore-ground — is in sharp focus. Therefore, extreme telephoto lenses "see less."

- To get the wide-angle forced perspective look of Figure 5.2 or the telephoto forced perspective look of Figure 5.3, the camera has to be moved in relation to the objects in the frame: closer for the wide-angle look and further away for the telephoto look.

- The expanded, rounded perspective of the wide lenses lends itself to that which is geographical and architectural. Big, wide-open exterior spaces — vistas, if you will — are made to look more like vistas by the rounded dis-tortion of the ultrawide lenses. Buildings and interior spaces — courtyards, rooms, etc. — take on added depth and seem more spacious and habitable when shot with a wide lens.

- Telephoto lenses diminish depth and therefore bulk. Because of this effect, these lenses lend themselves to close-ups and tight shots of the human face and body.

- Film is movement. By altering the way movement appears in the frame, lens-es offer a director yet another way to shape the medium of film to meet his artistic ends. Learn your lenses if you want to become a filmmaker in the fullest sense.

- If there is movement in a shot, then in order to select the right lens for that shot, you have to give the greatest weight to how that lens will affect the look of the movement.

- As soon as you have finished reading this chapter, you must go out and play around with telephoto and wide lenses and a camera. This is the only way to guarantee that you remember the principles of lens selection long enough to use them when you get your breakthrough directing assignment.

PART THREE:
PERFORMANCE

CHAPTER 6 | DIRECTING ACTORS – IT TAKES ERUDITION AND INTUITION

Directing actors is a demanding, specialized skill. When a director turns from his producer or his cinematographer to his actors, he has to put on a very different hat. With the producer and the higher-ups, the director must be politically adept, diplomatic, and at times cunning. Working with the cinematographer will challenge the first time director on a technical, mathematical, and aesthetic level. To get his actors to do their best work, the director will use some of the people skills that will serve him well with the producer and anyone else on the crew. Few directors who are not natural leaders have much success.

But it takes more than leadership or people skills to be a good director of actors. You also have to be a great student of human nature. Directing actors requires a very specific understanding of how human beings act and react emotionally to each other and to different sensual stimuli. To be a good actor or the kind of director who can help an actor, you must have an astute instinctive or intellectual understanding of what exactly sparks the entire gamut of human emotions. One would think that anybody with an advanced degree in psychology would have this understanding. Yet it takes more than a grasp of a psychological understanding of exactly what triggers different human emotions. My belief is that the one ability required to be a good director of actors is a good instinctive or intellectual awareness of one's own emotions and what triggers them. In my experience, this is what the director comes back to again and again in helping actors prepare for their roles.

Almost all actors in America are trained in the Method. If a director is going to help a Method actor, he has to help the actor come as close as possible to actually experiencing the feelings that the character the actor is portraying should be experiencing at any particular moment in the character's development in the drama. In other words, the actor cannot be acting. As much as he can, the actor has to actually be experiencing the feelings appropriate to the character he is portraying. In *The Godfather*, when Sonny Corleone (James Caan) is machine-gunned to death and Don Corleone (Marlon Brando) visits the morgue and weeps at the sight of his dead son, Brando is not weeping because he is trying to *act* sad. Brando, as a great practitioner of the Method, is not *acting*. He is actually transfused with real grief, to the point of tears.

If the Method actor is having trouble crying, a good director of actors must reference that which in his own life makes him cry. He then has to describe to the actor that which moves him, the director, to tears in terms that the actor can understand and use to move himself to the point of tears. Therefore, in addition to an understanding of what triggers all his own feelings, the good director of actors has to have the ability to translate that understanding into language that a Method actor can employ to summon up all of those feelings in himself. A great part of being a good director of actors comes from being able to use language effectively — not necessarily grammatically, but clearly. The kind of language that helps an actor can be grammatically incorrect, slang, or semi-literate. But it must provide the actor with a clear pathway to achieving specific behaviors in himself.

To help an actor evoke specific feelings in himself, you have to have a very special kind of understanding of what evokes those same feelings in yourself. Although this kind of understanding cannot be taught, what can be taught is the ability to translate what understanding you do possess into language that an actor can use to evoke those feelings in himself.

Judith Weston's book, *Directing Actors*, will teach you almost everything that you would ever need to know about directing actors. There are many other good books on this subject, such as Harold Clurman's *On Directing*, and a forthcoming book, *Friendly Enemies: Maximizing the Director-Actor Relationship*, from Delia Salvi, a world-renowned teacher of directing actors who is a professor in the film school at UCLA. If the first time director is serious about getting the best performances out of his actors on his breakthrough project, he must read one of these books cover to cover. He must have a full and subtle understanding of the acting process and everything a director can do to help an actor, if he is going to win the complete trust of his actors, and if he is going to be able to do everything that he possibly can to help them give their best performances.

On your breakthrough project you inevitably will end up having to work with some actors who cannot consistently deliver a credible performance. If you are not paying your actors, this is absolutely guaranteed. If you are paying your actors out of a budget that has been severely compromised because you are a first time director, then it is highly likely. In either case, you have to be able to help these actors deliver a credible performance. It is never easy to do. On the set of your day-late-dollar-short production, you will probably be working under immense pressure. Because you will be working with second-rate equipment and an inexperienced crew, things will be constantly going wrong. Then, all of a sudden, on top of all that, out comes a performance that fools no one. If the actor who fools no one is playing Vito Corleone viewing the bullet-riddled body of his eldest son, he will be trying very hard to appear to be grief-stricken to the point of tears. He will be **indicating** that he is grief-stricken to the point of tears ("indicating" being the conventional term used to describe a performance that does not seem real), but it is evident that the actor is not feeling any real grief, or certainly not as much as the story calls for. This performance could come out of the lips of an actor who was excellent in all of the many rehearsals you had. But more likely than not, this unbelievable performance will be delivered by an actor who in the first couple of quick rehearsals you have had on the set has been unable to convince you that he was having the feelings that he should be having to play his part, and you have just been too distracted by the general chaos around you to come up with a solution. But now you must, or this mediocre performance will, by itself, render everything else that is being done on the set at the same time useless.

This goes back to everything that I said in Chapter 2 about content. Content *is* everything, and the performances and the story make up the content. If the actor who is playing Vito Corleone is trying to act as if he is grief-stricken to the point of tears and the audience watching the finished film can tell that he is acting — if his emotions seem the slightest bit feigned or lacking authenticity — then the all-important spell that you are putting the audience under is broken. If this actually happened on the set of *The Godfather*, if when Brando had to be moved to point of tears his performance had lacked credibility, then all the time and effort expended to put that scene on film, every dime spent on film, equipment, costumes, props, sets, cast, and crew would have been for naught. Unless the director can help the actor make his mediocre performance believable, then he might as well not even run the film through the camera.

There is one other absolutely essential task that a first time director must undertake: Take an acting class. This may be extremely difficult and run against your basic nature, but you must do it. It will take time, so starting tomorrow you must find and enroll in an introductory level class. You must study acting until you are competent enough to get yourself cast in a significant part in a professional quality production that ends up on tape or film. True, some working directors of the first rank have never done this, but they would be better directors of actors if they did it, and they know it. Trying to help an actor improve his performance if you have never acted is like trying to teach someone how to swim when you cannot swim. It would be like trying to help a golfer improve his swing when you have never hit a golf ball. If you have never stood in an actor's shoes and gone out in front of a camera and crew on a working set and tried to deliver a performance, then you have no idea what the actor is up against, and you are not fully prepared to help him overcome the obstacles that he encounters.

In fact, in the process of working as an actor, you must experience an actor's hell. More than once, and the more times the better, you actually must sink into the deepest hole that an actor can sink into, and have a director help you out of it. You must personally experience that moment described above when the director says "Action" and the actor opens his mouth and out comes a performance that fools nobody. But in this case, the actor should be you. And after this initial moment of failure it should get worse and worse, with you and the director trying everything to improve your performance, but repeatedly failing. Ideally, you should be on the verge of complete emotional collapse, and then something the director tells you clicks, and suddenly your performance comes to life. The more times you, yourself, go through that actor's hell and receive a piece of direction that snaps you out of your paralysis and makes your acting fresh, the better prepared you will be to deliver that kind of performance-saving direction for your actors.

Historically in Hollywood, actors have been relegated to the status of second-class citizens. The rap against actors is that they are all children. When I was at Universal Studios in the late '70s, the dean of all television directors was Virgil Vogel. At that time, he was directing many hours of a miniseries, *Centennial*, based on the novel of the same name by James Michener. You could not land a much more prestigious TV directing gig than *Centennial*. Virgil Vogel was famous for saying "All I say to actors is 'Action.'" This is not right. No working director should be allowed to trumpet that kind of disregard and disrespect for actors and their craft.

But directors have historically gotten away with it. In fact, so many directors use the cop-out excuse, "I don't give acting lessons on the set," it has become a cliché. There are many reasons for this. The Hollywood set has long been one of the most macho environments in the world, and — the feminist revolution notwithstanding — it still is. (Many of the women in Hollywood today survive by just being more macho than the men.) Most actors are not very macho. Being able to act macho should not be confused with being macho. Acting is not a macho endeavor. It demands sensitivity and emotional nakedness, hence the disrespect for actors and acting among the macho crowd.

In addition, Hollywood has long been a place where money and technology were the tools of choice. True artistry is usually thought of as a sort of backup, at least by the "suits." Better if you have got it, but, bottom line, it's not essential. Few would deny that the film business in this country has always been a business first. Businessmen are not inclined to depend on artistry to ensure the quality of their products. They would much rather rely on money and technology. Acting is commonly referred to as a craft, but to me this seems to be misnomer. It is much more an art.

Unfortunately, as time has gone on, the film business has come to depend more and more on money and technology to deliver quality in film. The big budget, heavy-on-special-effects films which are favored by the major studios today are driven by money and technology, and those directors most proficient at handling the money and technology are the most successful and the most in demand. Powerful agencies have reinforced the system whereby quality in acting is guaranteed by money, with the best actors going to the highest bidders. In many instances, a director's responsibility toward the actors now hardly extends beyond casting. Once a director is on the set, most of his energy and creativity will be sucked into mastering the complex technology, and the actors will be left on their own. All of this has reinforced the perception among aspiring directors that to succeed in the industry today they do not have to be an especially proficient director of actors. They do not have to understand actors and their craft. If they want an actor to be happy, they can tell him to act happy, and they expect that such direction will suffice.

True, you could get away with this attitude if your breakthrough gig was a major studio film. But unless you are a film star or a top-tier screenwriter, your breakthrough will be a day-late-and-dollar-short production. Even if you are a hot young thing and you land a moderate budget indie film for your breakthrough and you get to cast second-tier, name actors as your principals, your indie producers are going to expect you to get performances out of them that are every bit as brilliant as what Meryl Streep or Jack Nicholson would deliver for a hefty chunk of the budget. Chances are you are going to have to work with an actor who seemingly cannot deliver a credible performance, and enable him to do so, perhaps for the first time in his life. Or you are going to have to be able to help your cast morph their very good performances into great or near great performances. You are going to be handicapped in your efforts to do this unless you have studied acting and worked as an actor. The last thing you want to do is admit is that out of fear of embarrassing yourself in an acting class, you did not acquire the skills that you must possess to get the best out of every actor.

Breaking Down the Script
Step One: The Spine of the Film – The Spine of the Characters

Because in all likelihood you will have no rehearsal time with your actors and because the only opportunity you will have to improve a weak performance will be between the first run-through on the set for the camera and the time the set is lit, you must over-prepare to help your actors. The only way you can come to the set armed with all the silver bullets you will need to kill all the bad performances you might encounter in the course of a day's work is to anticipate that every performance will be a disaster. There is no way you can foretell exactly what line in what scene is going to be the little trapdoor which is going to drop one of your actors into actor's hell. Nor can you accurately predict which of your cast is going to be the victim. Your best, most reliable actor can get spooked and have a horrible day, or hit a losing streak and be consistently unable to deliver a credible performance. Actors must work with emotions and emotions are not necessarily predictable. Therefore the director must come prepared for every contingency. If you get lazy and do not fully prepare, and it turns out that inconsistent performances prevented your first real directing job from becoming your breakthrough, then you will have only yourself to blame. Being a good director requires much hard work. Like most creative endeavors, it is 90% perspiration and 10 % inspiration.

This kind of thorough preparation requires that you come to the set prepared to fix every line in the script. This is not overkill because one bad line uttered by one actor and the spell is broken. To come up with the right direction to fix every line, you must analyze the script from the top down, in detail, before you start shooting and/or rehearsing. You need to understand the big picture concerns first: what message the film as a whole is trying to convey. Only then will you understand how each character's part in the drama advances that central idea. You must arrive at that understanding before you are ready to shape that actor's performance, line by line.

All the gurus of directing actors agree on this. Harold Clurman states that the first and most important step in a director's preparation is to determine "the spine" of the piece he is directing. According to Clurman, Constantin Stanislavsky, the granddaddy of the Method, called it "the superproblem." I follow Clurman and call it the **spine of the film**, but I find it helpful when trying to identify it, to think of it as the **theme**. Every moment in every good film reinforces one central idea. This is, in effect, the theme of the film. In *The Godfather*, the central idea is that "for all Corleones, the Corleone crime family comes first." In *Cast Away*, the theme or spine would be that "to survive you have to adapt." All of the film *American Beauty* supports the concept that "to find fulfillment in life you must be true to yourself." *Back to the Future* says, above all else, "if you believe in yourself you can do anything." In *Crimson Tide* the theme is a bit more complex, but I would say that it is "in the nuclear age a thinking warrior is better than a fighting warrior." The actual words you use to describe the spine are not that important. What is important is that those words accurately identify what, above all else, the film is about.

The first time director has to determine what the spine of his breakthrough project is for reasons far more important then preparing to help his actors with their performances. If he does not make this determination, the film will lack coherence. He has to know exactly what he is trying to say in the film before he can make an informed decision about how to best go about saying it. Once he has decided what the theme or the spine is, it will color and influence every decision he makes about every aspect of the film. It will inform how he casts the film and how he rewrites the script, and, in that, it will give the final shape to the most important component of the film: its content. It will also be the key factor in determining the look of the film and so will influence his choice of cinematographer, film stock, lighting style, lenses, camera movement, graphic effects, art director, art direction, locations, set dressing, props and so forth. The list is endless, but every detail in the finished film should contribute to a more effective articulation and validation of the theme of the film. And so the first time director, before he makes any one of the millions of decisions he will make to put his mark on his breakthrough project, must determine precisely what the spine or the theme of the film is. This determination will color every other decision he makes.

Once the spine of the entire project has been arrived at, the director can move on to decide how each character in the film works to support that central spine. That which defines an individual's behavior is what he wants out of life: his goal, the end to which all of his actions are directed. Almost all teachers and practitioners of The Method call this the **spine of the character**. In a well-written script each character has a specific central need. It is what he wants more than anything else. It informs all his behavior. His moods may shift. The tactics he chooses to satisfy that defining need may change and even contradict each other. But in the final analysis, it is clear that everything he does throughout the course of the film is to achieve this objective.

Perhaps one of the best written, self-contradictory characters in the history of cinema is the main character of *Casablanca*, Rick — unforgettably portrayed by Humphrey Bogart. Throughout much of the film, Rick seems like a bitter, disillusioned man. He says he "sticks his neck out for no man." Many of his actions seem to support this claim. But we learn that before the war Rick ran guns to the Ethiopians, who were desperately trying to defend themselves against the cruel and opportunistic Italian invasions led by Mussolini. And when the Nazis who patronize his nightclub drown out everyone else in the club by singing chauvinistic songs in German, he tells his bandleader to play the egalitarian French national anthem, *La Marseillaise.*

Rick is clearly a man at odds with himself. When his old lover Ilsa (Ingrid Bergman) walks into his nightclub with her husband, the freedom fighter, Victor Lazlo, Rick goes on a drinking binge which ends with him bitterly denouncing her and their weeks of bliss together in Paris before the war. Rick is terminally angry at Ilsa because she mysteriously and suddenly abandoned him. But between the lines it is easy to see that the person who Rick hates most is himself. Ilsa has come to Casablanca with Victor to try to escape the Nazis. Ironically, it turns out that the key to their freedom lies with Rick, because, by chance, he has come into possession of two letters of transit to Portugal. With these letters of transit in hand, Victor and Ilsa can escape. Ilsa now approaches Rick to beg for the letters. He attempts to selfishly manipulate the situation to win Ilsa back for himself. It becomes obvious that her love for him never died and she breaks down and agrees to abandon Victor and leave Casablanca with Rick. Then, in the final scene at the airport, Rick unexpectedly gives the letters of transit to Victor and Ilsa. Finally, he assures their successful escape by killing the commandant of the Nazi garrison as he attempts to prevent Lazlo from boarding the plane to Lisbon.

Rick seems truly all over the map with his feelings and actions. By turns he is bitter and romantic, heartless and compassionate, degenerate and noble, selfish and self-sacrificing. But on closer examination, it becomes clear that all of his moods and actions are driven by his need *to find out if Ilsa really loves him* — because if he finds out that she does, he can *believe in himself again*. Either of these motivations could be used as the spine of Rick's character. When Ilsa, the one love of his life, seemed to walk out on him and their love, Rick lost faith in himself. He came to see himself in a negative, self-loathing light. This drives him to verbally denounce all of the high-minded principles he truly believes in, while — intermittently, through his actions — he stands up for the underdog and does the right thing. He actually uses the letters of transit in a manipulative and seemingly self-serving way to break Ilsa down and make her confess that she loves him more than Lazlo. Ironically, by winning Ilsa back, Rick regains his sense of self-worth and acquires the strength to let her go. In this, Rick re-embraces the noble agenda that he once lived by.

In the film *Crimson Tide*, the commanding officer on the U.S.S. Alabama, Captain Ramsey (Gene Hackman), demands 100 % loyalty and subservience from everyone under his command. The spine of Ramsey's character is *to be obeyed*. His second in command, Lieutenant Commander Hunter's (Denzel Washington) actions are driven by his overwhelming desire *to use his superior intelligence to determine the best course of action*. Hunter is the sort of super-smart, take-charge guy who thinks he is always right and that everyone should do what he says. When the screenwriter, Michael Schiffer, wrote *Crimson Tide*, he must have quite deliberately shaped the character of Hunter so that Hunter would be driven by his need to use his superior brain power to guide those around him. No doubt, Schiffer just as deliberately shaped the character of Ramsey so that Ramsey would be obsessed by being obeyed by everyone under his command — because this is a perfect recipe for a titanic conflict. Conflict is the essence of drama. Schiffer is a talented screenwriter; to drive the drama and the story of *Crimson Tide* he concocted these two main characters who, from the minute they stepped onto the same boat, are destined to end up at each other's throat.

When the first time director, in preparation for helping his actors, seeks to identify the central desire that drives each of the characters, he is not imposing some sort of arbitrary structure on the story. He is merely identifying the organizing principles of good drama that the screenwriter, in his wisdom, used to shape the screenplay.

What motivates all of a character's actions is always a goal — the end towards which he is constantly working. The only way to reach the goal is through action. Therefore all character spines are verbs. They describe what the character systematically does to reach his goal. Nick in *Casablanca* wants *to regain faith in himself*. Hunter in *Crimson Tide* wants *to use his superior intelligence to determine the right course*. Ramsey in *Crimson Tide* wants *to be obeyed*. Marty in *Back to the Future* wants *to get back to the future*. The other main character in *Back to the Future*, Doc Brown, wants *to prove that he is a great inventor*.

The Actor's Objective – An Overview

In his essay, "The Principles of Integration," Harold Clurman concludes an explanation of how to determine the spine of a character by stating, "Since drama is action, it is better that these basic motivations or spines be stated in the form of a verb: the desire is an action; the things it prompts the character to do are further actions." This is the logic on which the most fundamental idea of the Method is based — the idea that the actor's role is made up, not of lines of dialogue or a pattern of behaviors, but a series of **actions or objectives**.

The first time director need not be overly concerned with the logical viability of the principles underlying the Method. What he should stay focused on is the fact that the best way a director can help his actors improve their performances is by providing them with **playable objectives** that work for them. In my experience, I always found good objectives to be the most effective tool at a director's disposal for fixing performances. Sandy Meisner, one of the most respected practitioners and teachers of the Method, also trumpets good objectives as the key to achieving good performances.

After the first time director has locked down the spine of his project and determined the spine of each character, he is ready to begin the most important phase of his preparation for directing his actors: breaking each actor's performance down into good playable objectives.

Here is how Clurman lays it out: "How do you determine an actor's objective? Ask yourself, bottom line, what it is that the character wants. When a character enters a scene everything he says and does has to be driven by a fundamental want. What he wants is his objective. What he wants — his objective — is going to motivate him and drive him until he succeeds in getting what he wants, in which case his needs will shift, he will want something different, and at that point he will have a new objective. Or he could be thwarted by circumstances or another character's wants (in which case we have conflict and drama) and be forced to give up that initial want.

As soon as he gives up, a new want will take the place of the old want and he will have a new objective. Each time the character changes objectives, the beat changes."

In *Back to the Future*, the main character, Marty McFly, is accidentally transported back to 1955 in a time machine invented by his best friend, the eccentric town inventor, Doc Brown. The trip back to 1955 expends all the fuel in the time machine, so Marty is essentially a kid from 1983, trapped in 1955. He wants to get back to his life in 1983, and figures that the only person in town who can help him get the time machine working again is Doc Brown. He goes to Doc Brown's house and knocks on the door (Figure 6.1 – page 153). The following scene then takes place:

EXT.   DR. BROWN'S HOUSE — NIGHT

The house at 1640 Riverside Drive is huge, beautiful.
Marty checks the address against the phone book page: It matches.

He recognizes the garage as the same one as we saw in 1985, except
in much better shape. (In 1985, the house has been torn down and
a fast food stand put up.

Marty rushes to the front door of the house.

EXT.   BROWN'S FRONT DOOR — CLOSER ANGLE

Marty runs up and pounds on the door knocker.

We hear a BARKING DOG from within; then YOUNG DOCTOR BROWN opens
the door. He's wearing an OUTRAGEOUS CONTRAPTION on his head, a
bizarre conglomeration of vacuum tubes, rheostats, gauges, wiring
and antennas; but there can be no doubt it's the same Dr. Brown,
some 30 years younger. Beside him is another DOG.

Marty stares at Brown's weird head gear. Brown yanks him inside.

INT.   BROWN'S HOUSE — NIGHT

                            BROWN
                  Don't say a word!
                       (to the barking dog)
                  Quiet, Copernicus! Down, boy!

Brown attaches a suction cup to Marty's forehead which is con-
nected to a wire into Brown's contraption.

                         MARTY
          Dr. Brown, I really---

                          BROWN
          No, don't tell me anything: I'm
          going to read your thoughts.

Marty indulges him.   Brown flips a switch on his "Brain Wave
Analyzer." Tubes hum to life, and sparks jump up from antenna to
antenna.   Brown concentrates, as if he's picking up brain waves.

                          BROWN
          Let's see now...you've come here...
          From a great distance....

Marty nods, wondering if maybe the thing does work.

                         BROWN (continuing)
          ...because you...want me...to buy a
          subscription to Saturday Evening
          Post!

                         MARTY
          No---

                         BROWN
          Don't tell me!
                  (takes another moment)
          Donations! You're collecting donations
          For the Coast Guard Youth Auxiliary!

                         MARTY
          No.

                          BROWN
          Are you here because you want to use
          the bathroom?

                         MARTY
          Dr. Brown, listen: I'm from the
          Future. I came here in a time
          machine you invented---and now I
          desperately need you to help me get
          back to the year 1985.

Brown stares at him in utter amazement for a moment.

> BROWN
> My God. Do you know what this means?

He pauses dramatically, then removes the contraption from his head.

> BROWN
> That means that this damned thing
> doesn't work at all.
> (throws the machine down)
> 6 months labor for nothing! Where
> did I go wrong?

> MARTY
> Dr. Brown, you've gotta help me!
> You're the only one in the world who
> knows how your time machine works!

Brown knits his brow and rubs a BANDAGE ON HIS FOREHEAD.

> BROWN
> Time machine? I haven't invented
> any time machine.

> MARTY
> You will. Look, I'll prove it to
> you...
> (pulls out his wallet,
> shows contents)
> Look, here's my driver's license.
> Expires 1987. See my birthdate? I
> haven't even been born yet!
> (pulls out a color snapshot)
> Here's a picture of me, my sister
> and my brother. Look at her
> sweatshirt: It says "Class of '84."

Brown looks the items over.

>   BROWN
>   Pretty mediocre photographic
>   fakery---they cut off your brother's
>   head.

>   MARTY
>   Please, Doc, you've gotta believe
>   me! I'm telling the truth!

>   BROWN
>   Then tell me, "future boy," who's the
>   President of the United States in
>   1985?

>   MARTY
>   Ronald Reagan.

>   BROWN
>   Ronald Reagan, the actor?

Marty nods. Brown rolls his eyes.

>   BROWN
>   And who's the Vice President?
>   Jerry Lewis? That's the most
>   insane thing I've ever heard.

Brown picks up the Brainwave Analyzer blueprints and
rushes out the back door.

A beat, then Marty runs after him.

EXT. BROWN'S HOUSE & GARAGE (PASADENA) — NIGHT

Brown runs across the lawn, toward the garage, with the Brainwave
Analyzer blueprints in hand.

Marty chases after him. Brown's Packard is parked in the drive-
way.

                              BROWN
                    I suppose Jane Wyman is first lady,
                    and Jack Benny is Secretary of the
                    Treasury.

EXT.   BROWN'S GARAGE DOOR (STAGE) — NIGHT

Brown runs up to the garage door and opens it.   Marty comes up
behind him.

                              MARTY
                    Please, Doc, listen to me!

Brown turns around and faces him.

                              BROWN
                    I've had enough of your practical jokes
                    for one evening. Good night, "Future Boy."

Brown slams the door in his face. We hear it lock.

Marty stands there for a moment, then gets an idea. He yells at
the closed door.

                              MARTY
                    Dr. Brown---that bruise on your head!   I
                    know how you got it! It happened
                    this morning! You fell off your toilet
                    and hit your head on the sink! And then
                    you came up with the idea of the
                    Flux Capicator, which is the heart
                    of the Time Machine!

                              MARTY
                    Doc, how else could I know that
                    unless I was from the future?

                              BROWN
                    Take me to this time machine.

After a moment, we hear the door unlock. Brown opens the door,
looks at Marty with new interest and rubs his bandaged head.

As soon as Marty is pulled into the house and realizes that the person who lives in that house is indeed the same Doc Brown who was his friend in 1983, albeit 30 years younger, he has only one want. He wants *to get Doc Brown to help him*. Everything he says and does throughout the entire scene is motivated by that want. When at the very end of the scene Doc says, "Take me to this time machine" (Figure 6.8), Marty has achieved his objective; the scene ends and the film moves on to another scene.

When Doc Brown pulls Marty into the house and sticks a suction cup on Marty's forehead that leads to the Brain Wave Analyzer (Figures 6.2 and 6.3), all Doc's actions are being driven by his desire *to test the Brain Wave Analyzer*. This is his objective, and he pursues it, in rapid succession, in a number of different ways. But the Brain Wave Analyzer does not work, so ultimately Doc abandons this objective, at which point he takes the Brain Wave Analyzer off his head and asks out loud, "Where did I go wrong?"

After that, Marty gets Doc to forget about the Analyzer by insisting that Doc will invent a time machine in the future. And it just so happens, that very morning in 1955, Doc Brown hits his head on the sink and the blow somehow inspires him to come up with a breakthrough idea, unlocking the key to inventing a viable time machine. (Of course, this coincidence is a plant, put there by the two talented writers of *Back to the Future*, Bob Zemeckis and Bob Gale.) When Marty delivers the line "You're the only one who knows how your time machine works!" Doc rubs the bandage on his forehead. (Figure 6.4). He has got to be thinking, "That's too much of coincidence! I think of how to invent a time machine, then a few hours later this kid shows up and tells me he came here in a time machine I invented!" This thought leads Doc Brown to his next objective: *to get Marty to reveal his true purpose*. Brown interrogates Marty (Figure 6.5), demanding, "Who's the President of the United States in 1985?" When Marty matter-of-factly replies, "Ronald Reagan," the answer strikes Brown as so patently absurd he runs out of the house and locks himself in the garage (Figures 6.6 and 6.7). Thus Brown has attained his second objective. The impossibility of Marty's answer has revealed that Marty is nothing more than a kid from the neighborhood playing a practical joke.

This discovery propels Doc into his third and final objective in the scene: *to get rid of Marty*. This is his new objective. He will pursue it by ridiculing everything Marty subsequently says and locking himself in the garage.

So to summarize, the theme or spine of the film *Back to the Future* is that *if you believe in yourself, you can do anything*. The spine of Marty's character is *to get back to the future*. The spine of Doc's character is *to prove that he is a great inventor*. Each objective serves the spine. What the character wants to do will move him a step closer to attaining his overall objective: what he is striving to attain, the spine of his character. By determining the spine of the film and the spine of each individual character, the first time director provides himself with a framework in which he can structure everything that he communicates to the actors. As he works to discover the key pieces of direction that he will use to inspire and guide the actors — which is to say, as he hunts for the most playable objectives to give his actors to work towards in each scene — he can reference each objective he assigns to a character against that character's spine.

How Objectives Work
Get-from or Do-to Objectives + Conflict = Reality

What is it above all else that makes an objective playable?

It is hard to discuss what makes an objective playable without discussing how the Method works — how it enables a Method actor to deliver a successful performance. And this is hard to describe to anyone who has never studied the Method, or worked as a Method actor. The first time director's understanding of what makes an objective playable will increase immeasurably once he has studied acting and worked as a Method actor. Nonetheless, one useful explanation is that an objective becomes playable if it gives the actor something to do. It should engage him and become emotionally all consuming. If the objective is playable, then as soon as the actor starts to play the objective, he will not have to think about having the emotions he is required to have in the scene. The activity of the objective will actually evoke those emotions within the actor. He will not be acting. He will be actually experiencing the emotions called for in the scene. He will be "in the moment," living as the character he is portraying.

The reason the Method works is because it is virtually impossible to voluntarily evoke a true feeling or emotion. As Judith Weston points out in *Directing Actors*:

> An actor caught trying to have a feeling is not believable....Bad actors, as well as much of the general population, go to great lengths to make the world believe they feel something that they don't actually feel, but most of the time no one is fooled.

If you are trying to feel angry and at the same time you are watching yourself to see if you are succeeding, you will not be convincingly angry. The Method relieves the actor of the task of trying to consciously evoke specific emotions, because this almost never works. In my experience as an actor, I found it almost impossible to think of more than one thing at a time as I was acting. Almost every actor I have worked with has corroborated this observation. The Method works because it limits what the actor has to think about to one specific thought. He must focus all his being on doing what his objective requires him to do. As an actor, I observed that the more effectively I

Figure 6.1

Figure 6.2

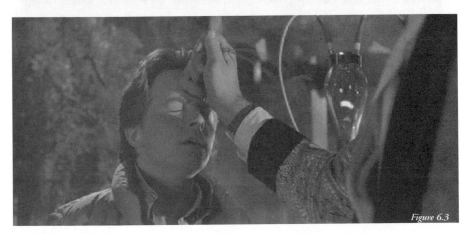

Figure 6.3

could give myself over to my objective, the more all consuming it became, the better my performance got. I have consistently observed this in every actor I have directed. The industry term for this is **committing to the objective.**

A playable objective is one that an actor can successfully commit to and thereby experience the emotions that are called for in his character at that moment in the script. The actor is the ultimate arbiter of whether an objective is playable. It is up to the director to provide the actor with an objective that the actor finds playable. The actor has to respond to the objective. It has to turn him on. It has to give him something to do that he can throw himself into wholeheartedly, spontaneously, and unthinkingly. If he cannot commit to the objective, it is up to the director to find an objective that the actor can commit to. This puts a certain burden on the director, but if a director truly wants to help his actors and improve their performances he must not shirk from this responsibility.

Therefore, the director must tirelessly strive to find an objective that the actor can commit to and make playable. If the director shirks this responsibility, it will weaken the actor's performance in almost direct proportion to the extent to which he fails to do so.

In my experience those objectives that most actors can commit to most successfully are the ones that require the actor to interact in a specific way with another actor in the scene — those objectives that require the actor to *get something from or do something to* the other actor in the scene.

For example, in the above scene from *Back to the Future*, Marty's objective is to get Doc Brown to help him. This is a **get-from objective.** The actor playing Marty wants a specific kind of help that he knows he can only get-from Doc Brown. All his energy should be focused on getting that help. Doc Brown wants *to test the Brave Wave Analyzer.* This objective, in fact, is not the best example of a get-from or do-to kind of objective (for reasons I will discuss later). However, the last two objectives he plays in this scene — namely, t*o get Marty to reveal his true purpose* and *to get rid of Marty* — are both objectives that are more playable because they tell the actor playing Doc what he has *to do-to* the actor playing Marty.

There are a number of reasons get-from or do-to objectives are more playable. For one, they always have to be an active verb. Every interpreter of the Method affirms the theory that a playable objective is almost always expressed in the form of an active verb. From Clurman to Weston to Salvi, they make the point that by requiring an actor to fulfill an objective which is phrased as an active verb — for example, berate him, torment her, warn him, mock her, jeer at him, lecture to her, bait him, cajole her

Figure 6.4

Figure 6.5

Figure 6.6

— the director gives the actor an action to perform, something to do. A get-from or do-to objective takes this a step further by focusing the action the actor has to perform on another actor in the scene. This is better because it forces the actor who is being directed to interact with another actor.

In order to fulfill his objective of getting Doc to help him, the actor playing Marty — from the minute he walks in the door — has to focus all his energy and attention on the actor playing Doc. If the actor playing Marty is committed to playing his objective, then as soon as he comes in contact with "Doc Brown," "Marty" is going to start feeling genuinely frustrated. The actor will not have to pretend to be frustrated. He will not have to think about trying to act frustrated. He will *be* frustrated. This is because the writers of the script understand that conflict is drama. And so they have written as much conflict as they can into the scene. Marty has come there for Doc's help, but thanks to the way the writers have written the scene, Doc Brown thwarts him every single step of the way. First, he totally bullies Marty into being his guinea pig. Then he ignores him while he tries to figure out why the Brain Wave Analyzer does not work. Then Doc sits back and shoots holes in every proof Marty offers that he is from the future. Finally, Doc runs away from Marty and locks himself in another building, all the while heaping ridicule and scorn on everything Marty says.

Almost every well-written scene will have this much conflict in it, although it is rarely as overt. But either outright or between the lines, there is almost always an abundance of conflict in every good scene. Where there is little or none, the experienced director of actors invents it. This is because get-from or do-to objectives + conflict = reality. The conflict is virtually a given in every scene. By giving his actors get-from or do-to objectives, the director forces them to interact and to come smack up against their conflicting agendas. Suddenly, magically, no acting is needed. If the actors' emotions are readily accessible, when they start to tangle with each other and sort out their conflicting agendas, they will be flooded with real emotions. They will not be acting. They will be truly feeling. This experience is what every Method actor comes into every scene hoping that he will experience. It is called being **in the moment**.

Sometimes the emotions that come swimming up, un-summoned and real, are not quite appropriate to the scene. Then the director must tinker with the objective, or give the actor an adjustment (I will describe adjustments in detail later) that enables the actor to go back, recommit, reengage with the other actor, and then find himself in a real-life conflict that produces a similar, but slightly different array of emotions. Ideally, after the director's input, the feelings the actor is actually experiencing are more appropriate to the scene.

Figure 6.7

Figure 6.8

Figure 6.9

Another reason why get-from or do-to objectives always work better is they keep each actor focused on the other actor in the scene. In order to successfully play his objective, an actor has no choice but to home in on the other actor and how he is responding — this is the only way he can tell if he is making progress toward his objective. And this is good. Because by concentrating on how his actions are affecting the other actor, the actor exposes himself that much more directly to the conflict that is written into the scene. Thus, his natural human response to this conflict is what fuels his feelings and drives the Method.

Since Method actors don't actually know what they will do or say until they do it — since they are not acting, but being — they will often modify their performance from take to take. The director must make sure these modifications do not go outside of the bounds of what is called for by the script. So long as they do not, they are good. Spontaneous modifications in performance make the actor's performance seem fresher and more real, both to the actor himself and to the camera. The director should do everything he can to help the actors feel like they are not acting. They have to buy into the fictitious reality they create between themselves. The more they buy into it, the more relaxed they will feel, and the more natural and believable their performances will become. If an actor responds spontaneously to something the other actor did unexpectedly, the actor will actually surprise himself a little. This is what you as the director want. If he surprises himself, the actor's performance will feel fresh and real. He can never completely forget that he is acting. But these surprises can help him forget. The more he forgets, the more he buys into the fictitious reality he is creating between himself and the other actor, and the better his performance gets. Get-from and do-to objectives keep the actors focused on each other and enable them to respond to the unexpected things they each may do.

Physicalization of the Objective

One absolutely sure-fire way of helping an actor get into the moment is to allow the actor to physicalize the objective. Since the most-playable objectives are interactive, then physicalizing the objective usually means getting touchy-feely. For example in the above scene from *Back to the Future*, the stage directions state that Doc Brown "yanks" Marty inside the house, and then "attaches a suction cup to Marty's forehead." In this case, the director is fortunate. The stage directions actually call for the actors to touch each other. The director is fortunate because when the actors start to interact physically, and put their objectives into actions that result in physical contact, then they are more easily affected by the formula: get-from or do-to objectives + conflict = reality.

In the above scene, the director hopes that the actor playing Doc Brown will seem frantic, obsessed, and maniacal about finding out if his Brain Wave Analyzer really works.

The director should want to give the impression that Brown just finished assembling it, put it on his head, and was about to rush out the door to find someone — anyone — to be his guinea pig and find out if his invention works. After all, this is in keeping with the spine of his character: *to prove that he is a great inventor*. And from reading the entire script, you cannot miss the fact that Brown is ultra high energy, excitable, and uninhibited. The director should want to give the impression that Marty is freaked out about being trapped in the past, and that getting Doc Brown to help him is almost a matter of life and death. The spine of his character is *to get back to the future*, so his behavior in this scene is yet another manifestation of what drives Marty. He has got to seem both desperate and determined at the same time. To my mind, Marty's objective — *to get Doc Brown to help him* — and Doc Brown's objective — *to test the Brain Wave Analyzer* —are good playable objectives.

But perhaps, to the director's eye, Doc Brown does not seem sufficiently frantic, and Marty does not seem convincingly desperate and determined. The script requires the actors to be full of emotion from the first line. It is not unusual for actors to start out a little flat, but the director wants the actor to be in the moment as soon as he calls "Action." This is very difficult to achieve. The script calls for physical interaction between the two actors from the very beginning of the scene. To help the actors get into the moment, the director could intensify the extent to which the actors put their objectives into physical action. He could tell the actor playing Marty to offer resistance when Doc Brown "yanks" him inside the house. He could also tell Marty to swat away the suction cup when Doc tries to stick it on his forehead. This would probably prolong this part of the scene, but you could tell the actors to adlib whatever lines come to their head to cover the stall. And the opening exchange between the two actors — in which Marty tries to say "Dr. Brown, I really..." but the Doc interrupts him, saying "No, don't tell me anything"— could be repeated several times if necessary to cover this same stall.

If Marty resists Doc Brown's efforts to pull him in the house, then Doc will have to work harder to achieve his objective (*to test the Brain Wave Analyzer*). For the sake of clarity, let us assume that, just as was the case in the movie, Michael J. Fox is playing Marty and Christopher Lloyd is playing Doc Brown. As Lloyd pulls on Fox, if Fox resists and pulls back, Lloyd cannot help but start feeling annoyed. Lloyd wants to play his objective and Fox is making it more difficult in a way that is immediate and tactile. Lloyd can channel his annoyance right into his character. He may also feel impatience, anger, frustration, and anxiety. All of these feelings are real. The actor is having the feelings right then and they will draw him into the moment. When Lloyd channels these real feelings through his objective, hopefully they will all make his Doc Brown seem believably frantic, obsessed, and maniacal.

If, when Lloyd tries to attach the suction cup to Fox's head, Fox swats it away a couple of times, Fox is going start feeling a range of very real emotions, which might include — but probably will not be limited to — frustration, annoyance, impatience, confusion, anxiety, and even fear. Exactly what emotions he feels depends on the individual actor and his mood. But Fox will not have to act to feel these feelings. The physical interaction with Doc Brown will make them undeniably present, right then in the moment. Fox's objective is *to get Doc Brown to help him*. This requires co-operation from Doc. Therefore, when Fox channels the feelings set off by the physical exchange between him and Lloyd through his objective, he will have to temper his feelings in such a way as to make them acceptable to Lloyd/Brown, otherwise he will never win the co-operation he needs to succeed. The real feelings of annoyance, confusion, anxiety, and fear sparked in Fox by the physical interaction may come out as desperation and anxiety, tempered by Fox's acting instrument — his winning personality — into a sort of puckish annoyance, as called for in the script.

As demonstrated above, the right choice of physical contact between the actors can help an actor commit to his objective and make it playable and real. By introducing an appropriate choice of physical contact into the scene, a director can jumpstart an actor who is stuck and cannot seemingly commit to his objective. This is very helpful in the day-late-dollar-short world of breakthrough projects. Because of the lack of rehearsal time, the first time director needs a gunbelt full of silver-bullet quick fixes to kill unconvincing performances. Physicalizing an objective is about as surefire a quick fix as they come.

Even if the script does not call for the actors to touch, if it is in keeping with the story, the first time director should go ahead and have the actors get physical to make an unconvincing performance real. Hopefully, the higher-ups will not object to this sort of script change. They should be able to understand that a slight departure from the script is a small thing to sacrifice, especially if, in the process, an embarrassing performance is made believable and the entire illusion of the film is maintained

If having the actors come into contact physically truly violates the sense of the story, the first time director can still use another quick fix to save a performance. This alternative application doesn't always work, but it is worth a try. In *Back to the Future*, Fox and Lloyd never interacted physically in any of the ways I described above. Since Zemeckis co-wrote the script, I would say he could be judged to be the ultimate arbiter of how the scene should play, so if he chose not to have them touch in the ways I have suggested, that is probably the way the scene should play. But if Zemeckis had trouble getting Fox or Lloyd to commit to their objectives and deliver a credible performance — a highly unlikely event that I will explore hypothetically — then he could tell them in rehearsal to physicalize their objectives in the ways that I describe above, and then when it came time to shoot, he could tell them to do everything short of actually touching.

An actor can usually go back to an emotion or a state of being once he has been there. Getting there the first time is the hardest part. Almost every actor I have worked with always doubts that he can hit all the emotional high notes called for in his part. But once he's hit them, his inhibitions abate, his self-doubt diminishes, and so long as it stays fresh, he can do it every time. An actor's greatest enemy is his self-consciousness. He must not be watching himself as he attempts a performance. The extent to which he does so will detrimentally affect his performance. Once the director has proved to the actor that the actor can have the feelings called for in the script, the actor tends to stop watching himself. He can then commit to his objective and has a much greater chance of being in the moment. If the actor is having trouble committing to his objective, the director can make it much easier for him to do so by physicalizing the objective. This can thrust the actor into the moment. So the first time director can use the quick fix of physicalizing the objective in rehearsal on the set before the take, and the actor can often duplicate the same performance without physicalizing the objective once the cameras roll. This technique is always worth a try.

Identifying the Most-Playable Objective

After the director has determined the spine of his breakthrough film and the spine of each actor's character, he is ready to break down each scene in the script to find the most-playable objectives for each character. He should stick to get-from or do-to objectives. In *Directing Actors*, Judith Weston walks the reader through a huge variety of playable objectives. These objectives are also listed in an appendix at the back of the book. The first time director should read her book and look through these lists and see how each of these objectives gives an actor something to get-from or do-to another actor. This will heighten his understanding of what makes an objective playable. When he breaks down the script of his breakthrough project, he will never go wrong if he sticks to objectives on Weston's lists or selects objectives that instruct an actor to get something from or do something to another actor in the scene.

Besides being playable, an objective should also accurately identify what the character wants at that particular moment in the script. In the scene from *Back to the Future*, the objective *to get Doc Brown to help him* is truly an accurate description of what motivates all of Marty's actions in the scene.

The other reason why *to get Doc Brown to help him* is a good objective for Marty in this scene is because he can play it for the entire scene. When the first time director breaks down the script of his breakthrough project, he should try to come up with objectives that (1) are playable, (2) accurately describe what is motivating the character, and (3) can be played for as long a beat as possible.   Again, when the objective changes, the beat changes, so the longer the beat, the better the objective — provided it is truly playable.   The fewer times the actor has to change objectives, the more intensely he can concentrate on each individual objective.   This will make it easier for him to truly commit to the objective.   If the actor is in the moment, things are happening spontaneously.   In order to stay in the moment, the actor has to stay focused as intensely as possible on the emotional interchange between himself and the other actor.   In order to remind himself to change his objective, the actor has to momentarily take his mind off of this emotional interchange.   This tends to break his momentum. It can throw him completely out of the moment.   For a talented, trained actor staying in the moment and changing objectives is not overly difficult.   But the first time director is advised in his preparation to prepare for the worst.   Better to be prudent and make it as easy as possible for your actors to commit to their objectives and stay committed.   This is truly the purpose of a director's homework: to come to the set prepared to handle the worst.   This is the logic behind digging to find the objective that can be played the longest.

In the scene from *Back to the Future*, Marty can play to get Doc Brown to help him for the entire scene.   This objective is playable; it is an accurate description of what Marty wants for the entire scene.   On the other hand, what Doc wants — what motivates his actions — shifts several times in the scene.   The first objective that I selected for Doc Brown in this scene — *to test the Brain Wave Analyzer* — is not a get-from or do-to objective.   But, to my mind, this is a better objective than the logical get-from or do-to objective — *use Marty to test the Brain Wave Analyzer* — because the actor playing Doc can play the former objective for several lines longer.   This is because as soon as Doc realizes the Brain Wave Analyzer does not work, he almost forgets about Marty and focuses all his attention on his failed invention.   In other words, after he asks Marty "Are you here because you want to use the bathroom?" and before he responds to Marty's assertion that in 1985 he will invent a time machine by stating, "Time machine?   I haven't invented any time machine," Doc Brown is so obsessed with trying to figure out why the Brain Wave Analyzer does not work, he could not possibly play the get-from or do-to objective.   This would focus him on Marty instead of his failed invention and is a perfect example of the sort of trade-off a director has to make to come up with an objective that an actor can play for the longest beat possible.

To some it might seem unimportant to find an objective that an actor can play for two or three more lines.   But this is not the case. *Back to the Future* is a comedy.   The three extra lines that I am concerned with contain a joke.   Timing is everything in comedy, and precision timing and nuance in delivery have to be achieved in order for funny lines to come off as funny.   The following excerpt contains the setup and pay off of the joke.

                    MARTY
          Dr. Brown, listen: I'm from the
          future. I came here in a time
          machine you invented — and now I
          desperately need you to help me get
          back to the year 1985.

                    BROWN
          My God. Do you know what this means?

He pauses dramatically, then removes the contraption from his
head.

                    BROWN
          It means that this damned thing
          doesn't work at all!
                    (throws the machine down)
          Six months labor for nothing! Where
          did I go wrong?

For the joke to play, it has to be believable that the actor playing Doc is so focused on trying to figure out why the Brain Wave Analyzer does not work, he actually fails to comprehend the amazing news that he will successfully invent a time machine in the future. By this point in the film, the audience is well acquainted with Doc's character. They have to be aware that the spine of his character is *to prove that he is a great inventor*. Marty tells Doc that he got there in a time machine that Doc will invent in the future, and Doc responds "in utter amazement" as the scene description informs us, and says, "My god. Do you know what this means?" In these lines the audience is being set up to think that he will say something of great portent, like, "I'm going to realize my life's ambition." — something with the same ring of importance as "One small step for man. One giant step for mankind." Instead he comes out with the prosaic, everyday complaint, "It means this damn thing doesn't work at all!" For the joke to play, the actor portraying Brown has to believably tune out the actor playing Marty. This means that he must be playing an objective that can divert his focus away from Marty, such as *to test the Brain Wave Analyzer*. It will help the actor portraying Brown if he can get a running start and play this objective from the top of the scene, instead of having to switch to a new objective right as he is setting up the joke. The chances that the joke will get a laugh will be that much better. And a comedy director lives and dies by how many real laughs he can get out of an audience.

If the first time director goes to the trouble to select those objectives that can be played for the longest possible beat, he will be making it easier for his actors to prepare and to deliver their best performances. A good director of actors is the kind of director who goes the extra mile for his actors. The actors can tell when he does. They will appreciate this and usually repay the director handsomely. Working with actors works a lot like any human relationship. What you put into it is generally what you get out of it. Coming up with playable objectives that the actor can play for the longest possible beat is always worth the extra effort required.

This brings up another necessary component of being a good director of actors: **simplification**. Before I studied acting and worked as an actor, I talked my actors to death. I gave them all my thoughts about a character, how they could prepare to play that character, and all the things they could do after I called "Action" to bring the character to life. This was a big mistake. As described above, after the director calls "Action!" it is very difficult for the actor to think of anything. He should focus as much of his attention as possible on *doing*. He should work to achieve his objective and stay free to respond fully to the feelings that are evoked by the emotional interchange between himself and the other actors in the scene. Every time he has to interrupt this spontaneous interplay between himself and the other actors — every time he has to stop *doing* so he can *think* of something you told him — he risks losing his connection to the flow of emotions in the scene. Therefore, the less you tell him and the less he has to think about, the better. Because of this, it is essential the first time director on his breakthrough project remember that he must simplify, simplify, simplify. The fewer directions the director gives an actor, the better. This rule applies to many aspects of the director-actor relationship. A good director of actors governs his actions by it. In this instance, as is so often the case in the world of film, less is truly more.

Ultraplayable Objectives

When I break down a script in preparation for helping my actors with their performances, I select two objectives for each beat. First I select the objective that accurately describes what the character that the actor is portraying wants at that moment in the script. Then I go back and reevaluate the scene looking at it on a different level. Under each objective, I write a second, alternate objective. I think of this second objective as the **ultraplayable objective**. In determining this objective I am not concerned with accuracy. The want that I identify may not be something that the character in the story actually wants. The criteria for the ultraplayable objective are that (1) it would be the easiest for the actor to commit himself to and (2) once the actor has committed himself to this objective, it would leave him the most exposed to the conflict in the scene and so evoke the most powerful emotions in him.

For example, the ultraplayable objective that I could think of for Marty would be *to get him to put his arms around you*. This is not what Marty wants, but I think it will be easier for the actor playing Marty to commit to this objective. To get help from someone is much more abstract than to get someone to put their arms around you. Michael J. Fox can imagine in his mind's eye exactly what he wants Christopher Lloyd to do if his objective is *to get him to put his arms around you.* My experience as an actor revealed to me that if I could picture in my mind's eye exactly what I wanted to get-from the other actor, then often that image would produce feelings and attitudes in me that enabled me to commit more fully to the objective. What is also good about this ultraplayable objective is that the image that it enables Fox to conjure up in his mind's eye is a powerful image. A hug is not only concrete, it is also something that most of us have very good associations with. If a young actor like Fox imagines wanting a hug from an older male actor, this will almost inevitably summon up images and memories of when, as a child, it felt great for Fox to get a hug from his father. This should feed Fox and give him a more evocative emotional context in which to work, provided that he had a normal, loving relationship with his father. Again, the actor is the ultimate arbiter of whether an objective is playable or not, so the director must be responsive to this and adjust accordingly.

In addition to being more concrete and so potentially a more potent source of evocative images that will feed the actor's imagination, the objective *to get him to put his arms around you* is more playable because it exposes the actor more directly to the conflict written into the scene. Doc Brown rejects Marty throughout the scene. First he manhandles and shouts him down. Then he ridicules everything Marty is telling him and then he runs away from him. The objective *to get him to put his arms around you* is going to make Fox as a human being more vulnerable to this stream of rejection. Ideally this will trigger feelings of hurt, despair, desperation, panic in Fox, all of which the actor can use to fuel his emotional life and inform the role with authenticity. Marty does not want Doc Brown to put his arms around him, but he should seem believably desperate, anxious, and perhaps taken aback and hurt by the way Doc treats him. Marty's situation is one of life and death. This is essential to the story. If Fox as Marty cannot convince the audience that he is believably freaked out about being trapped in 1955 and sees Doc as his only hope of saving himself, then the scene will not play and advance the story.

Of course the character of Marty, in addition to being desperate, vulnerable, and needy, is also amazingly clearheaded, patient, and tenacious. But the director need not be so concerned with this, for these are the feelings with which Marty suppresses his fear and anxiety. What the director must help the actor to do is to get to the feeling at the bottom of all his feelings. In the above scene, Marty's fear and desperation are at the bottom of all his feelings. That's what has driven him to seek out Doc Brown and to ask for his help. The actor has to start with the feelings that, bottom line, are driving him. The other feelings that he uses to suppress or control those feelings can be layered on top. In the case of this scene, much of this layering comes from the script. The words that the writers have put in Marty's mouth cannot help but make him seem clever, quick-witted, determined, and patient. The objective to get him to put his arms around you will expose Fox to Lloyd's rejections and drive him as far as he can go in the direction of his character's neediness. Then the words in the script, coming out of Fox's mouth, will reveal how the character uses his wit, determination, and patience to control his gut-level fear and desperation.

Going for an ultraplayable objective will not only make Marty's most basic primal feeling seem more real — Fox will seem to be believably freaked out and frightened — it will also give authenticity, strength, and definition to all the feelings the actor summons in himself, and everything the script gives him to say and do to stay on top of those primal feelings and not let them overwhelm him. So an ultraplayable objective is more playable because it both rigs the game against the actor and also raises the stakes of the game. Fox goes in wanting more. He will get less, but wanting more, he will be driven to work twice as hard for the little he gets.

I call this the efficacy of impossibility. The director gives the actor the objective he is least likely to get. The actor goes into the scene wanting much more than the character he is playing. The writer has written conflict into the scene. By going in wanting more than what Marty wants, Fox makes himself that much more vulnerable to the abuse that Lloyd is dishing out. This often seems to produce the right amount of real emotional life in the actor. Fox cannot be as emotionally invested in this scene as Marty. For Marty it really is a matter of life and death. For Fox it is just a scene in a film in which he is acting. The ultraplayable objective hopefully will make Fox react to what Lloyd says as Marty would to Doc, which is to say, completely freaked out and desperate, knowing that if Doc does not help him, he might die.

After coming up with an ultraplayable objective for one actor, the director should go back and select ultraplayable objectives for the other actor or actors in the scene. The way to expose Lloyd to the conflict in the scene is to take the objectives that the director has already selected for Lloyd and then bump them up a notch so they are more abusive of Marty.

Doc hopes that Marty is telling him the truth about the time machine, but he is guarding against the possibility that he is not. To do this, Doc is testing Marty by feigning abusiveness. By giving Lloyd an excessively abusive objective, the director exposes him to Fox's charm. Ironically, this will make it difficult for Lloyd to play the ultraplayable objective. But he can channel all of this difficulty into his performance. Since the ultraplayable objective calls for the actor to be excessively abusive of Marty, Lloyd will probably feel a little guilty or forced or phony as he pursues this objective. This is good because these are all feelings that Doc should be having. Lloyd should allow himself to feel these conflicted feelings because they will make his portrayal of Doc seem that much more complex and real. Here again, the efficacy of impossibility will work for the director. So at the head of the scene, the director could tell Lloyd: Instead of playing the objective of trying *to test the Brain Wave Analyzer*, he could play the ultraplayable objective of *use him as a guinea pig or treat him like a piece of meat*. Similarly, the director could replace the next objective for the character of Doc Brown — *get Marty to reveal his true purpose* — with the ultraplayable objective of *make him feel stupid*. The final objective that I identified earlier for Doc in this scene is *to get rid of Marty*. The director could require Lloyd to ratchet up the abusiveness yet another notch by replacing *get rid of Marty* with *make him cry*. Again, these are not accurate descriptions of what Doc wants. They are objectives that could be more playable for the actor playing Doc, because they exploit the fact that the two characters in the scene are at cross-purposes.

These three ultraplayable objectives for the character of Doc Brown also fulfill the criteria specified earlier: They all employ imagery that should feed Lloyd's imagination and make it easier for him to commit to the objective.

The conflict that is written into almost every scene is the director's greatest ally in his effort to wring the best performance out of his actors. The more directly he can expose the actors to the conflict, the easier it will be for them to summon real emotions and make the scene come to life. At 7:00 a.m. or at the end of a long day of shooting, the director may need a little rocket fuel to get the actor up to the emotional level called for in the scene. Ultraplayable objectives often prove to be just the silver-bullet, quick fix a first time director needs to give a scene that added boost.

Adjustments

The director preparing to help his actors by breaking down the script prior to the start of shooting begins by working out each actor's objectives (both playable and ultraplayable) in a scene. Then he moves on to determine, in advance, the adjustments each actor can make in the course of pursuing his objective. I use the term adjustment in the same manner as Harold Clurman, and slightly differently than Judith Weston. Weston uses the term adjustment to refer to what she calls a "what if" direction. She gives as an example a situation in which the director wants Actor A to show respect for Actor B in a scene — a special kind of respect bordering on fear. So the director would give Actor A the adjustment to play the scene "as if" he knew "that B carries a weapon, and has been known to shoot people he feels are disrespectful of him." She goes on to state that an adjustment can be thought of as an imaginative subtext.

Clurman is much more specific about just what an adjustment is. In *On Directing*, Clurman describes how when breaking down a scene from a script he first determines an actor's objective, which he refers to as "the basic action," and then goes on "to set down the manner in which the basic action is to be carried out." He specifically relates how in his "director's work script" he puts a blank sheet of paper in the script opposite the page on which the scene is written and then divides this blank sheet of paper into columns. "The first column states *what* is to be done, the second *how* it is to be done. Actors speak of the instructions in the second column as *adjustments* (italics are Clurman's)." In the examples he then supplies, it is clear that Clurman uses the term adjustment to describe the numerous ways that an actor can go about trying to reach his objective. For example, in the scene from *Back to the Future*, Marty has but one objective: *to get Doc Brown to help him.* But throughout the course of the scene he tries dozens of different, very specific tactics to get what he so desperately wants. At various moments in the scene Marty sticks to some of these tactics, or adjustments, for several lines. But at other instances he changes the way he is going about trying to reach his objective with every exchange of dialogue. Of course, Doc Brown switches adjustments just as frequently, in the same manner. Following Clurman, I identify each time an actor changes the way he is going about trying to reach his objective as an **adjustment**.

So when Marty comes through the door, his objective is to get Doc Brown to help him. But before he can get more than a few words out, Doc Brown "yanks him inside," sticks a suction cup which is wired into the Brain Wave Analyzer onto Marty's forehead, and commands, "No, don't tell me anything. I'm going to read your thoughts." The only thing that Marty wants is to convince Brown that he came back to 1955 in the time machine that Doc invented, and to persuade Doc to get the machine running again. But at this point in the scene, he chooses to pursue this objective by *doing nothing*. As the scene directions tell us, when Brown manhandles Marty into place and orders him to shut up, "Marty indulges him." Marty wants something from Doc Brown, so rather than risk offending him at the initial moment of their encounter, he chooses to get what he wants *by playing along* with Doc's game. His objective is *to get Doc Brown to help him*. And at the top of the scene, *the manner* in which he chooses to get what he wants — the tactic that he adopts — is to ingratiate himself with Doc *by playing along*. This is his adjustment. When it becomes clear to both Marty and Doc that the Brain Wave Analyzer is a failure and does not work, Marty quickly shifts from passive to aggressive and delivers the following string of statements of fact:

MARTY

Dr. Brown, listen: I'm from the
future. I came here in a time

```
        machine you invented — and now I
        desperately need you to help me get
        back to the year 1985.
```

He hopes these announcements will shift Doc's focus off of the useless Brain Wave Analyzer and onto fixing an invention that actually does work: the time machine. Now Marty is trying to achieve his objective *by leveling with the Doc*. This tactic clearly is a total failure. Doc seems to have not heard a word.

Again, let's assume that Christopher Lloyd is playing Brown and Michael J. Fox is playing McFly. As I noted above, a good objective for Lloyd to be playing at this point in the scene is *to test the Brain Wave Analyzer*. It has become evident that the Brain Wave Analyzer does not work. This is a huge disappointment to Brown, so he preoccupies himself with looking at the machine and *trying to figure out why it doesn't work*. Lloyd can use this as his adjustment because it describes exactly how he is going about continuing to try *to test the Brain Wave Analyzer*. As I pointed out, the more preoccupied Lloyd can appear, the better the joke will play. The source of the joke is the irony in the fact that Marty gives Doc Brown the amazing news that he will realize his life's ambition in 1985, and it has no affect on him. Doc's response is as follows:

```
                    BROWN
        My God.  Do you know what this means?
```

```
He pauses dramatically, then removes the contraption from his
head.
```

```
                    BROWN
        It means that this damned thing
        doesn't work at all!
                (throws the machine down)
        Six months labor for nothing!  Where
        did I go wrong?
```

Because Brown seems to have not even heard what he said, Marty switches tactics. He goes from trying to get Doc Brown to help him by delivering a startling piece of news, to trying to get Doc Brown to help him by impressing Doc with the life and death nature of his dilemma. He is trapped in the past and only Doc Brown can help him. He is now trying to realize his objective by *pleading with Doc*.

> MARTY
>
> Doc Brown, you've gotta help me!
> You're the only one in the world
> who knows how your time machine works!

Brown's reaction to this amazing piece of news is mixed. He hopes that Marty is telling the truth, but he suspects that Marty is putting him on, because the kids in the neighborhood think Doc is crazy and make a practice of playing practical jokes on him. For the moment, Doc is willing to suspend judgment, because just that morning he hit his head on the toilet and the blow somehow gave him the idea for the heart of the time machine: the flux capacitor. So maybe, when Marty talks about a time machine Doc will invent, it is not just a fortunate coincidence. The writers tip us off that this is what Doc is trying to figure out (Figure 6.4 – page 155) by telling us in the scene description that Doc "knits his brow and rubs the bandage on his head." Rather than reject Marty out of hand as a practical joker, Doc decides *to get Marty to reveal his true purpose*. This is his new objective. When he unstrapped the Brain Wave Analyzer and put it down, he gave up his first objective of trying *to test* the Brain Wave Analyzer. Now he has to deal with Marty and the way he goes about it at first is *by testing Marty*. That is his tactic in the lines:

> BROWN
>
> Time machine?   I haven't invented
> any time machine.

Doc is testing Marty, who jumps at the opportunity to pass the test. In so doing, he changes tactics yet again. This makes the third time in a row that McFly responds to Brown by adopting a different strategy. The actor therefore can prepare by playing a different adjustment. Marty still desperately needs *to get Doc Brown to help him*. So the actor playing Marty can stick to this objective, but now he is trying to achieve the objective *by presenting evidence* that he hopes will dispel Brown's doubts. He whips out his wallet (Figure 6.11) and tells Doc:

> MARTY
>
> Look.   Here's my driver's license.
> Expires 1987.   See my birthdate?   I
> haven't even been born yet.
>   (pulls out a color snapshot)
> Here's a picture of me, my sister
> and my brother.   Look at her
> sweatshirt: it says "Class of '84".

Brown responds to this display of hard evidence by taking an even harder line. Initially he pursued his objective *by testing Marty*, but now he takes it one step further and starts *putting Marty down*. This is his adjustment in both of the next exchanges of dialogue.

Figure 6.11

> BROWN
> Pretty mediocre photographic
> fakery — they cut off your brother's
> head.

> MARTY
> Please, Doc, you've gotta believe
> me! I'm telling the truth!

> BROWN
> Then tell me, "future boy," who's the
> President of the United States in
> 1985?

When Doc challenges Marty to prove that he really is from the future by revealing who the President of the United States will be in 1985, the words in themselves could be taken as a straight-ahead question. In other words, as if by asking this question, Brown's purpose was merely *to get the information*. This would lead one to think that the proper adjustment for the actor playing Brown to make when he says these lines would be *to get the information*. But by addressing Marty as a "future boy" in the middle of this question, it is clear that Brown is implying that Marty is lying to him about being from the future. So by delivering this line, Doc Brown is exposing Marty as a liar and imposter and in so doing, *putting him down*. (Figure 6.5)

In response to Doc's put downs, Marty at first goes back to *pleading with Doc*. When breaking down this scene, a director could select that as the proper adjustment for the actor playing Marty as he delivers the lines:

> MARTY
> Please, Doc, you've gotta believe
> me! I'm telling the truth!

But when Marty moves on and answers Doc's question as to who the President of the United States in 1985 is, he changes tactics yet again. The director breaking down this scene has to ask himself, how would anybody like Marty (who, as of 1985, had lived through five years of the Reagan presidency) answer this question and conclude that you cannot live in the United States for five years without becoming painfully aware of who the President is — so you would answer this question with complete certainty. You would have to be living under a stone not to know the answer to this question with as much certainty as you know your own name, or where the sun will come up tomorrow. Therefore the proper adjustment for the actor playing Marty to make when delivering the line: "Ronald Reagan" is *by stating the obvious* (Figure 6.12).

This shocks Brown. He cannot believe what Marty has just told him. Had Marty answered, "Buffalo Bob" or "Mickey Mantle" or "Groucho Marx," Brown's reaction would have been the same: shock and disbelief. He repeats Marty's answer because he cannot believe it (Figure 6.12). He is still pursuing his objective of trying *to get Marty to reveal his true purpose*, but now his tactic and therefore his adjustment is *by double checking*. When Marty nods his head, confirming in all certainty that Ronald Reagan, the actor and star of *Cattle Queen of Montana* in 1955 will be the President of the United States in 1985, Brown decides that he has heard enough. Now, he knows for certain that Marty is *not* from the future, but rather, a kid from the neighborhood who is playing a practical joke on him. Now, his wants change dramatically. After this line, Brown has only one intent: *to get rid of Marty*. He is playing a new objective. The first *manner* with which he goes about pursuing this objective is *by mocking Marty*. He does this in the first half of his next line (Figure 6.13):

> BROWN
> And who's the Vice President?
> Jerry Lewis? That's the most
> insane thing I've ever heard.

Figure 6.12

Figure 6.13

In the second half of the above line — "That's the most insane thing I have ever heard" — Doc again changes the manner in which he is trying to achieve his objective: *to get rid of Marty*. He now is *putting Marty down* or *ridiculing Marty*. The director breaking down this scene should note these adjustments and be prepared to give them to the actor to help improve his performance.

"The More Adjustments, the Better" – How Come?

When I was laying out the ground rules for selecting objectives, I advocated the principle that "less was more" and stated that the first time director should look for objectives that (1) are playable, (2) accurately describe what is motivating the character, and (3) can be played for as long a beat as possible.   I went on to claim that the longer the beat, the better the objective, provided it is truly playable. The opposite can be said of adjustments. In the case of adjustments, more is better. The more adjustments you can find while breaking down a script, the better.   In the following lines, Doc Brown shifts tactics in the middle of the line.

BROWN

And who's the Vice President?
Jerry Lewis?   That's the most
insane thing I've ever heard.

The actor playing Brown can use two adjustments while delivering this line: *by mocking Marty* and *by ridiculing Marty*. Both adjustments can be made while the actor keeps his focus on his objective, which is *to get rid of Marty* — a do-to objective.

If I were getting ready to direct the above scene and breaking down my script in preparation for helping my actors improve their performances, I would do just as I have advocated in the above paragraphs and write down a different adjustment for Marty to make each time he speaks, starting after he gives up his first adjustment: *to play along* and continuing on through the line "Ronald Reagan." To some this may seem unnecessary, or as Benny Colman, the octogenarian DP on *The Fall Guy* used to say whenever people got obsessed by details and seemed to lose sight of the big picture: "Pickin' fly shit out of pepper." I consider this to be the very least a first time director should do in preparing to direct his breakthrough project.

Yes, I am telling the first time director to be over-prepared. Because only by being over-prepared will he be ready to cope with the challenges he will confront trying to coax the best performance possible out of his actors on the set. He can be assured that his cast will not be comprised solely of actors who can consistently deliver believable performances. And he will be further handicapped by the fact that, in all likelihood, he will have no time or very little time to rehearse his actors prior to shooting. Therefore, he must be over-prepared. He must be able to help his actors nail each and every line, even though he will have practically no time on the set, and no time prior to the day of shooting to prepare his actors. To do this, he has to identify every subtle shift in *the manner* in which the character the actor is portraying goes about trying to achieve his objective.

For example, the line "Ronald Reagan" is a setup for a joke. The joke comes in Doc's reaction to Marty's claim that Ronald Reagan will be the President in 1985. For the joke to play, it has to be set up and paid off properly. This requires a very precise, spot-on delivery of these lines. The first time director will not be working with comedians as talented as Michael J. Fox and Christopher Lloyd. He had better be ready to make *all* of the jokes play in his breakthrough project. The best way to be ready to get a precise reading of a line out of a Method actor is to have identified every different way that the actor can go about working towards his objective. The best way to do this is by having noted every possible adjustment while breaking down the script prior to the start of shooting. This is why when I broke the scene down in the above paragraphs I found four different adjustments to be played by the two actors in the seven lines that set up and the pay off the joke.

The fewer directions the director gives an actor, the better. This is always the case. So how can I reconcile "the more adjustments, the better" with "the fewer directions, the better"? Easy. Do not give an adjustment to an actor unless he needs it. If it ain't broken, don't fix it. If you are serious about launching your directing career with your breakthrough project, you must come to the set with every possible adjustment identified. Only this way will you be ready to quick-fix every reading of every line that you do not think comes up to the mark. If you break down your script figuring that the more adjustments you can find the better, then you will be able — working under intense pressure and without adequate rehearsal time — to fine-tune a performance.

Say, for example, that the actor playing Marty gave a reading that did not set the joke up properly. The joke turns on the irony that Marty *and the audience* take the fact of the Reagan Presidency for granted. Yet even though Marty is 100 % correct, what he states matter-of-factly seems absolutely preposterous to Doc Brown. This is called **dramatic irony** and it works because the audience is in on the joke. They know Marty is right. They know more than Doc. Therefore they are happy to laugh at Doc when he flips out and ridicules Marty's answer. This makes them feel powerful and they enjoy that. *Back to the Future* is peppered with these kinds of bits of dramatic irony that turn on the special understanding shared by Marty and the audience at the expense of all the other characters in the film. For the joke to play — for the dramatic irony to pay off — the setup has to be delivered as if Marty is *stating the obvious*. If the actor cannot come through with the precise delivery, the only way the director can make the pinpoint fix needed to correct the way the actor says these two words is with an adjustment.

That is unless the director wants to try to fix the problem by giving the actor a **line reading**. This would be a big mistake. Because in the world of the Method (and as I stated above, with a few very exceptions, all actors working in this country come out of the world of the Method) line readings are a big no-no. In the world of the Method, a director who delivers a line out loud to an actor and tells him "Try it like this" or words to that affect, is unschooled in or oblivious to the bedrock principles of the Method. The Method works from the inside out. The actor is not acting, which to say he is not working from the outside in, pitching his voice and screwing up his face in a way that he thinks will convince the audience that he is having the feelings that the script calls for. The actor is working from the inside out. By giving the actor a line reading the director is asking the actor to mimic him, like a parrot. This is very clearly working from the outside in, and runs counter to principles of the Method.

Giving an actor a line reading is not going to destroy his performance. Many successful directors refuse "to give acting lessons on the set." They come right out and tell their actors precisely which emotions they want to see at exactly what point in each scene. To their mind, they have the right to tell the actor to be happy, sad, mad, glad, and if the actor is worth what he is being paid, he will do whatever it takes to be believably happy, mad, sad, or glad. But these are successful directors whose reputations are established, and they have a track record to prove it. They can get away with flouting the Method. The actors are generally lulled into submission by the director's track record.

But the first time director who flouts the Method by delivering a line reading for an actor is giving the most petty and insecure of his actors a knife with which to stick him in the back and ruin his rapport with his entire cast. The first time director does not have a track record. The actors will come to the set worried whether he has what it takes to make them look good. They must look good. If they cannot deliver a believable performance, they will fool no one. The director has to prove to them that he can help them. If he does, they will embrace him, even worship him. Every working director and actor I know agrees this is the dynamic between the first time director and his actors.

To win this trust, the first time director must be consistently helpful. His command of the Method cannot be hit and miss. If he falls down and gives the actors direction that does not help them or that they cannot understand, their trust may vanish. Therefore, he must consistently exceed their expectations.

Most actors will be reasonable and fair in judging the director. But the first time director can almost be certain that among his cast he will have one or two mediocre, insecure actors. They will be the first to turn on him. They will try to justify their inadequacies to themselves and their fellow actors by dismissing the director as incompetent. The minute the first time director delivers a line reading on the set, he gives the most petty and insecure members of his cast that backstabbing knife. Line readings — like result directions (telling the actor to be happy, sad, mad, glad) — are reviled in every Method acting class. All Method actors learn that working from the outside in like this is bad, bad, bad. If you ask them to do it, you run the risk of destroying their confidence in you. But if you come to the set having identified every possible adjustment an actor can make in the course of achieving his objective, you will have no need to deliver line readings. You will be prepared to do what delivering a line reading is intended to do — help an actor deliver a line in a very specific way — and you will be helping the actor according to the Method's bedrock principles.

Some people prefer to work under pressure. They may reason that it is overkill to think up and write down every possible adjustment an actor may need to deliver every line in a very specific way. But by not thoroughly breaking down the script and thinking up every possible adjustment in advance, the director leaves himself open for error. He might not be able to make a joke play or a crucial line seem believable if he does not come up with the right adjustment for the actor. If he can eliminate or drastically reduce the possibility of such an error by sheer hard work and diligence, he is foolish not to avail himself of this protection. He has a great deal to gain through such preparation — consistently believable performances, the respect and trust of his actors, harmony and happiness on the set — and very little to give up — a few more hours of sleep, an extra hour or two with his significant other. Anybody who is not willing to make that sacrifice, to my mind, does not have the self-discipline and work ethic needed to breakthrough as a director.

All Adjustments Are Gerunds or Adverbs

The adjustments I selected for the above scene from *Back to the Future* — by pleading, by testing, by presenting evidence, by putting him down, by stating the obvious, by double checking, by mocking him, by ridiculing him — are all phrased as an active verb in the "ing" form. The "ing" form of a verb is also known as a **gerund**. Adjustments can also be phrased as adverbs. For example when Doc Brown asks Marty: "And who's the Vice President? Jerry Lewis?" he is trying to achieve his objective *by mocking Marty*, or *mockingly*, or *sarcastically*. So in this instance the adjustment can be stated either as a gerund or as an **adverb**. They say almost the same thing in two slightly different ways.

Judith Weston and other authorities on directing actors caution against the use of adverbs, which is understandable. Adverbs can be used to deliver result directions. For example, a director could tell an actor he wants him to deliver a line "happily." That clearly gives the actor only a description of a state of being — happiness — and asks the actor to impose that state of being on himself from the outside in. This is a dangerous trap.

The way I see it, a good adjustment always gives the actor something specific *to do*. An adjustment stated as a gerund will do just that, and so keep the actor working from the inside out. In the above scene, I would tell the actor playing Marty that, above all else, he has to stay intent on trying to get Doc Brown to help him. If in the course of playing his objective, the actor could not nail the setup line "Ronald Reagan," then I would tell the actor, in this line you are *trying to get Doc Brown to help you by stating the obvious*. By employing the "ing" form of the active verb *to state*, the adjustment keeps the actor focused on an activity, not a state of being, and so avoids being a result direction.

Similarly, an adjustment that uses an adverbial form of an active verb will always give an actor something specific to do, and so keep him working from the inside out. When Marty tells Doc that the President of the United States in 1985 will be Ronald Reagan, Brown decides that Marty is pulling his leg and decides to get rid of him. The very first thing that he says to Marty in an attempt to get rid of him is: "And who's the Vice-President? Jerry Lewis?" The actor playing Doc should deliver this line as if he is *trying to get rid of Marty mockingly*. The adjustment, *mockingly*, is the adverbial form of the active verb, to mock. So it gives the actor a very specific tactic to employ in the pursuit of his objective. He is to mock Marty in an effort to hurt his feelings and get rid of him. Accordingly, the first time director is advised to make sure that his adjustments, whether they are gerunds or adverbs, are always derived from active verbs — verbs that describe an activity and so give the actor something to do.

Improvisation

Notes on possible improvisations are the last component of a complete script breakdown. Sometimes all the carefully thought out objectives and adjustments will not bring a scene to life. This calls for a good improvisation. A good improvisation can crack a scene open for the actors. So a first time director, when breaking down a script, should devise one or two good "improvs" for the actors to play. The improv is strictly a rehearsal tool. When the actors improvise, they use their own words and they play themselves. Ideally, acting out the improv will enable the actor to summon up some or all of the feelings he will have to exhibit in front of the camera. The theory is that the improv has helped him to go to the emotional place he has to go. If, while doing the improv, he can hit all the emotional notes he knows he has to get to, he will stop watching himself. He will relax and, if all goes well, when the cameras role he will be able to commit to the objective, get into the moment, and hit all those same emotional notes while he is in character.

Improvs cheat a little, making it easier for the formula "Get-from or do-to objectives + conflict = reality" to work. They cheat in three ways. First, they allow the actor to be himself and to use his own words. The big picture goal of acting is to enable the actor to make it real. It is always easier for the actor to believe what he is doing is real — to be in the moment — if he can use his own words. Having to stop and intellectually retrieve the scripted lines from his memory continually reminds the actor that he is not being himself, but trying to be someone else — someone who uses words differently than he does, words that don't come to him unthinkingly. As soon as he can start using his own words, spontaneously, any old way that they come out, this wall of a scripted, specific, somewhat alien behavior is eliminated. He can believe that what he is doing is real. The stronger this belief, the more in the moment he is, the better his performance becomes.

Second, improvs jack the conflict up to the max. The kind of improv that I find most useful is one that puts the actors on a head to head collision course, or as close to a collision as possible, without distorting the true nature of the conflict. It's a setup game of "chicken" with the wheels locked. The essence of all good drama is conflict. But there is conflict and then there is CONFLICT!!!! Most conflict in most dramatic scenes is between characters whose separate agendas do not put them directly in opposition to each other. They are opposing each other on a tangent, not head to head. In the scene from *Back to the Future*, Marty and Doc have conflicting agendas, but their agendas never are in direct opposition to each other. As the scene progresses, their conflict escalates. Doc goes from *suspecting* that Marty is not from the future to *being certain* that he is not. They start out coming at each other on an angle and they end up almost on a collision course, but they never quite get there, mostly because Doc's final tactic is to run away and hide in the garage.

Third, improvisations prolong the conflict. The scene is only as long as the number of its lines. Playing an objective that puts an actor at odds with the other actor in the scene is supposed to evoke real feelings inside the actor. But what if the actor only has 10 lines in the scene and he needs 20 or 30 lines of dialogue playing that objective to reach the level of frustration, or anxiety, or desire that is called for in the scene? Just playing the objective for those 10 lines may not get his juices flowing and enable him to really start feeling the volcanic, matter-of-life-and-death feelings the script calls for him to have. An improv cheats because it also lets the actors go at each other for an indefinite period of time — for as long as it takes for them to start disturbing or angering or exciting each other as much as the script calls for.

To devise a good improv for a scene, you need to imagine a parallel situation in which the clash of agendas is more head-on and the stakes are higher. Ideally, by playing out the roles of the characters in your parallel situation while being themselves and using their own words, the actors will be transported emotionally to the same place where you want them to go when they do the scene.

In coming up with a good improv for Michael J. Fox and Christopher Lloyd to play when rehearsing the above scene from *Back to the Future*, I would suggest the following:

To Christopher Lloyd:

1) You are at LAX. You have just boarded your flight to Kennedy.
2) This is your carry-on bag. (I give him a knapsack or a briefcase.) In this carry-on bag is $1 million worth of diamonds.
3) You are flying to New York to ransom your [most precious loved one] who has just been kidnapped.
4) When you get to Kennedy, a limo driver will meet you at the gate. You have to get in his limo, and then get out wherever he delivers you, leaving the bag in the limo. Or else your [loved one] will be killed.
5) The stewardess has warned you that a delusional paranoid schizophrenic is known to be in the area. This schizophrenic believes that he is an FBI agent.
6) You are worried about the very real threat of terrorists trying to blow up this flight, especially since it is a cross-country flight, full of fuel.
7) Your objective is to deliver your carry-on bag to the limo driver at Kennedy.

To Michael J. Fox:

1) You are an FBI agent following a terrorist bomber, Mustafa X. This terrorist's MO is to put a bomb in a brand-name knapsack or handbag and then find a passenger about to board a plane with the identical bag. The terrorist then switches bags. The bomb is timed to go off as soon as boarding is complete, while the plane is still on the ground.
2) Just one minute ago you saw Mustafa X switch his bag with Christopher Lloyd's bag, just before Lloyd boarded this flight to Kennedy.
3) It just so happens that Christopher Lloyd is your favorite camp counselor from camp [a camp Fox went to as a kid], who you have not seen in 10 years.
4) Your objective is to get Lloyd to give you his carry-on bag so you can dispose of it and prevent everyone on the plane and yourself from being blown up.
5) You have two minutes before the bomb explodes.

When the actors go to act out the improv, Fox will have to work very hard and very fast to try to convince Lloyd that 1) he is an FBI agent, 2) he and Lloyd have a prior, close relationship as camper and counselor, and 3) there is a bomb in the bag that is going to blow up in a matter of seconds and kill them all. Lloyd is going to have to work very hard to disprove everything that Fox is trying to convince him of, because 1) he is going to immediately suspect that Fox is the delusional schizophrenic that the stewardess warned him about, 2) as far as he is concerned the bag he is carrying has never been out of his hands and it contains the precious diamonds, and 3) his priority is just to get to Kennedy with his bag and give it to the limo driver. He knows if he doesn't do that his most precious loved one is going to be killed.

If the actor playing Fox truly goes after his objective, he is going to have to muster every ounce of charm, credibility, and authority in his person to win Lloyd over quickly before the bomb blows up. If the actor playing Lloyd truly commits to his objective, he is going to have to summon all of his intellectual acumen and masculine authority to make Fox prove his story.

The circumstances of the improv are such that during the improv, each actor is going to be doing something very much like what he is called upon to do in the scene from *Back to the Future*. In the improv, the stakes have been jacked up as high as they can go for both actors. It is a matter of immediate life and death for both actors in the improv, whereas in the scene, it is only a matter of life and death for Fox — and even then, it is not immediate, he still has some time to avert his death (by getting his parents to fall in love to guarantee that he will born). The conflict has been made head to head in the improv. Fox just wants to take the bag away from Lloyd, while Lloyd just wants to hang onto it. The words are not going to get in the way, since they can use any words that come to mind. So when the director says "Action!" each actor is going to be able to throw himself wholeheartedly into doing more or less what he is called upon to do in the scene. Because their objectives have them on a collision course, and because the stakes are so high, each actor should very quickly and very intensely start to feel the same emotions as Marty and Doc. Fox is going to be desperate, frustrated, freaked out, hurt, and rejected. Lloyd should feel defensive, put upon, indignant, angry, scornful, and vulnerable. This is precisely what the director hopes for. These feelings are the planned emotional fallout of the improv — the product of the actors having the freedom to play themselves in very similar circumstances to that of the scene with the conflict and the stakes jacked up to the max. The improv sets up a parallel universe that the actor can enter and go right to the emotional place that he wants to get to in the scene. Ideally, he can step out of that universe long enough for the camera to roll and the director to say "Action," and then step right back in again.

Script Breakdown – Layout

Harold Clurman, in *On Directing*, describes how, when he is breaking down a script, he inserts a blank sheet of paper in between each page and then records his choices of objectives and adjustments on this sheet, immediately across from the location of the line of dialogue where the objective or adjustment changes. I have followed

Clurman's advice on every project I have directed and found it to be absolutely indispensable. The first time director should do as Clurman recommends if he is serious about being able to help his actors improve their performances. Logic dictates that the director should put his script in a three-ring binder to accommodate these extra pages. This way when the director is in the middle of a rehearsal or on the set, and he needs to refresh his memory and recall any one of the great ideas he dreamed up while breaking down his script, all he has to do is open his script to the scene — which he can do quickly because all the scenes are numbered. On the facing page, on the left side of the ring binder, will be all of his handwritten notes, immediately across from the scene itself.

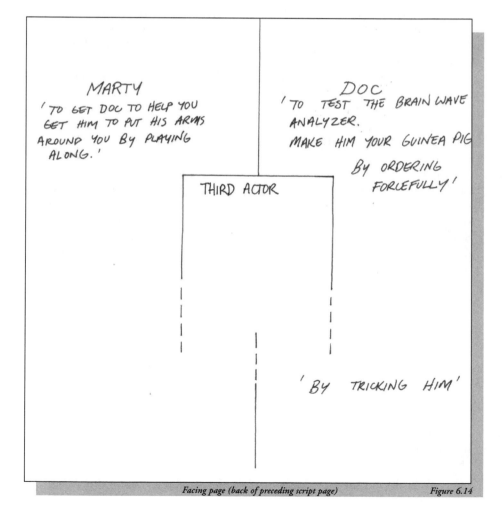

Facing page (back of preceding script page)   *Figure 6.14*

Clurman's advice makes particularly good sense when it comes to keeping track of the many adjustments that the director should come to the set with so that he is certain that he can help his actors improve every line that they have to deliver. Since it is not unusual for an actor's adjustment to change with every speech he makes, or several times within a two-or three-line piece of dialogue, that makes for a lot of adjustments. But should the director need to refer to his script in order to recall a particular adjustment, he can find it quickly if he breaks his script down in the way that Clurman recommends.

Clurman directed only one motion picture (*Deadline at Dawn*). His many illustrious credits are in theater. Accordingly, his book focuses on breaking down a script prior to directing a play. Everything Clurman says about getting a performance out

```
EXT. BROWN'S FRONT DOOR - CLOSER ANGLE

Marty runs up and pounds on the door knocker.

We hear a BARKING DOG from within; then YOUNG DOCTOR BROWN
opens the door.  He's wearing an OUTRAGEOUS CONTRAPTION on
his head, a bizarre conglomeration of vaccuum tubes,
rheostats, gauges, wiring and antennas; but there can be no
doubt that it's the same Dr. Brown, some 30 years younger.
Beside him is another DOG.

Marty stares at Brown's weird head gear.  Brown yanks
him inside.

INT. BROWN'S HOUSE - NIGHT

                    BROWN
          Don't say a word!
               (to the barking dog)
          Quiet, Copernicus!  Down, boy!

Brown attaches a suction cup to Marty's forehead which is
connected to a wire into Brown's contraption.

                    MARTY
          Dr. Brown, I really---

                    BROWN
          No, don't tell me anything:  I'm
          going to read your thoughts.

Marty indulges him.  Brown flips a switch on his "Brain
Wave Analyzer."  Tubes hum to life, and sparks jump from
antenna to antenna.  Brown concentrates, as if he's picking up
brain waves.

                    BROWN
          Let's see now...you've come here...
          from a great distance....
```

Script page

of an actor who is working in a play is equally valid for actors working in front of a camera. But how the actors are blocked — their movement on the stage — is very different from how actors are blocked for a camera. Accordingly, I have modified Clurman's method of laying out his breakdown notes on the facing page of each page in the director's script so that it works effectively for a director who is breaking down a film script.

My method is to draw a line down the middle of the facing page dividing it into two columns. At the top of one column I write one actor's name, for example, "Marty," and at the top of the other column I write the other actor's name, "Doc." Then on the far left side of the "Marty" column I write Marty's objectives, and on the far right side of the "Marty" column I write the different adjustments. Of course both are written immediately across from the scene description or the line in the script where the objective or the adjustment changes (Figure 6.14). Then I repeat the procedure for Doc Brown in the column under "Doc."

Nine out of 10 pages in a film script contain dialogue between no more than two characters. If a third character has lines on that page of the script, then I make a box in the middle of the facing page, taking up half of each of the two columns, and on the left side of the box I write the third actor's objectives and on the right side of the box I write their adjustments.

When Clurman broke down a script he noted objectives, adjustments, and blocking directions. I have embellished on Clurman's method by adding ultraplayable objectives (in addition to most-playable objectives), physicalization of the objective, and improvisations. So, if I were breaking down the scene from *Back to the Future*, I would make my two columns, one under "Marty" and one under "Doc" on the facing page, directly across from the slug line at the very top of the scene: EXT. BROWN'S FRONT DOOR – CLOSER ANGLE. On the far left side of the "Marty" column, at the top of column, I would write the most-playable objective: *get Doc Brown to help you* and under that I would write the ultraplayable objective: *get him to put his arms around you.* (Figure 6.14) Then in that same column, on the right side across from where the scene description states that, in response to Doc Brown's demands that Marty play the guinea pig, Marty "indulges" him, I would write down the first adjustment: *by playing along.* In the column under "Doc," on the left side of the column, directly across from the scene description "Doc yanks Marty inside," I would write Doc's most-playable objective: *test the Brain Wave analyzer.* Right under that I would write his ultraplayable objective: *make him your guinea pig.* Next, on the right side of the column under "Doc," I would write down Doc's first adjustment: *by ordering, forcefully,* directly across from where Doc's first line of dialogue falls in the script. (Figure 6.14)

In this fashion I would continue to record my selection of objectives and adjustments. On this first facing page, there would be no need to record any new objectives, since neither Marty nor Doc changes objectives. In fact, the only other note that the director would need to record on this first facing page of the scene would be the one change in adjustment that Doc Brown makes when he starts trying to pursue his objective *by tricking Marty* with lines like:

BROWN

Let's see now... you've come
here... from a great distance...

This leaves plenty of space on the facing page to record notes for physicalization of the objectives.

The director should record his ideas for the improv on a separate blank sheet of three-hole-punch paper that he would insert in his director's three-ring notebook before the first breakdown sheet for the scene. The sheet with the notes for improv on it must be inserted in the notebook before the breakdown sheet on which are noted the objectives and adjustments, so that when the notebook is opened to a specific scene, the adjustments and the objectives can be found on the facing page right across from the scene description of the line of dialogue where the objective or adjustment changes. The notes for the improv should describe the most relevant circumstances of the parallel situation in which the two actors are to imagine themselves, and a clear objective for each actor to play. The notes need not go into more detail than mine on page 180.

A great deal of what determines a first time director's success is dependent on chance. Therefore, wherever he has a modicum of control he must seize it and exploit it. If the director breaks down his script thoroughly using all the steps I describe above, he will be prepared to exert the maximum amount of control over the acting process and get the best possible performances out of his cast.

CHAPTER 6 | SUMMARY POINTS

■ The one ability required to be a good director of actors is a good instinctive or intellectual awareness of one's own emotions and what triggers them.

■ Almost all actors in America are trained in the Method. If a director is going to help a Method actor, he has to help the actor come as close as possible to actually experiencing the feelings that the character the actor is portraying should be experiencing at any particular moment in the character's development.

■ On your breakthrough project, you will inevitably end up having to work with some actors who cannot consistently deliver a credible performance. Unless the director can help the actor make his mediocre performance believable, then he might as well not even run the film through the camera.

■ Directing actors is every bit as complex as the human psyche. No mortal can fathom all of the infinitely complex ways that human beings are moved to feel the way that they feel. Therefore nobody knows everything they need to know about directing actors. The first time director is advised to go to work immediately starting to gain some mastery of this subject. The more he understands about it, the better his films will be.

■ You must find and enroll in an introductory level acting class. You must study acting until you are competent enough to get yourself cast in a significant part in a professional quality production that ends up on tape or film.

■ The first time director, before he makes any one of the millions of decisions he will make to put his mark on his breakthrough project, must determine precisely what the spine or the theme of the film is.

■ To prepare for directing his actors, a first time director on his breakthrough film must analyze the script in detail, breaking down every scene, devising and recording:

   1. The spine of the character:

   What motivates a character's actions is a goal — the end towards which he is constantly working. The only way to reach the goal is through action. Therefore, all character spines are verbs. They describe what the character systematically does to reach his goal.

2. The most-playable objective:

How do you determine an actor's objective? Ask yourself, bottom line, what it is that the character wants.

A playable objective is one that an actor can successfully commit to and thereby experience the emotions that are called for in his character at that moment in the script. The actor is the ultimate arbiter of whether an objective is playable. It is up to the director to provide the actor with an objective that the actor finds playable.

In my experience, those objectives that most actors can commit to most successfully are the ones that require the actor to interact in a specific way with another actor in the scene — in other words, those objectives that require the actor to get something from or do something to the other actor in the scene.

Get-from or do-to objectives + conflict = reality.

3. Ultraplayable objectives:

Ultraplayable objectives are those objectives that (1) it would be the easiest for the actor to commit himself to and (2) once the actor has committed himself to this objective, it would leave him the most exposed to the conflict in the scene and so evoke the most powerful emotions in him.

4. Physicalization:

When the actors start to interact physically and put their objectives into actions that result in physical contact, then they are more easily affected by the above formula: get-from or do-to objectives + conflict = reality.

5. Adjustments:

Each time an actor changes the way he is going about trying to reach his objective as an adjustment.

All adjustments are gerunds or adverbs.

6. Improvisations:

To devise a good improv for a scene you need to imagine a parallel situation to the situation in the scene, but one in which the clash of agendas is more head-on, and the stakes are higher. Ideally, by playing out the roles of the characters in your parallel situation while being themselves and using their own words, the actors will be transported emotionally in themselves to the same place where you want them to go when they do the scene.

- The first time director should look for objectives that can be played for as long a beat as possible. The longer the beat the better the objective, provided it is truly playable.

- The more adjustments you can find while breaking down a script, the better.

- Do not give an adjustment to an actor unless he needs it. If it ain't broken, don't fix it.

- Simplify, simplify, simplify. The fewer directions the director gives an actor, the better.

CHAPTER 7 | REHEARSAL

Preparation

When I broke through in episodic television and low budget features, all the rehearsal time I ever had was between the first run-through on the set for the DP and the time the set was lit. It is not likely you'll be afforded more of a luxury. Even so, you should be prepared to make the most of whatever time you do have to rehearse.

Come to the rehearsal with as much of the script broken down as possible, using the method I have recommended in Chapter 6. Logic dictates that you should have at least broken down the scenes that you are going to rehearse; if you have broken down the entire script, you will have a more complete understanding of the spine of the film and the spine of each character. This big-picture awareness of the film and the characters will inform all the little decisions you make spontaneously in the course of the rehearsal and give them coherence.

As much in advance of the rehearsal as possible, inform the actors that they must be completely **off book**: They must have all of their lines memorized, cold. The Method only really works if the actor never has to think what his lines are. He should be able to rattle them off so quickly they are unintelligible. They should be ingrained in his memory as indelibly as anything else he has had memorized all his life: his social security number, the Pledge of Allegiance, the lines: "Mary had a little lamb, whose fleece was white as snow, and everywhere that Mary went the lamb was sure to go." The reasons for this are inherent in the way the Method works. As soon as the actor has to pause and stop to think what his next line is, he cannot focus on his objective and, even worse, he is reminded that what he is doing is not real, but staged. This stops him from buying into the reality of what is happening between him and the other actors. It throws him out of the moment.

So it is almost pointless to have a rehearsal unless the actors know all the lines they will have to say, completely by heart, without having to think about them for an instant. Announce this and, at the risk of making a complete pain-in-the-ass out of yourself, remind the actors and their agents of this again and again. All too frequently, professional actors will come to rehearsals, or, even worse, to the set, without having thoroughly memorized all their lines.

This means that you have to start the rehearsal with a clandestine, polite test to discover if the actors know all their lines (of the scenes you intend to rehearse). When they walk in the door, engage the actors in some polite chitchat to put them at ease. Hopefully you have had a couple of informal meetings with them or at least talked on the phone, so you have had a chance to somehow convey to them your admiration for their work. You must make every member of your cast feel that you are glad he is in your film. Even if you really wanted another actor and are ambivalent, or, at worst, disappointed about the fact that he has been cast to play the role they are playing, I would advise strongly against revealing any of your ambivalence or disappointment. In my experience, the only way to get an actor to do his best work for you is to make him feel that you fundamentally like his work, that you are happy to be working with him, and that you are on his side and want him to do his very best. If he believes that you are on his side, he will listen to your constructive criticism and respond to your suggestions for improving his performance. Generally speaking, actors who suspect that you do not believe in them will see you as an adversary. If this is the case, they shut you out and try to direct themselves. Avoid this situation at all costs.

So, after putting your actors at ease with a little friendly chitchat and gentle praise, find out if they have done as you had instructed and thoroughly memorized their lines. To do this, seat them across from each other where they can all look at each other eyeball to eyeball and ask them to "Just say the lines, without any feeling... as if you are reading a laundry list." Of course, no scripts should be out or visible. If the actors cannot rattle their lines off, seemingly unthinkingly, without a flub, you cannot start rehearsing. You will have no choice but to burn up precious rehearsal time helping them memorize their lines.

You want to make sure you spend at least half of the time set aside for the rehearsal actually rehearsing, so don't bite off more than you can chew. If, in the worse case scenario, one actor knows none of his lines, then try to gauge how much of the scene or scenes he can memorize in half the rehearsal time, and then just focus on helping him memorize those lines. This way you can at least spend the second half of the rehearsal doing what you came there to do.

To help the actor memorize enough lines to give you something to rehearse, tell the actors, "Since we are not off book, as I had hoped, let's just run the lines, with the scripts in hand to see how much we can do without looking at the script. But again, no feeling, just say the lines flat, like you are reading a laundry list." The actors will have a good idea of what you are asking them to do. They are all practiced at playing scenes with scripts in hand. After all, this **cold reading** technique is what they do every time they audition for a part. If they were not extremely accomplished at being able to play a scene very believably, with almost all the right inflections and emotions, when they still do not know the lines and must hold the script in front of them, they would never be cast in a part, and would have no track record. So they will take out their scripts and when you say, "Action," they will launch themselves into the scene; in all likelihood, even though you told them "no feeling," they will give it to you with as much feeling as they can convincingly muster.

This is because they are actors. They feel it is their job — their calling — to put the right feelings behind the lines. Hopefully all of your actors will be very good at putting all the right feeling behind the lines. (If not, you better go back and start recasting.) Because they are good at it, they exult in it. They are like race-horses. They love to run. So even though you said "No feeling," they will read the lines with feeling. At which point you will have to admonish them gently and urge them to say the lines "completely flat." You can also offer them an explanation. Tell them you don't want any feeling because you "want them to be fresh when you start rehearsing." Experienced actors will understand the subtext of this explanation — namely, that if they had come to the rehearsal ready to rehearse, with their lines memorized, this little drill with the scripts in hand would not be necessary. Either consciously or unconsciously, they will get the point. You are punishing them, albeit lightly, by depriving them of the pleasure of doing what they do well — reading the lines with feeling — because they did not come to the rehearsal with all the lines memorized as you had instructed them. If they are relatively inexperienced actors, it might be a good idea to rub it in their face a little to make the point. After you tell them that you don't want them to say the lines with any feeling because you want them "to be fresh when we start rehearsing," add: "Because you know the Method doesn't work unless you never have to think of a line. So we can't really rehearse until you have the lines down cold."

Make them continue to run the lines of the first scene you want to rehearse, in this fashion — without any feeling, keeping the scripts in hand for reference — over and over. After running it four our five times this way, they will start to get bored at the monotony of the drill and try to slip a little more feeling in with each run-through. Stay alert to this covert effort to usurp control of the rehearsal and admonish them every time they inject a little feeling into a line.

The more the actors run through this drill, the more the pattern of the words and the rhythm of the lines will become ingrained in their memory; they will begin to glance less frequently at the scripts in their hands for the cues that they have not yet committed to memory. When you notice this, ask them to turn the scripts over and only pick the scripts up when they forget a cue. Do this over and over until they can do the scene and say all the lines without ever having to pick up a cue using the script. Once they have done it two or three times in succession without having to refer to the script, instruct them that they can now do the scene with feeling. This should come as a reward. If you have been strict and have not let them start slipping in a little more feeling with each repetition, they should now — when they are finally given the opportunity to do what they are good at and came there to do — throw themselves wholeheartedly into the rehearsal. Ideally this will enable you to make up for the time lost getting them ready to really rehearse.

Credibility versus Interpretation

Once the actors have the lines down cold, they can play the scene with feeling. They should still be sitting across from each other, so that blocking is not an issue. As they act out the scene, focus on what they are doing that you do not like. There will be moments that you do not like because they seem unconvincing or less real than other portions of the performance, and there will be moments that you do not like because, even though they are convincing, they are not to your mind the correct interpretation of the role — they do not seem appropriate to the character. For the time being, forget the moments that you do not like because of interpretation. Concentrate on the moments that are unconvincing. As I have explained earlier, these are the moments that will destroy the illusion of reality and so seriously undercut the overall effectiveness of your film. These have to be eliminated.

Often you can kill two birds with one stone. Moments that are unconvincing may also be slightly off in terms of line reading or interpretation. When you go to work on them, you might be able to correct both problems simultaneously. Put credibility ahead of interpretation, but take advantage of chances to eliminate problems in both areas. Unless each member of your cast is a proven professional, each actor will have at least two or three unconvincing moments in each scene. Pick the most offensive moment and go to work on it. Forget the other moments when the actor fails to be believable. Focus on those lines where his performance is weakest and try to bring them up to the level of the best parts of the performance. Devote no more than two or three more run-throughs of the scene to fixing this most offensive part. Don't get stuck. Try a couple of different plans of attack, and if they all fail, move on. Go to work on the second most unconvincing portion of the performance and try to fix it. Devote two or three run-throughs to fixing it, and then move on. If, before the rehearsal time is over, you have enabled the actor to deliver a performance that is completely convincing from beginning to end, then you can go to work on moments that you do not like because you feel the interpretation is not ideal.

I believe in this approach to rehearsal for first time directors for two reasons. First of all, it keeps the rehearsal simple. The director works on one part of the performance at a time, and one part only. He gives the actor one new tactic to try for each run-through. Frankly, my experience as an actor, and later as a director, taught me that only the best actors can correct more than one problem area in their performance each time they run a scene. The actor has to be very good to focus on the one new thing you have told him to try to help his performance *and* concentrate on everything that he was doing to get into the moment before you gave him one more thing to do. Remember in giving direction to actors: simplify, simplify, simplify!

The other reason I favor giving the actor one new tactic per run-through and focusing first on those moments which are unconvincing, is that trying to change the actor's entire interpretation of the part on a line by line basis is usually more trouble than it is worth. This sort of micro-management is a luxury few first time directors can afford. If the actor is way off in his interpretation — if he is playing Marty McFly as a sulky, morose adolescent, or Michael Corleone as a hyperkinetic extrovert — then you have to sit him down and talk about the spine of the movie and the spine of his character. That is why you have done your homework and know just what these fundamental, defining measuring sticks are. Once you and the actor are in sync about the spine of the character, I would advise the first time director to let the actor deliver the lines the way that sounds right to him, especially if his delivery is convincing and credible. The bottom line with an actor's performance is if it ain't broken, don't fix it. If the actor delivers a line or a speech convincingly, but it sounds a little weird to you, because he did not deliver it just the way you heard it in your head when you wrote the line or when you were pouring over your script the night before when you broke it down, just chill! What's important is: Do the actor's emotions seem real? Is he believable in the part? If so, that's great! Cut! Print! Walk away from it! Because that's what's going to sell your film and make your script realize its potential.

First time directors, especially those who have also written the script of their breakthrough project, tend to obsess about line readings. They demand that the actors deliver the lines just the way they hear them in their heads. This is a deep pitfall. There are two excellent reasons to avoid this pitfall. First, when you start messing with line readings, you may win the battle and lose the war. When you're done, the actor may be delivering the lines the way you want to hear them, but the credibility has gone out of his performance. Congratulations! Credibility is paramount, so now you are worse off than when you started. If what the actor is doing reinforces the spine of his character, and it sounds real, buy it. Second, with actors, fixes are like favors. With each actor, you only have a certain number of favors in the bank. Some actors are always open to advice and eager to try anything to improve their performance. But in my experience, most are only receptive to a limited amount of constructive criticism, especially from a first time director. When you have made films as good as Stanley Kubrick, you can ask for 60 takes. Until then, don't risk expending your actor's good will and understanding on line readings.

There still may be instances when a first time director needs to use up some very valuable rehearsal time working on a line reading. If your breakthrough film is a comedy, it might be essential that the actor deliver the line in a very specific way — just the way the director hears it in his head — in order to make a joke play. In the case of a comedy, making the jokes play is a top priority. The more jokes that play, the better the film. This is why Irving Thalberg let the Marx Brothers take *A Night at the Opera* on the road before it was shot. They fine-tuned all the jokes in front of live audiences before they put them on film.

In rehearsal, the first time director working on a comedy will have to prioritize his fixes. Certainly the reading of a line that pays off or sets up a joke is crucial. A good example of such a was cited earlier in the scene from *Back to the Future* in which Marty McFly answers Doc Brown's question as to who the President of the United States will be in 1985. Marty has to answer "Ronald Reagan" as if he were stating the obvious. This sets up the irony in Doc's over-the-top incredulous reaction. The actor playing Marty has to nail the line for the joke to play. A first time director would be wise to make sure he got the delivery of all crucial joke lines just right, even if it meant letting a few slightly unconvincing readings slide by unfixed. This is especially true if the director knows he has enough coverage to cut around the unconvincing lines. The director must be the final arbiter of which lines are most crucial to success of the film and so which lines should be prioritized and fixed first.

Objectives and Adjustments in Rehearsal

I approach the task of improving a performance as a boxing match. What you don't like in the actor's first delivery of the scene is your opponent. You take the opponent on with your left jab or your right hook. The adjustments are your jabs. The objectives are your hook. The jabs are sharp and precise. They wear your opponent down little by little. The hook is your knockout punch. Usually the way I work is to set my opponent up with a couple of jabs and then try to KO him with my hook. If the performance in the first read-through is strong, then the opponent is weak. A couple of more read-throughs and the scene will be fixed, the opponent eliminated. In such cases, you just throw a couple of jabs — an adjustment in the second read-through and another adjustment in the third read-through — and, bang, he's down and out. If the performance is fair, then a couple of jabs and then a hook; a couple of more jabs and down he goes. Five or six read-throughs — four changes in adjustment, one change in the objective. If the performance is weak, the opponent is a monster. You start with a couple of jabs and then you throw a hook. That hardly fazes him, so you repeat that combination, once, twice, three times, and so on, until you bring him down; or, more often than not, the bell rings, and you're out of time. Rehearsal is over. The set is lit. Ready or not, you've got to put it on film.

As I said above, your most effective tool for shaping a performance is finding the right objective and getting the actor to commit to it. But, unless the performance is awful, you want to avoid diving in and immediately questioning your actor's choice of objectives right after the first or second read-through. As a first time director working with a professional cast, you had best show respect for your actors and give them a lot of rope to hang themselves with. You're going to come off like a kid with a new toy if you are perpetually grilling them about every objective they're using. Some of the best actors can't even articulate what they are doing to summon feelings. It is not like playing the piano. You don't hit a key and get a note. It's very intuitive and hard to describe. It's like they're trying to juggle while walking on a tightrope. You may just be trying to be constructive, but if you start criticizing their juggling right from the get-go, they might just fall off the tightrope. So let your actors work on it themselves. Let them do at least two or three run-throughs before you discuss changing their objective. The first run-through is usually a warm up. If after the third or the forth run-through, 15 to 20 % of the feelings are still not totally believable, go to work on the objective. Again, if it ain't broken, don't fix it.

You can only wait to the fifth run-through to work on the objective if you are rehearsing prior to the start of shooting. If you are squeezing in a rehearsal on the day of shooting while the set is being lit, the same theories apply, but you have got to work at least twice as fast, if not faster. If you are rehearsing on the set, remind the actors that time is precious and there is no such thing as a warm-up. When you tell them to do the scene with feeling, that means full-bore, 100 %, no holding back. Then, after two or three run-throughs, if it still is 20 % unbelievable, you had better go to work and come up with a better objective.

Again, the objective is your weapon of choice. The adjustments are your jabs. They enable you to make more precise, surgical improvements while you are (hopefully) lining up the opponent for your knockout blow. So right after the first run-through, pick the part of the performance that you find most unconvincing, and check your script for the adjustment for those lines from your script break-down. This is why it is essential that you thoroughly break down the script, writing down all the adjustments, well before the first rehearsal. Say you were directing the scene from *Back to the Future*, when Marty first introduces himself to the younger Doc Brown in 1955. If the part of Marty's performance that you like the least is when he announces to Doc Brown that Ronald Reagan, the actor, will be the President of the United States in 1982, then you would find that the adjustment for those lines is "by stating the obvious."

The adjustment "by stating the obvious" is a tactic that Marty is using to achieve his objective — *to get Doc Brown to help you*. Giving the actor this adjustment to play for these lines should help him make his performance more believable. It gives the actor something precise to do while delivering those lines, and so should give him yet another means to commit to the objective.

This adjustment will be the first piece of direction you give the actor during this rehearsal — your first piece of constructive criticism. Before you criticize the actor, show him, yet again, that you fundamentally believe in him and you are on his side (even if you have grave misgivings about his abilities). A little bit of praise will go a long way. So, pick the best part of the actor's performance and praise him for it, and in the next breath, give him the adjustment. Tell him, "In these lines this is what I think your character is trying to do – he is *stating the obvious*. On this next run-through, try doing that when you deliver these lines," or words to that effect. Hopefully this will fix his delivery on those lines. If it does, then you can move onto the part of his performance that you have identified as his second least believable moment.

Continue working this way with each actor through four or five run-throughs. If the performance is still more than 20% unbelievable, then launch into a discussion of the actor's objectives for the scene. Refer to your script breakdown and give him one or two of the most-playable objectives to try. For example, if the actor was playing Marty in the above scene, you could tell him "I think what Marty wants is *to get Doc Brown to help him*. That is his one objective. That's what he wants when he knocks on Doc's door, and he keeps on trying to get that until the last line of the scene." The actor may want to play more than one objective or he may disagree that what Marty wants is *to get Doc Brown to help him*. Be respectful. Listen to the actor's ideas. But in the end, insist on him trying it your way. You are the director. All set etiquette gives you the right to politely insist. You should be able to bolster your argument in support of your choice of objective using all of the reasoning processes that you went through when you broke down the script. This means that you should have thought it through as thoroughly as I did in the section above when I gave my reasons for selecting *to get Doc to help you* as a good objective for Marty in this scene — in which case, you should easily be able to muster a very convincing argument.

If it was the actor playing Doc Brown who was still 20% unbelievable by the fifth run-through, you could suggest to this actor that he try using the objectives *to test the Brain Wave Analyzer* and *to get Marty to reveal his true purpose* up through the point in the scene where Marty insists that the President of the United States in 1982 will be Ronald Reagan. The point of giving him just two of his three objectives for the scene is to keep it simple and not give him too many new strategies to try in each run-through. But objectives seem to be linked. The choice of objective often depends on where it starts and ends, so once you change one objective for an actor in a scene, you may automatically have to change all his objectives.

When I talk to an actor about his objective, I like to do it one on one, out of earshot of the other actors. This is not by any means absolutely necessary, but I find it helpful — most importantly because, again, drama comes from conflict. So the actors will have conflicting agendas. The conflict may not be head to head, but it will be there. When they go to play their objectives, they are going to encounter some form of resistance from the other actors. The frustration, anxiety, despair, scorn, or glee that this resistance triggers in the actor is one way the Method works to help actors embody real feelings. If the actor does not know exactly what the other actor's agenda is — which is to say, what objective he is playing — then his reaction to the resistance posed by this conflicting agenda will be more spontaneous, more real. For this reason, I like to keep the actors in the dark for as long as possible as to what objectives the other actors in the scene may be playing.

It is also helpful to think of acting and creating a performance as a form of play. It is not just a coincidence that the term "play" has long been used in the English language to describe actors acting together on a stage. If, just before you run the scene to test the new objectives, you take each actor aside briefly, and whisper to them the new objectives, and then step back and, say, "Okay, let's try it again with some new objectives," there should be a little thrill of anticipation in each actor at encountering the unexpected. We're not talking a huge thrill here. It's just a little treat to get the actors excited and keep the spirit of the rehearsal and the entire enterprise of crafting a performance upbeat and positive. Up until the last moment, before trying the scene with new objectives, I keep everybody in on the conversation and discuss all the actors' objectives, in general, in front of everyone at the rehearsal. This makes the rehearsal feel inclusive and familial. It should feel that way because it is a team undertaking. But when you give the actor the precise objective, whisper it in his ear to introduce a little constructive gamesmanship.

If, after the fifth run-through, the performance was on the whole weak and you felt compelled to change the objective or objectives, then after the sixth or seventh run-through there should be a noticeable improvement. That is the best-case scenario. A new objective can make a scene come to life and in one fell swoop knock out all the unbelievable moments. If this is the case, all you may need to supply the actor is a couple more adjustments and the scene is working — believable and credible from beginning to end. In the worst-case scenario, the new objective does not work. Say, for example, I was rehearsing the scene from *Back to the Future*. After the fifth run-through, I told the actor playing Marty to try using the objective *to get Doc Brown to help you*. But, during the sixth run-through, I saw no change. Then, as soon his performance sagged during the seventh run-through, I would shout out loud, "Play the objective! Get him to help you. You need his help. You'll die without it!" If after shouting out, I still notice no improvement, I will try it again. This time I may say, "Play the objective! You want him to help you! Show me how desperately you want him to help you!"

This old-fashioned, ballet-teacher-with-the-cane or maestro-with-the-baton approach can sometimes suddenly focus the actor and get him to commit to the objective. It may seem a little heavy handed, but as an actor, I have found that it helped, and I was actually grateful to the director for shouting at me. It is so hard to think of anything and act at the same time. As an actor you may think you are playing the new objective, but you have not committed to it. Your thoughts have not affected your behavior. Having the director shout the objective to you suddenly reminds you what you are doing. It gives you something to do. You do it, and suddenly you are playing the objective.

Unfortunately, sometimes the new objective changes nothing. After three or four more run-throughs, you may have to change the objective a second time. You want to give the actor at least three shots at making the new objective work. There is no rule that says the actor has to successfully commit to a new objective on the first try. It's like starting a lawn mower with a starter cord. Sometimes it takes a couple of pulls before it kicks over and comes to life. Even if the actor cannot commit to the new objective in the course of run-throughs seven, eight, and nine, at least try to inch him closer to a better performance by giving him a new adjustment after each run-through to improve that part of the scene that sticks out as the weakest. You can think of this as a double-pronged approach to making the performance credible.

Giving him a new adjustment to try on run-throughs seven, eight, and nine also helps disguise the fact that you still do not like his performance and are just pulling the starting cord three more times, praying that the actor will commit to the new objective and make what he is doing seem believable for the first time.

That's all the more reason to come to the rehearsal with every possible adjustment written down. You can vamp by just throwing out adjustments for the actor to try.

If up to 20% of the performance is still unbelievable after nine run-throughs, then you need to try to make it come to life by changing the objective for the second time. Do not mention to the actor that you are changing the objective again because he seems to be having trouble committing to any objective. Accentuate the positive and say to him, "Okay, that was good, but I want to try something a little different from here on." If you were working with the actor playing Marty, you could now give him the ultraplayable objective that you wrote down in your script underneath the most-playable objective when you broke down your script: *to get him to give you a hug*. This is why I recommend writing down two significantly different objectives for every beat of the scene. Often your actor cannot successfully commit to the first change in objective that you make. The ultraplayable objective is your back-up defense.

When you give your actor an ultraplayable objective, it may shock him a little and he may question the validity of playing such an objective. Even actors who are very familiar with the Method may never have played an objective that works the way an ultraplayable objective works. The ultraplayable objective does not refer directly to what the character in the drama wants. Rather, it is something the actor playing that character wants. In this it does not conform to Harold Clurman's or Lee Strasberg's definition of how an objective works. Still, the change of pace — the novelty of trying something a little out of the ordinary — may be just what an actor needs to make his performance come to life.

The beauty of ultraplayable objectives is that they seem to tap into very useful reservoirs of feelings within the actor which objectives, as defined by Clurman and other authorities on the Method, may leave untouched. For example, the ultraplayable objective — *get him to give you a hug* — may be easier for the actor playing Marty to commit to emotionally because it might lead him to successfully project the image of his own father on the actor playing Doc Brown, and it might then evoke within him the powerful feelings of longing, neediness, and desirability that most boys feel in relation to the prospect of a hug from their dad. Hopefully, this would make the actor playing Marty seem more desperately in need of some sign of affirmation coming from the actor playing Doc Brown, and so, more flustered, hurt, and desperate when the other actor spews out an endless stream of doubt, ridicule, and rejection. It might then, after ten run-throughs, finally enable the actor playing Marty to seemingly actually be experiencing the feelings called for by his role, when one change in objective and seven or eight changes in adjustments had failed to help him deliver a credible performance.

By the same token, an ultraplayable objective might give an emotional boost to an actor who, very early on in the rehearsal — say after the second or third run-through — was delivering a solid, credible performance.   By tapping into the same untapped reservoirs of feeling, it might enable that actor to deliver a performance that exceeded being merely credible and approached being entirely good or even great.   Logic dictates that if the director regards the actor's performance as fully credible and likes his interpretation of every line of dialogue, he could then give the actor the ultraplayable objective as a means to help him take his performance to a higher level.   That is exactly how it should be presented to the actors.   In the case of the scene between Marty McFly and Doc Brown, the director, after two or three run-throughs, might say to the well-prepared, gifted actor portraying Marty, "I love what you're doing.   It's all very believable and good, but this time through, why don't you play the scene as if what you want, more than anything else, is to get him to give you a hug?   I think it might bring out some interesting colors or take the scene to a higher level."

Physicalization As a Rehearsal Tool

When a director breaks down a script, I recommend that he also think up and write down ways that the actors can work to achieve their objectives that would involve touching each other or interacting physically.   This **physicalization** of the objective is effective because when the actors are allowed to resort to physical means to achieve their objective, they are more easily affected by the formula of a get-from or do-to objective + conflict = reality.

For example, after Marty tells Doc Brown that Ronald Reagan will be the President in 1985, Doc decides Marty is playing a practical joke on him and gives up testing whether Marty is actually from the future.   His objective becomes *to get rid of Marty*.   So he runs out of the house and locks himself in his garage.   Marty is still playing his objective — *to get Doc Brown to help you*.   Marty runs after Doc, shouting at him along the way, still trying to convince Doc that he really is from the future.   The director can tell Marty to follow right on the heels of Doc and to try to slow him up by reaching out and trying to grab him by the wrist or the shirt sleeve or whatever he can get his hands on.   The director should tell the actor playing Doc to keep yanking his arm free and twisting out of Marty's grasp, so as to make sure he gets to the garage ahead of Marty.   The two actors both have get-from or do-to objectives — what they are both trying to do is to get something from or do something to the other actor.

There is conflict written into the scene because they are at cross-purposes: Doc wants to get rid of Marty while Marty wants Doc to stop and fix his problem.

Because each is dependent on the other to get what he wants and because they are at cross-purposes, they are going to frustrate and annoy each other. This frustration is a real feeling that each actor will feel, and it will be exacerbated by the other actor's behavior. This is the means by which get-from or do-to objectives plus conflict equal reality. Each of the characters — both Doc and Marty — at this point in the film are meant to be are extremely annoyed and frustrated, so for the actors to actually be feeling these feelings is entirely appropriate, and in fact will heighten the credibility of their performances.

Physicalization of the objective is a very effective rehearsal tool for the first time director. He can use it to jumpstart a performance that is having difficulty coming to life. Perhaps the rehearsal has progressed through ten or more run-throughs. The director has given the actor or actors seven or eight adjustments to try, as well as both the most-playable objective and the ultraplayable objective, and, still, the performance seems weak and not all together credible. The director could then ask the actors to physicalize their objectives in the hope that they could finally get into the moment and make their performances real.

My experience as both an actor and a director has taught me that most good acting takes place on a purely physical and emotional level. Physicalizing the objective works strictly on this level, so it sometimes is effective when all other approaches have failed. I would say it is the most simple, most accessible directing tool I have ever encountered. It almost always produces results. Those results might not be just what the director hoped for, but they usually are quite real.

The director might also use physicalization of the objective as a means of strengthening an already strong performance. More or less duplicating the same scenario by which an ultraplayable objective could be used to this same end, the director would suggest to the actor, who very early in the rehearsal was delivering a solid, credible performance, that he try physicalizing his objective — in the hope that this might enable him to tap into some untapped reservoirs of feeling and take the performance to a higher level. That is exactly how it should be presented to the actors.

In the case of the above scene between Marty McFly and Doc Brown, the director, after two or three run-throughs, might say to the well-prepared, gifted actor portraying Marty, "I love what you're doing. It's all very believable and good, but this time through, when he runs away from you, stay right on his heels and keep grabbing his clothing or his wrist and try to get him to stop, turn around, and deal with you. I think it might bring out some interesting colors or take the scene to a higher level." Of course, to keep the level of conflict high — and make sure that the physicalization of the objective would feed the actor playing Marty with all the hoped for feelings of rejection, frustration, and panic — the director would also tell the actor playing Doc Brown to keep moving and stay far enough ahead of Marty so he can make it to the garage with room to successfully close the door in Marty's face.

The director might ultimately decide that when he puts the scene on film, he does not want the actors to touch or to interact physically in any way — hugging, kissing, hitting, etc. — because it is not true to the characters and/or misconstrues the story. In *Back to the Future*, Marty and Doc never interacted physically in any of the ways that I have suggested. This would seem to provide strong evidence that these forms of physical interaction are not appropriate for their characters or in keeping with the spirit of the story. But this does not mean these suggested physical interactions could not be used in rehearsal as a way to help the actors access the emotions needed to deliver a credible or inspired performance.

Improvisation As a Rehearsal Tool

Improvisation, like physicalization, is a very effective rehearsal tool for the first time director. It can be used as a last resort to jumpstart a performance that a director is having difficulty making come to life.

In the case of this scenario, the rehearsal might have progressed through ten or more run-throughs. By that point, the director would have given the actor or actors seven or eight adjustments to try, as well as both the most-playable objective and the ultraplayable objective, and still the performances seem weak and not all together credible. The director could then suggest to the actors that they try an improvisation. He can tell them that while in the improv they get to play themselves and use whatever lines of dialogue come to their head. They just have to obey the circumstances of the improv and work to attain their objective. The other rule of improvisation is "no denial" and "no obligation." This means that if, in the course of the improv, one actor decides to elaborate on the circumstances laid out by the director, the other actor cannot "deny" the reality of these added circumstances, no matter how far-fetched they may be. After all, the improv is an entirely fictitious situation, but just because one actor says it is so, doesn't mean the other actor must also say it is so. He is under "no obligation" to confirm what the other actor claims. He just should not come right out and deny it or put it down.

The improv is going to work best if each actor is completely unaware of the other actor's agenda. This makes their reactions to the conflict more spontaneous and real.

So the director should attempt to lay out the improv to each actor, individually, in private. He could either ask the other actor or actors to leave the room. Or, if it were easier, he could take one actor into another room or into the hall. Once alone, he would refer to his ideas for an improv for this scene that he had prepared while breaking down his script. If he were working on the scene between Marty and Doc, once he was alone with the Christopher Lloyd, he would lay out the circumstances for the improv that affect him and his objective. So the director would explain the situation to Lloyd, just as on page 180. And then, in private, he would tell Michael J. Fox the circumstances under which he should be operating during the improv and his objective, again as on page 180.

The director would then bring the two actors together. Lloyd, since he is playing the tourist on the plane, should be seated. The director can then create a space to act as the set, using more chairs and a couple of moveable flats, or anything else that could stand in for the body of the plane. The director should then remind the actors of the basic rules: They can use their own persona in the part of tourist or FBI agent, they can use their own words, they can touch the bag, and they can touch each other, but no pulling or pushing or trying to achieve the objective by simply overpowering the other actor.

The final rule that I give is the most important one. I learned this little trick from Delia Salvi. I have seen her use it dozens of times to great effect, and I myself have used it countless times to jumpstart a performance that refused to come to life. I tell the actors that when I say, "Action," they should start the improv. And when I clap my hands, they should go into the scene we are rehearsing on such and such a line and go into the characters that they are playing in the scene. If we were rehearsing the scene from *Back to the Future,* I would tell them to go into the scene at the top for their first exchange of dialogue when Marty says, "Dr. Brown, I really…" and the Doc cuts him off, saying, "No, don't tell me anything," because he just wants to start his Brainwave Analyzer test.

It's important that the circumstances of the improv are devised so that during the improv, each actor is going to be doing something very much like what he is called upon to do in the scene in the film. In the improv, the stakes have been jacked up as high as they can go for both actors: It is a matter of immediate life-and-death. The conflict has been made head to head. Fox just wants to take the bag away from Lloyd, while Lloyd just wants to hang onto it. The words are not going to get in the way, since the actors can use any words that come to mind.

So when the director says, "Action!" each actor is going to be able to throw himself wholeheartedly into doing more or less what he will be called upon to do in the scene. Because their objectives have them on a collision course, and because the stakes are so high, each actor should very quickly and very intensely start to feel the same emotions they will be called upon to exhibit as Marty and Doc. Fox is going to be desperate, frustrated, freaked out, angry, and rejected. Lloyd should feel defensive, put upon, indignant, angry, scornful, and vulnerable. The circumstances also dictate that they will be feeling these feelings while they are doing almost the same thing that they are called upon to do in the scene for the film. Fox is going to be using charm, reason, and authority to convince Lloyd of an unlikely scenario involving the bag, and Lloyd is going to be using reason, scorn, and masculine authority to get Fox to leave him alone.

Ideally, the improv will enable each actor to put himself into the exact mental, psychological, and physical state that he wants to be in to best play the scene in the film. When the director claps his hands, as the signal to go from the improv into the scene, the actors should be in the moment and almost in character. All they have to do is say the lines and the scene should come to life.

This is the best rehearsal tool I have ever come across in all my experience as a director. I have found that when nothing else worked, this would finally get the actors into the moment as much as was humanly possible and make the scene come to life. It can be tricky to get the improv to work just right. Actors are not machines and so it is impossible to predict exactly what they will do. Even though their agendas have them on a collision course and the stakes are high, they may not confront each other as vigorously and wholeheartedly as the director hopes for.

Other directors may use improvs differently; my interpretation of how to use an improv depends on the actors getting very confrontational, very quickly. If an actor is non-confrontational by nature, he may hide behind the instruction that the director has given him prior to the improv "to play himself" and use it as an excuse to avoid fighting against the other actor's conflicting agenda. Such an actor's disposition may undermine the effectiveness of the improv.

For example, in the above improv, if the actor playing the FBI agent senses that the actor playing the tourist is going to vigorously deny and ridicule the idea that he is an FBI agent, it may not spur him to press his point. He may just give up or back down or press his point gently. If he does this, the improv will not work as intended. The success of the improv is dependent on Fox aggressively confronting Lloyd, coming up hard against Lloyd's conflicting agenda, and experiencing feelings of anger, frustration, rejection, and fear in the face of Lloyd's resistance.

If the director notices one of the actors avoiding the confrontation that is written into the improv, then he should stop the improv and go over the circumstances and the objective. In the case of the above scene, he would remind Fox that he must convince the tourist to turn the carry-on bag over to him in two minutes or the bomb will go off and kill everyone. The director can start the improv again, and if the actor playing the FBI agent still refuses to aggressively pressure the tourist into handing over the bag, the director can use the ballet-teacher-with-the-stick approach and shout at the actor, "Play your objective! If you don't get the bag, you're dead!" Even this may not work, and the director may be forced to stop the improv and discuss it further.

Making Weak Actors Believable and Good Actors Great – Improv As a Versatile Tool for Rehearsal

Improvisation is one of the three silver bullets that a first time director can use to make a weak performance come to life or to turn a good performance into a great one (an ultraplayable objective and physicalization are the other two). He can use any one of the three to save his ass if he is rehearsing a scene with actors who are short on talent and cannot, after multiple run-throughs, deliver a convincing performance. And, if by some incredible stroke of luck or through a series of industry connections, the first time director ends up with a good, solid cast, he can use these three bullets to make his good actors look great and actually make the splash he dreams of making with his first film.

It should be noted that this particular improv for this scene from *Back to the Future* will start the scene off too strong. This is often the case. Because the actors' emotions shift, sometimes quite dramatically in the course of a scene, the transition from improv to scene is most seamless and perfect at one particular point in the scene. In the case of this improv, the perfect transition point comes about two thirds of the way through the scene — after Doc tries to get rid of Marty by running out of the house and locking himself in the garage, while Marty runs after him pleading his case. Marty at this point is feeling desperate, misunderstood, and full of apprehension and dread. Doc is angry with Marty and angry at himself for ever listening to Marty. The improv is designed to get the two actors into this intense, semi-hysterical emotional space.

Still, the improv can be used successfully as a rehearsal tool for the entire scene. If the actors are having difficulty evincing credible emotions, an improv that might be overkill in any other case may be just the sort of powerful stimulus needed to help such actors summon up some of the necessary feelings. In such an instance,

206 first time director | bettman

the director makes the actors repeatedly jump from the improv into the top of the scene. Every time they do this, the weak actors might be able to bring some reality to yet another part of the scene in which they had previously been consistently weak and unconvincing. By discussing the scene and helping the actors understand what sort of emotional transactions between them and the other actors had finally enabled them to hit these true notes, the director should be able to help them hit all those notes again, on cue, when the cameras roll. In this way the director uses the improv as a tool to help the weak actor get into the moment at different places in the scene, in the hope that in the end, he will be able to get into the moment at the top of scene and play it in the moment all the way through. Usually the director runs out of time before he can help a weak actor cobble together a performance that works for the entire scene. But rehearsing this way, the director can enable a weak actor to come close enough to delivering a consistently believable performance and perhaps prevent the weak actor from holding back or doing serious damage to the director's breakthrough film.

With a talented actor, the director's approach is almost the opposite. Instead of trying to amplify and multiply the real feelings that the actor carried from the improv into the scene, the director works with the actor to tone down and be more selective in his use of these real emotions. In the case of the scene from *Back to the Future*, the director might tell the actors to go straight from the improv into the top of the scene. Afterwards he would identify for the actors where the feelings evoked by the improv were right for the scene, but too strong, too "over the top," in the hope that the next time through, the actors would be able to go back to those same places emotionally, but suppress those feelings — "hold them back" or "feel them without showing them."

From my own experience as an actor, I know it is not difficult to suppress a feeling. What's difficult is to actually achieve the feeling that needs to be suppressed. It is not hard for an actor to hold back anger. We do this all the time in everyday life. We are good at using our intellect to control our emotions. On the other hand, we are not good or experienced at summoning up specific emotions on call. Only a small cadre of gifted working actors can actually do that. So the fact that going from an improv into a scene might generate emotions that are too strong for the scene and have to be suppressed by the actors is actually a very good thing. Better to have the feeling big-time and be required to hold it down, than only have a little of the feeling or not have it at all.

Going from the improv into the scene might also cause the actors to experience feelings that were appropriate for one part of the scene but not the other. For example, if the improv made the actor playing Doc angry with Marty, once aware of that, a gifted actor could go back to that anger for the last third of the scene where he needs to be angry with Marty. In any case, an improv that evokes feelings that are especially appropriate to one part of a scene can always be used productively as a rehearsal tool for the entire scene. Whether the actors are weak or strong, the improv helps them access real emotions that can become very good raw material to put into their final performance.

Preparation Is Everything

By this point, it should be absolutely clear to the first time director why — before coming to a rehearsal — he must break down all of the scenes he is going to rehearse. He should have written down in his work script legibly and in great detail all of the objectives and adjustments the actors might play. As noted above, there will be a few crucial objectives, but a great many possible adjustments, and the director should have taken the trouble to identify all of them. He should have figured out exactly how the actors could best physicalize their objectives and written down notes to himself on this. He should have devised an improv that parallels the circumstances of the scene, such as the one involving a bomb and some carry-on luggage, and he should have written down the circumstances of the improv and each actor's objectives in the improv, going into as much detail as appropriate. If the first time director does not go to these lengths to prepare for the rehearsal, and the rehearsals do not succeed in making every performance of every actor noticeably, if not remarkably better, then the first time director has only himself to blame. He has squandered a great opportunity — a chance to make sure that his breakthrough film catapults him into the ranks of working directors.

Very few people think on their feet well enough to make all of the many precise judgments and subtle distinctions a director must make when he breaks down a script. Even if the rehearsal is held prior to the start of shooting, so the director can come to the rehearsal clearheaded and energetic (unlike the rehearsals on the set where he will be frazzled and exhausted most of the time), it is unlikely that he would be able to think with enough precision to see that Doc Brown shifts tactics in the middle of the following lines.

                          BROWN
            And who's the Vice President?
            Jerry Lewis? That's the most
            insane thing I've ever heard.

Even if the first time director is quick enough to see that in the middle of the above line Doc Brown changes tactics, he would need to have a great command of the language to be able to come up with just the right words to describe that shift in tactics. Language is an important part of helping an actor with his performance. The director has to find the words that will alter and guide the actor's behavior. When coming up with objectives and adjustments that work — that effectively shape a performance and make it credible — my experience has always been that if I came up with all the right words and wrote them all down prior to rehearsal, I always got much better results in the rehearsal.

Even if the first time director is an incorrigible last-minute artist, he should still write down as much as the spirit moves him before coming to the rehearsal. There are instances when even the most conscientious directors are caught by surprise and do not have enough time to fully prepare for a rehearsal that has been called at the last minute. The bottom line is: The more you prepare, the more notes you can scribble down on the facing pages of your script, the better the performances will be when the rehearsal is over.

If the first time director is a risk taker and wants to cut some corners, or if the rehearsal is called at the last minute and he does not have time to fully prepare, then he can dispense with identifying every single adjustment and thinking through the improv in as much detail as I recommend. If something must be sacrificed, it should be the adjustments. Similarly, once the director has the broad strokes of a good improv, he can fill in many of the necessary details spontaneously when he lays out the improv for the actors, or between subsequent run-throughs. In the improv for the scene from *Back to the Future*, the essential elements are that the actor playing Marty must believe that he is an FBI agent and feel certain that the tourist has a soon-to-explode bomb placed in their carry-on luggage, while the actor playing Doc Brown must believe that he is required to get the bag to New York to save his loved one, and that a fast-talking delusional, schizophrenic who thinks he is an FBI agent is in the area. If the director had written that much down, he could embellish it as he gave it to the actors or between run-throughs.

Even if you do not go into the same amount of detail, even if you do not write down all of the adjustments, even if you do not create an improv that is as intricate as the one involving the bomb, you should at least write down (1) the most-playable objectives, (2) the ultraplayable objectives, (3) some ideas for physicalizing the objectives and (4) an improv for each scene. This way you can come to the rehearsal with all of the silver bullets for killing a bad performance in your gunbelt. Again, acting is an intuitive business and so there are no hard and fast rules. What works great with some actors under certain circumstances, fails utterly with different actors under different circumstances. The director's best defense against this unpredictable component of the acting process is a variety of weapons with which to kill a bad performance.

Now that you've written down the four items in the preceding paragraph, use them in the following order to work on improving a performance: (1) change the most playable objective, (2) try an ultraplayable objective, (3) try physicalizing the objective and last (4) try an improv. This order is not carved in stone. The director should rely on his instincts and judgment. But the logic of this order is that it saves the most powerful weapons for the last. If the director can make the performance come to life by just changing the most playable objective and a couple of adjustments, he should quit there. He can save the strong stuff for the set. The less ammunition you use up in rehearsal, the better. This way you have new fixes for the actors to try if their performances start to falter in front of the camera. In acting, as in life, that which is new and inexperienced contains the power of renewal. You want to save as much of this power for when it really counts: on the set. But you do not want to leave the rehearsal without at least feeling that you have made the performance believable. At best, you should feel that the actors were great in rehearsal and that you have the power to make them even better on the set. So, no matter what, you want to come fully armed. You never know exactly which bullet will work, so you must have them all. The only way to do this is to think it all through and write everything down beforehand.

CHAPTER 7 | SUMMARY POINTS

■ The first time director — before coming to a rehearsal — must break down all of the scenes he is going to rehearse. He should have written down in his working script all the objectives and adjustments the actors might play. He should have figured out exactly how the actors could best physicalize their objectives and written down those notes. He should have devised an improv that parallels the circumstances of the scene; he should have written down the circumstances of the improv and each actor's objectives in the improv.

■ As much in advance of the rehearsal as possible, inform the actors that they must be completely "off book." They must have all of their lines memorized, cold. It is almost pointless to have a rehearsal unless the actors know all the lines they will have to say, completely by heart, without having to think about them for an instant.

■ Start the rehearsal with a clandestine, polite test to discover if the actors know all their lines (of the scenes you intend to rehearse).

■ In my experience, the only way to get an actor to do his best work is to make him feel that you fundamentally like his work, that you are happy to be working with him, and that you are on his side and want him to do his very best.

■ For the time being, forget the moments that you do not like because of interpretation. Concentrate on the moments that are unconvincing, will destroy the illusion of reality, and seriously undercut the overall effectiveness of your film. These have to be eliminated.

■ Focus on those lines where the actor's performance is weakest and try to bring them up to the level of the best parts of the performance.

■ If, before the rehearsal time is over, you have enabled the actor to deliver a performance that is completely convincing from beginning to end, then you can go to work on moments that you do not like because you feel the interpretation is not ideal.

■ In giving direction to actors: simplify, simplify, simplify!

- If what the actor is doing reinforces the spine of his character, and it sounds real, go with it.

- There still may be instances when a first time director needs to use up some very valuable rehearsal time working on a line reading. If your breakthrough film is a comedy, it might be essential that the actor deliver the line in a very specific way — just the way the director hears it in his head — in order to make a joke play.

- Right after the first run-through, pick the part of the performance that you find most unconvincing, and check your script for the adjustment for those lines from your script breakdown.

- Pick the best part of the actor's performance and praise him for it, and in the next breath, give him the adjustment.

- The ballet-teacher-with-the-cane or maestro-with-the-baton approach can sometimes suddenly focus the actor and get him to commit to the objective.

- Work on improving an actor's performance in this order: (1) change the most-playable objective, (2) try an ultraplayable objective, (3) try physicalizing the objective, and (4) try an improv. Accordingly, the first time director should at least write down (1) the most playable objectives, (2) the ultra playable objectives, (3) some ideas for physicalizing the objectives, and (4) an improv for each scene.

PART FOUR:
SET POLITICS

CHAPTER 8 | ON THE SET

Getting Ahead by Getting Along

The director has absolute power on the set. If the producer or those more exalted than the producer have a clue about filmmaking, they will never question the director's judgment on the set. This gives the director the power to be a little Hitler, but, in spite of that, he should do his best to be a great guy — a big mensch. If he is a mensch, he makes a better film and has a better time doing it. This is especially true if he is a first time director. Once he has an established track record, he can get away with being a little Hitler; there are lots of them who work all the time. But I doubt if even the little Hitlers were like that their first time out.

If the first time director gives the crew a reason to dislike him, they will. The first time director can be certain that there are dozens of people on the set who feel that they are more qualified to direct the picture than he is. If he throws his weight around to get his way, they will foment mini-rebellions. Consciously or unconsciously, they will sabotage the director's game plan. The grips or the electric crew may take the hustle out of their game. Or the 1st Assistant Director may forget to suggest sending part of the crew ahead to pre-light the next location. It will all be subtle and invisible, but it will add up to a drag on how effectively the crew functions. The first time director's margin of error is very small. If some of the crew is pulling against him, it could have fatal results: He could fall significantly behind schedule and get fired, or other dire scenarios could take place. At the very least, a first time director cannot do his best work with a crew that is not giving its all.

Therefore, even though he can dictate, he should always *ask*, with as much warmth and enthusiasm as he can muster. A director does not have to be charming and warm with the entire crew. So when he is, they generally are appreciative and will repay him for his kindness many times over. The director is the king, but if he is a kindly king, his subjects will do more than obey him, they will serve him.

It has been my good fortune to have known the director Arthur Hiller for many years. If you do not genuinely like Arthur Hiller, there is something wrong with you. Anyone who has worked with him loves him. He is exceptionally intelligent. He is decisive and cool-headed. And at the same time he is a complete teddy bear. He exudes sweetness and warmth. When you are on an Arthur Hiller set, you feel like you are in Santa's workplace. Everyone is busy, busy, working their butts off and having a great time. Arthur gets the very best out of his crews. For almost 30 years he was one of the most sought-after directors in Hollywood, and I am certain that his genuine warmth as a human being was a big contributing factor. The first time director would do well to emulate Arthur Hiller. You should always seem upbeat and poised. That way, by emulating you, the crew will work more efficiently and enable you to make the best film you possibly can.

First time directors must also exude self-confidence. You cannot begin to inspire confidence unless you always know exactly what you want and how to get it. You must never think out loud or seem unsure of yourself. You must perform credibly as the alpha dog, with certainty about your ideas, or the pack will turn on you.

This brings to mind a trick I learned when I was breaking in as an episodic television director. At Universal Studios throughout the '70s and '80s, Danny Haller was one of the busiest episodic directors. He must have directed at least 300 one-hour episodes of such shows as *BJ and the Bear, Sheriff Lobo, The Fall Guy, Knight Rider*, and *Battlestar Galatica*. Year in and year out, he worked on dozens of well-known series.

Shooting an hour episodic action show meant cramming about 10 days worth of stunts and story into a six- or seven-day shoot. There was no margin for error and things were always going wrong. The studio was continually pissed off about budget overages and threatening to fire *someone, anyone*. The stress was palpable. In the midst of all this chaos, Danny Haller moseyed along calmly, dodging bullets, unflappable, seemingly invincible. With a face like a road map and a gravelly voice to boot, he was a dead ringer for the cowboy star, Ben Johnson. The producer on *BJ and the Bear* once confessed to me that when the shit was really hitting the fan, he would pick up the phone and call Danny. "Talking to Danny Haller is like taking a Valium," he said.

You don't tell Lee Majors how to play *The Fall Guy* or David Hasselhoff how to be the *Knight Rider*. Ninety percent of what an episodic director does on the set is lay out the camera blocking for the cinematographer. The way that Danny went about this was part of his MO. After a good take Danny never just said, "Print." Or, "Print it." It was always, "Cut. Print, and we're over here." Then he would pop up out of his cowboy crouch, or jump out of his chair and walk straight to where he wanted to put the camera next. When he got there he would turn back and look at the crew a little impatiently, as if asking why the camera wasn't already set up where he was standing. Every single setup. After he said, "Print," there was never a millisecond of hesitation before he said, "And we're over here." Obviously, he always knew exactly what he wanted. In the midst of all the chaos, he was a rock of composure and confidence. The crews, the actors, the producers — they all loved him for that. He led. They followed. It was that simple.

In a private moment Danny revealed his secret to me. It may have seemed like he always knew what he was doing, but sometimes, given the amount of last-minute shuffling of schedules and adjusting for Murphy's law, inevitably — like any mortal — he was left completely clueless. But he always took pains to mask any uncertainty by resorting to a proven drill. Instead of calling "Print" after he knew he had good take, he would bluff and say, "Okay, let's put a hold on that take and we'll do a couple more." Then he would go sit in his director's chair and completely tune out everything that was happening on the set. His eyes would be open. He would seemingly be looking at the actors and the crew trying to hit all their marks and nail their lines, but he would only be thinking about one thing: where he was going to put his camera next. As soon as he figured it out, he would wait until the crew and the actors had finished going through their paces, and then he would shout, "Cut. Print. And we're over here." And off he would march, even though he had no clue as to the merits of the take he had just printed.

Later in the day, when no one was watching, he would slink over to the script supervisor and reverse his decision, instructing them to put a hold on the take that he had printed (but never focused his attention on) and to print the take that he had put on hold, even though he knew it was what he wanted. These were the lengths Danny Haller went to make sure that he never, ever, seemed to be in doubt — even for a fraction of a second.   And he probably had 300 hours of television to his credit, 300 *good* hours. Therefore, logically speaking, the first time director has to work *harder* than Danny Haller did to give the impression that he always knows exactly what he is doing.

Yet it behooves the first time director to always be open to suggestion. There is no inconsistency in this. It takes a strong man to admit that he is wrong and a wise man to concede that sometimes other people's ideas are better than his own. If a director insists on maintaining the fiction that he's the only one on the set who can have a good idea, he cuts himself off from a huge reservoir of talent. "Most successful directors are good thieves," Leonard Schrader (*Kiss of the Spider Woman*), the Oscar-nominated screenwriter whom I am blessed to have as a colleague at Chapman University, told me the other day. He then regaled me with a series of stories about how the spark of inspiration for some of the most acclaimed work of the best directors he has worked with — Martin Scorsese; Hector Babenco; and his brother, Paul Schrader — came from the fevered imagination of someone other than the director: actors, writers, and crew people who, in their effort to help the director, got a good idea and passed it along. Wisely, the director ran with it and built it into something truly memorable. And then, of course, he took all the credit for it. It is a collaborative business. The director who is a gifted collaborator — who is truly open to suggestion —will, given luck and talent, go the farthest.

Collaboration is a two-way street. You have to prove to your collaborators that you are open to their ideas before they will offer them to you, free for the taking. If you shoot down every suggestion you get, eventually the suggestions will stop coming in — maybe not all of them, because some people are not above giving the director advice for purely frivolous reasons. But the best ideas — the flow of gold — will dry up.

But really, who would be so stupid as to say, "No" to a great idea? Certainly not *you*, esteemed reader. Certainly not *me*, I told myself as I stepped on the set of my first professional directing gig. Wrong! Under the stressful conditions of the many day-late-and-dollar-short productions that I have directed, I have shot myself in the foot by hurriedly, unthinkingly waving aside many good ideas. Then I had to eat my heart out when I watched the dailies. Trust me, you don't want to go there.

Ironically, perhaps the only way a first time director will ever truly learn to avoid making this mistake is to make it once (or as many times at it takes), and suffer the heart-rending consequences. After that, after watching the dailies the next day and seeing something truly mediocre, frozen forever on film, because you, the fat-headed director, insisted on doing it *your* way... maybe next time you'll listen.

This is not to say that every suggestion the director gets from all the wannabe directors on the set is worth listening to. Far from it. Some very talented, well meaning people will bend the director's ear, ad nauseam, when, either consciously or unconsciously, they have no intention of helping him. A friend of mine who worked on *The Sting* told me that, generally, Paul Newman happily took George Roy Hill's direction. But on the days when Newman, for whatever reason, was in a funk and did not want to act, he was full of ideas about what his objective should be, and ready to debate them with Hill — until Hill would have to resort to any excuse to cut the debate off just so they got something, *anything*, accomplished.

The best way a director can inoculate himself against those who would bend his ear for no good reason is by making a speech at the production meeting announcing his policy on helpful suggestions. The gist of this speech should be that the director is not so stupid as to think that he is the only person on the set who can come up with a good idea. So he sincerely encourages everyone who is struck with an epiphany on any subject to come up and share that idea with him — on one condition: that he reserves the right to say "No," without an explanation. This way the director opens the door to the best, most helpful, most inspired ideas his cast and crew can come up with, and at the same time gives himself a way to slam the door on the garbage. He gets the upside with a minimum of the downside.

When the director says he retains the right to say "No," without an explanation, he should justify his right to do that by telling the crew that if he had to let everyone of them down gently, and politely, he would not have the time to direct. Any reasonable crew member can understand this. The stressful conditions of the set do not allow for the niceties of the everyday workplace.

Still, some people are better at saying "No" than others. As Mark Lichtman, a very successful Hollywood agent in the '80s and '90s said of Sherry Lansing, who at the time was running Fox, but moved on to run Paramount, "She gives great 'No.'" Some people can say "No," and make it feel like "Yes." (Sherry Lansing being one of them) Others cannot even say, "Yes, thanks for the great idea," graciously or ungrudgingly. The first time director is advised to emulate the Sherry Lansings of the world. This way, just like Sherry Lansing and most other successful studio execs, your diplomatic demeanor keeps you in everybody's good graces. You want to give everyone the impression that eventually you will say "Yes." This makes them feel empowered. They are not just meaningless cogs in the machine. They are collaborating with you, helping you make a better film. If the first time director is always a mensch like Arthur Hiller; always in control like Danny Haller; and always open to suggestions, but able to say "No," and make it feel like "Yes," like Sherry Lansing; then everyone on the crew will be pulling his oar in the boat as hard as he can, and the boat will go farther, faster.

Successful Collaboration

To succeed on the set a director must lead. Leadership comes in all different shapes and sizes. Leading men in the SAG actors directory are almost all handsome and fit. By contrast, so many successful Hollywood directors are balding, bearded, and slightly out of shape that, if you added a pair of shades and a baseball cap, you'd have the stereotype. Bottom line, the exterior counts for next to nothing when it comes to doing that which a director must do on the set in order to lead. The key to leading effectively, especially for a first time director, is to get his principal collaborators to willingly follow. The principal collaborators — the 1st AD, the DP, and the cast (there are others but these are the ones I am going to focus on) — are artists in their own right. If the producer is smart, he will surround his novice director with as many seasoned pros as he can. Therefore, most of the first time director's principal collaborators will generally have more experience in the business than he has. If they are any good at what they do, they will have a great deal of pride in their work. The director must lead and therefore must choose the destination and the direction to get there. But, if he can find a way to allow his principal collaborators to participate in those crucial decisions, he will find them following him enthusiastically, and if they are 110% behind him, almost everyone on the set will follow along. He can make the best film he possibly can and go on to become a regular working director only if he can empower his principal collaborators in this way.

Collaborating with the 1st AD

The director is the ultimate authority on the set, but if the 1st AD is any good, he will actually run the set for the director. Hitchcock was the director who perfected this division of labor. According to the legend, Hitchcock was not even called to the set until the shot was ready. This seems to have been the case, especially towards the end of his career. He would be summoned from his dressing room, like a movie star, say "Action, cut, print," and then exit.

What permitted Hitchcock to absent himself from the set while the shot was being ramrodded together by the 1st AD was his use of **storyboards**. Hitchcock had every shot storyboarded, and he never deviated much from what was on the boards. What the storyboards allowed the 1st AD to do was to read Hitchcock's mind, as it were, and literally see the shot that Hitchcock wanted. If there were some way a director could allow his 1st AD to read his mind, then the director would not have to step onto the set until the shot was ready. Good 1st ADs spend their entire working life, year in and year out, on a set, setting up shots. A first time director's experience on a set is going to pale in comparison to that. So if the 1st AD is experienced and good, he is probably more capable of working with the crew to set up the shot.

If the director lets the 1st AD work with the crew to set the shot, that frees the director to do what he can do that the 1st AD probably cannot do — namely, work with the actors to help them summon up their very best performances. The little windows of time during which the director can rehearse the actors on set pop up before the first shot of the day, during lighting setups, and during company moves. The director should seize these moments as golden opportunities to make those performances that are mediocre, good and those performances that are good, great.

How can a director walk away from the responsibility of blocking the camera and leave that up to the 1st AD? Like Hitchcock, he can storyboard every shot. But it is unlikely the budget of his day-late-dollar-short production will allow for that. No problem. A good, clearly written **shot list**, or overhead, football-play type diagrams, can actually give a 1st AD almost all the information he needs to figure out what shots the director has in his mind.

Everybody does shot lists and overhead drawings differently. The first time director should meet with the 1st AD during the preproduction period and make sure that the 1st AD can read the director's shorthand. As the production grinds on, the 1st AD will become quite expert at deciphering the director's hieroglyphics. Whatever information the 1st AD cannot glean from the director's shot list or shot diagrams, he should be able to deduce after watching the director do a walk-through for camera with the actors and the DP before each scene.

In today's technology-driven film business, there is a school of thought that believes that all a director has to do to get good performances out of his actors is to hire the best that money can buy. According to this school, the director should spend all or the majority of his time on the set working with the DP making sure that the shot looks great. This is how most directors who do studio movies work. They have the money to hire actors who don't need much help with their performances. Huge amounts of money are being spent to give the film a certain look. So the director lets the actors fend for themselves and focuses his energy on making sure the money ends up on the film.

Even though this has become the standard way of working on most studio movies, the first time director should not be seduced into thinking he can work this way — primarily because his budget in all likelihood does not allow for such a high caliber of acting talent. The first time director should take advantage of the fact that the 1st AD and the DP can set the shot on their own, so that he is free to apply himself to the more crucial business of getting the very best out of each actor.

A shot list also enables the 1st AD to help the director stay on schedule and make each day. The first time director has got to stay close to schedule and budget if he does not want the higher-ups breathing down his neck and getting in his way. The 1st AD can help the first time director accomplish this goal in two very important ways.

First, he can act as a governor on the director's creative impulses. He can keep the director from cutting off his nose to spite his face by devoting too much precious time to one particular setup or series of setups. One of the painful truths of film-making is that after the script is written, all you can do is fail. The finished film will never measure up to the script — especially the script as it is envisioned as a finished film by the first time director. The first time director sees this finished film as a masterpiece that will launch his career. Unfortunately, once he starts shooting his masterpiece, the limited budget and unforeseen difficulties will force the director to compromise his vision many times. His intense desire to succeed artistically will make it difficult, if not impossible, for the director to make these compromises. The 1st AD can help him make these hard choices, and make them well, but only if the 1st AD has a clear idea of each shot that the director intends to do in a day. The shot diagrams or shot list will help the 1st AD break down the day's work into setups. Given his experience, he should have a good idea of how much time can be devoted to each setup, while allowing enough remaining time to complete the day's work. If the director starts to exceed those limits, the 1st AD can be the voice of reason that pulls him back from the brink.

One of the best 1st ADs I ever worked with performed this role masterfully. His name was Jon Liberti, and I worked with him on *The Fall Guy*. Liberti, like most great 1st ADs, worked all the time. He was the 1st AD on a couple dozen television shows and then became a very successful unit production manager. Liberti was as soft-spoken and low-key as they come. He ran the set for me, but it was as if he were invisible. I was never aware of his presence, except when I was falling behind schedule. Then Liberti would magically appear in my peripheral vision. When I became aware of his presence, I would give him a look and sure enough he would make a little circling motion with his index finger. That was all. This was his way of telling me that I was in danger of falling behind and it was time to wrap up the scene. I knew him and his work well enough to know he was never wrong. I trusted his judgment, did as he suggested, and seemingly magically completed each day in the allotted $11\frac{1}{2}$ hours.

The second way the 1st AD can help the director make each day (provided the director supplies him with a shot list or shot diagrams) is by managing the crew's work hours more efficiently. People outside the film business who visit a motion picture set for the first time are always amazed by the number of people standing around seemingly doing nothing. What is not apparent is that everybody on a film crew works and works hard, but generally the work is intermittent. A good 1st AD can usually get more out of the crew if he can keep them working ahead of the director.

Once a set is lit, the only people who are working steadily are the director, the crew operating the camera, the actors, and the 1st AD. If the 1st AD knows that the director intends to shoot a lot of coverage to complete the scene, he can safely send the gaffer and the lighting crew on ahead to start roughing in the lighting for the next scene. If there is a company move coming up, all the equipment that is not being used to complete the shot can be packed up. If the company is going to be doing some insert car work later in the day, the grip and electric crews can get started rigging that. There are numerous other scenarios whereby those crew members who are not working to put the scene that is being shot on film can work ahead of the shooting company. But these decisions cannot be made hastily. Splitting the crew always generates a certain amount of confusion. That's the downside. But if there is a real upside — if there is enough downtime for part of the crew to get something substantial done by working ahead — then it's worth splitting the crew. The 1st AD cannot safely make this judgment call and others like it involving a division of the crew, unless he has an accurate idea of how the director intends to cover the day's work. If the director supplies the 1st AD with a shot list or shot diagrams, it should fill in the picture for him.

Of course, only rarely does a director end up shooting a scene just as he planned the night before or whenever he did his homework. His shot list and shot diagram are usually just starting points. His collaborators make suggestions during the first walk-through for camera. That's when the director takes the cinematographer's, the actors', and — if there are stunts involved — the stunt coordinator's suggestions and modifies his game plan to accommodate their input. While the director engages in this crucial give and take with his principal collaborators, the 1st AD generally hovers nearby so he can overhear all the decisions and figure out what the final game plan is. The information supplied during the final walk-through for camera is the final piece of the puzzle for the 1st AD. With the shot list or the overhead diagrams in hand, and the modifications hashed out between the director, the cast, and the DP during the final walk-through ringing in his ears, the 1st AD has the information he needs to do everything he can to help the director. So it behooves the first time director to keep the 1st AD parked by his side during the first walk-through. The director should make sure that the 1st AD knows exactly what was resolved between himself and his principal collaborators. The director should not take this for granted. If the director is going to let the 1st AD work with the crew to set the shot so the director can go off and fine-tune the performances, then he should talk through the shot with the 1st AD one last time before he surrenders the set to him.

The First Walk-Through for Camera

Of all the director's responsibilities on the set, the first walk-through for camera is the most challenging. Before it happens, the actors don't know their marks. They may not even know their lines. And generally, the cinematographer doesn't have a clue as to what kind of shot the director has in mind. After the walk-through for camera, the actors should know all their marks and the DP should be ready to set the shot. And if the walk-through takes more than 15 or 20 minutes, it has taken too long. For the first time director, those are 15 challenging minutes. After those 15 minutes, the director has made the majority of his contribution to the scene. After that, all he really has to do is keep pumping up the actors.

The fact that the director is responsible for everything — even that which he has no control over — makes directing a demanding and tiring job. First time directing is usually even more stressful and tiring because things go wrong more frequently with a comprised budget. This often leaves the first time director feeling like he barely has the energy to draw a breath. But during the first walk-through for camera he has to suck it up. During the first walk-through for camera the actor blocking and the camera blocking will be set. As soon as it's over, the crew is going to go into high gear to set the shot as fast as possible. If the director changes his mind 10 or 15 minutes later, it is going to put him behind about a half hour. The first time director does not have the luxury of being able to change his mind. If he does it frequently enough, his dailies better be fantastic, because, if not, he is running the risk of getting replaced. So the first time director should do whatever he has to do to make sure he is at his best during the first walk-through for camera. He should not think of it as a drill or a rehearsal. He should think of it as the moment when he puts his mark on the film.

Collaborating with the Cinematographer

During the first walk-through for camera there is an active exchange of ideas between the director and all the important collaborators, but the majority of the give and take is between the director and the cinematographer. This is when they have their meeting of the minds and settle on what the master is going to look like. After that a few finishing touches may be added, but the bulk of the work has been done. In Chapter 6, I described the collaboration between a director and a cinematographer as being comparable to working on a painting together. The cinematographer does all the painting, but you, the director, tell him what to paint — and in the end, you are responsible for the painting, which has to do more than look great, it also has to tell a story. You want the cinematographer to feel proud of the painting. If he is convinced this will be his masterpiece, then he will pour all of his talent into the work.

To paint this painting together, the director and the cinematographer have to successfully collaborate on three principal tasks: (1) lighting and exposure, (2) lens selection, and (3) camera blocking. The best way to make the cinematographer feel empowered is to allow him as much freedom as possible in the execution of these three tasks. For example, when it comes to the first task, lighting and exposure, once I have expressed my general ideas about the look of the film to the cinematographer, I never say anything more to him about lighting and exposure. This leaves a lot of the painting up to him. If I see something in dailies that I don't like, I tell him. More often than not, as soon as I mention whatever I saw that I don't like, he goes off on a tirade about how much he hates it too. Usually it's a mistake, not something that he intended.

That's because I'd made an effort to get on the same page with the cinematographer about the ultimate look of the film before I'd even hired him. I'd sat side by side with him and looked at specific scenes from his film, or scenes from films shot by other cinematographers both of us respected, and pointed at the screen saying, "That's it! That's the way it should look." It doesn't take much effort to set up such a joint viewing session with a prospective DP. But it is well worth the effort because it leaves no doubt as to what you expect the cinematographer to do. If you have shown it to him on as big a screen as possible, and he agrees with you and says that's the way he wants the film he will shoot for you to look, then you are on the same page. You can back off and let him be completely in charge of the lighting and the exposure. He'll get off on that. He'll work harder for you, and generally it proves to be a win-win deal.

When it comes to the second task, lens selection, as I described in Chapter 6, I try to give the DP as much freedom as possible, but in some instances, I insist on having it my way. Forcing perspective through the use of extreme wide-angle or long lenses can be a very effective story telling tool. This is especially true in scenes that are mostly visual — where the dialogue is limited and the story is told through images and montage: action sequences; dance sequences; scary scenes; love scenes; montages; scenes where physical actions have important dramatic significance, such as the last shot of *The Godfather* (a shot — seen through the door of Michael Corleone's office — of Michael leaning against his desk taking care of business, that ends with the door shutting on the viewer).

When working with some cinematographers, I have gotten into arguments about whether to force perspective at all, or how much to force it. I directed an episode of the updated version of *The Twilight Zone* that had a chase sequence in it featuring two police cruisers pursuing some teenagers in a stolen car. Bob Collins, the highly gifted DP, sometimes objected when I told him to use a wide-angle lens and put it where one of the speeding vehicles would pass close by. And even when he agreed, he would balk when I told him I wanted to use a really wide lens, like a 10mm, and put the car within a foot of the lens. Bob knew just as well as I did that the lens would make the car explode into the foreground and zip away into the background. But he felt that this effect should be used in moderation, and that my method of exploiting it to the max was ham-fisted and crude. Our disagreement sprang from a difference in taste. We both liked the effect. The question was how liberally to apply it.

When I find myself getting a little hissy with the DP over a lens, I just split the difference. I advise all first time directors to do the same. If you give in half way to your DP, he should appreciate the gesture. You have every right to insist and shove it down his throat. You are the king. He is your subject. So if you tease him a little and give in a little, he should come away from the confrontation not feeling as if his territory has been violated. That is the goal. You want to preserve and foster his feelings of ownership of the visual aspect of the film. That way he should keep pumping 110% of his talent into the film. This big picture objective is much more important to the first time director than whether a certain shot was made with a 9.8mm or an 18mm lens.

Another task that director and cinematographer collaborate on is camera blocking. In the post-Spielbergian era, how the director uses camera blocking and lens selection to tell the story has become critical. Most name directors have a signature visual storytelling style. When a studio hires Michael Bay to direct a film, it is because they figure his hyperkinetic visual storytelling style is especially appropriate for the project. A first time director on his breakthrough film should hope to execute his responsibilities as a visual storyteller with enough originality and flair to attract the attention of producers, agents, studio executives, and anyone else who has the power to hire him to direct his second project.

Up until this point, I have always implied that camera blocking is the sole responsibility of the director. And, given the fact that so much of the director's destiny depends on his command of visual storytelling (which is mostly made up of camera blocking), the director should approach camera blocking as if it were his sole responsibility. He should come to the set everyday with a fully developed, hopefully brilliant camera-blocking plan for every scene. This means he should have made up a complete shot list, shot diagrams, or story boards, and should have a rock solid idea of how he is going to shoot every master. Having prepared to control the camera blocking completely on his own, the director then collaborates fully with the cinematographer on all the crucial decisions involving blocking. He simply must, because when it comes to the visual aspect of the film, it is the DP who implements all the director's ideas.

Camera blocking is the most difficult and the most important task that the director and the cinematographer have to collaborate on. Because the director has so much riding on this part of the DP's job, he must micromanage it. If your producer is smart enough, he will team you as a first time director with a very experienced cinematographer who does not need to be micromanaged. How does a first time director deal with this contradiction? He and the cinematographer must either genuinely like each other as human beings, or they have to behave like perfect gentlemen. Otherwise, it will be hell for the director.

The good news is that cinematographers as a whole pride themselves on being able to work with anyone. Being able to implement the director's vision — no matter how big a jerk the director may be — is part of their job description, and those that do it best are the ones who succeed. If your producer has a clue about how to make a film, he will team you with an experienced cinematographer who can work well with anyone, even you at your worst. If the producer respects you as an artist, he might accept your suggestion on whom to hire as the DP or play matchmaker and let you interview cinematographers until you find one that you know you can work with.

In the world of episodic television, a director can get stuck with a DP who will fight him and make his life hell. This is because in episodic TV the cinematographers do every show, but the directors usually rotate in and out. As a first time director, you might get stuck in the rotation for one or two shows and come up against a DP who decides he doesn't like you. Most TV DPs have thoroughly ingratiated themselves with the star of the series and the producer. So if they don't like you or respect you, they might just act like an 800-pound gorilla because they can probably get away with it. I have been in this situation when I was doing episodic TV and it was hell. One day after I described a setup I wanted to this particular 800-pound gorilla masquerading as a DP, he folded his arms over his chest and in a very loud voice, dripping with sarcasm and incredulity, asked me, "So *that's* where you want me to put the camera?" I just had to gut it out. Fortunately, in TV the visual style of the show is set by the producer. The DP makes his living implementing the producer's vision and making the producer happy. So even if he chooses to defy you, don't fight him. You can't win and you'll just make a bad situation worse. Go ahead and defer to the DP in the area of camera blocking and rest assured that whoever is controlling the show will like the look of your episode. You may not like it. But if the producer likes it, that's what counts; that's what is going to get you hired back to do more episodes.

When collaborating on camera blocking, the moment of truth arrives during the first walk-through for camera. Generally speaking, if the director absolutely insists, the DP will do the shot exactly the way the director describes it to him, provided it is technologically feasible. But unless the director is an experienced cinematographer or a genius like Spielberg, he would be a fool to insist that the DP act like a puppet and do just as he commands.

Good DPs work all the time. Day in and day out, year in and year out, they set up moving masters. In contrast, only a few top directors work all the time, and when they do get a film, they are only setting up shots when they are in production — which comes down to about a third of the time they spend on the film. On his breakthrough film, the first time director should put the DP's experience with camera blocking to work for him. The director should describe the shot as he envisions it and let the DP improve on his good ideas and replace his bad ideas.

When you consider it from a scientific perspective, the odds are your DP can improve your shots. This is because there is never one absolutely correct way to set up a shot to cover a scene but rather a myriad of possibilities, many of them equally valid. The one master that you laid out in preparation for the scene may contain some of the best alternatives, but chances are it does not contain all of them. By accepting the DP's input, the director is probably improving his camera blocking.

The other factor that favors incorporating the DP's thinking into your camera blocking is the reality that all of your pre-conceived notions about what the best master for a scene should look like are largely done in the abstract. Only when you are actually standing where you are going to shoot the scene and watch the actors say their lines and hit their marks can you make any solid decisions about the best place to put the camera. And that moment does not arrive until the first walk-through for camera. The timing of the camera blocking is dependent on the actor blocking. The timing of the actor blocking is dependent on the location. The only way you can make rock-solid decisions about your camera blocking would be to rehearse the actors prior to shooting in the sets or on the locations where their scenes were to be shot, and it is extremely unlikely that you will be allowed the convenience of such a rehearsal on the set. Inevitably you will be relying on a certain amount of guesswork when you plan your blocking prior to the day of the shoot. If you are relying on guesswork, your plans are bound to be flawed here and there.

Usually these flaws will become apparent during the first walk-through for camera. When they crop up, let the DP step in and help you make the necessary fixes. In all likelihood, his fixes will be better than yours. And, during the first walk-through, you are going to have the added burden of helping the actors get comfortable with their blocking. This is a huge distraction. Actors are famous for driving directors crazy by quibbling over the details of their blocking. While you are babysitting them, your DP can be calmly coming up with brilliant solutions to all of the little problems in your camera-blocking plan.

Do your homework. Come to the set with shot diagrams or storyboards for every scene, but consider all of your plans a point of departure for a much better blueprint that you and the DP will devise together — after you have seen the first walk-through for camera and, for the first time, are able to factor in all the relevant data.

I have found that if I take this positive attitude at the start of production, and try to incorporate the DP's thinking into my camera blocking 1) my dailies usually end up looking better than I expected and 2) I succeed in empowering the DP, and he ends up pouring all of his energy and creativity into a film with my name on it.

Just like with directors and actors, there is no way for a director to predict exactly what sort of attitude will work best when laying out shots with his cinematographer. What works like a charm with one DP may drive the next one crazy. The director just has to keep his radar on and be sensitive to any signals, stated or unstated, that the DP may be sending him when they disagree on the look, lenses, or camera blocking. Always try to get ahead by getting along. Don't force the DP into doing something he clearly doesn't want to do. Keep him on your side and feeling personally invested in the project. If you pull rank and force him to accept your decision on lenses or camera blocking, you may have won the battle and lost the war. If you can't read his signs, but suspect he may be unhappy, invite him to air his grievances, and then ask him to tell you specifically what you need to do to keep him happy. Then modify your behavior as much as you possibly can without betraying the essence of the project as you envision it. You can't realize that vision unless you can get the DP to respond to you sympathetically and precisely.

Making Your Stars Shine During Production – Off the Set

Of all those individuals that the director must collaborate with on the set, the leading actors are the most important. This was even truer in the past. In his autobiography, *A Life*, Elia Kazan, one of the most respected directors of the '40s and early '50s, admits that when he directed his first feature he concerned himself only with the actors and their performances. He left all of the decisions that would control the look of the film, such as camera blocking and lens selection, to the cinematographer. He completely and willingly surrendered the same directorial responsibilities that, 30 years later while working on *Jaws*, Spielberg discharged with such brilliance that he managed to propel himself to the forefront of working directors.

In Kazan's day, films were generally filmed theater. The story was mostly told the same way as it was in Shakespeare's day: through the dramatic exchanges of the actors. In *Jaws*, Spielberg told about half the story that way, the old fashioned way — dramatically. The rest he told visually, innovatively selecting his lenses and masterfully manipulating his camera and what was in front of the camera. When movies were filmed theater, the director's creative responsibilities on the set were predominantly dramatic, whereas today they are about half visual and half dramatic. The balance shifts somewhat depending on the script. However, I think most directors would agree that it always feels as if one expends more energy working with the actors than with any of the other key collaborators on the set.

There are many reasons for this, the most influential being the nature of the work itself. What the director does with his DP and his AD is much more scientific, more nuts and bolts, more like any other job. You do your homework. You meet with your collaborators as often as possible prior to the day of the job. You get together on the given day and implement your plans. What a director does with his leading actors is more human, emotional, and intuitive. It is more like preparing and implementing a seduction or a dinner party at which you will introduce two sets of your friends who have never met each other. All the best-laid plans in the world can come to naught if the mood is not right.

A director coming to the set on a day when he has to get his leading lady to cry convincingly, or worse, his leading man to cry convincingly, is likely to be much more preoccupied with that task than anything else he will have to do that day. This is because there are many variables to the director's being able to elicit a genuine, passionate performance that do not even present themselves until the last minute. It all comes down to the moment when the actor has to cry, or otherwise emote, and how — at that moment — the actor is feeling about the director, the project, and life in general. The director's control over all of the above varies from limited to non-existent. This tends to worry or preoccupy even the coolest director.

There is also a lot of truth in the generalization that actors tend to be temperamental. They have to be. Their profession requires that they be able to go from zero to 60 emotionally on the word "Action." So their moods shift rapidly, and if the director rubs them the wrong way for any reason, real or imagined, it is going to make it hard for them to do what that director wants. If an actor is going to do his best, it usually is, in some part, because he wants to please the director. But if the director has alienated the actor, this dynamic will misfire. Because the cinematographer and the 1st AD are using their understanding of technologies — cinematography, physics, statistics, accounting, logistics, etc. — to do that which the director wants them to do, they can be royally pissed off with the director and still do a good job. But an actor works with his feelings. And if he is in a funk in general, or angry specifically at the director, it will make it very difficult for him to give his all.

Therefore, the first time director on the set of his breakthrough gig is advised to have his radar on and be extremely aware of all of the emotional currents flowing between himself and his leading actors. In this arena in particular, the best way to get ahead is to get along. The dynamic here is very much like a love affair. If the director wants to win the hearts of his actors, he has to turn on the charm — as much as he can muster and as genuinely as possible. Again, like in a love affair, you will get farther faster if you are real and unaffected. Most actors have an excellent crap filter. Expressions of emotion are their stock and trade, so they can usually distinguish the real thing from the fake.

The best way to keep things on a positive note with your actors is to find something in each of them that you genuinely like or admire and focus on that. Even if you find some of them genuinely detestable overall, you can rise above it if you just home in on the portion of their personality that you like and make that the departure point of all your interactions. There is a bit of Jekyll and Hyde in all of us. It really is not asking too much of the first time director to insist that he take the best and leave the rest in his interactions with his actors, especially when the success of his breakthrough film project hangs in the balance.

Bottom line, what happens between a director and an actor is really a matter of the heart, and it is hard to be scientific about such matters. Sometimes what should succeed doesn't and vice versa. I got a taste of this when working with Sylvester Stallone for a couple of days on a rock video to promote one of his least successful films, *Over the Top*. In the movie Stallone plays a truck driver who is a champion arm wrestler. Sammy Hagar cut a song (*Winner Takes All*) for the movie soundtrack, and since I was Hagar's director of choice at that time, I got to direct the video. It was a good little song, and Sammy came up with a sort of sweet, goofy concept that featured him arm wrestling with Stallone and beating him. Stallone went along with the idea and we spent a pleasant afternoon on a Hollywood soundstage shooting it. The shoot had the requisite amount of stress for a day-late-dollar-short rock video, but we got the day in and it went smoothly. Stallone was aloof with everyone on the set, except Sammy. He probably felt he was slumming to be working with a low-rent rock video crew.

I followed my own advice and focused on the fact that I have a tremendous amount of respect for what Stallone did in *Rocky*. (And yes, I know there is a school of thought that says that everything good in the final draft of *Rocky* was written by an un-credited script doctor, but so far this is just hearsay and I never put stock in hearsay.) It is undeniably one of the best sports movies of all times. And when the moment was right I told him so, which I am sure made no impression on him, because he has heard that a million times. But I went on to tell him specifically why I felt that way, which I am sure he has also heard before, but probably only a couple dozen times. What I told him was I thought his script for *Rocky* represented a real Hollywood milestone because in it he successfully solved the problem of how to write a sports film that doesn't telegraph its ending to the audience in the first 15 minutes. Up until *Rocky* and ever since, every sports movie is about the loveable underdog beating the heavily favored champion. That story was new when they wrote David and Goliath. Stallone had the smarts and the integrity to rewrite it so that the loveable underdog loses to the heavily favored champion. It truly was a stroke of brilliance and I told him so.

Maybe that's why he was tractable and willingly did everything I asked him to do that day on the set. Maybe I can feel proud of the fact that I got off on the right foot with Stallone and attribute it to focusing on the positive when collaborating with my leading actor. Because after that first successful day on the set, the monster in Stallone reared its ugly head and from that moment on the monster was all I saw. As is usually the case with rock videos, there was literally a week, maybe 10 days, tops, for all the postproduction. The editor, whom Stallone had approved, and I worked day and night to get a good assembly together. We sent it to Hagar, the record company, and Stallone. Everybody thought we did an excellent job and had some minor changes. Then the word came back that Stallone hated the video. Nothing more specific than that. Only that he hated it. This touched off much gnashing teeth and wringing hands in all quarters. It was announced that Stallone would come down from Mount Sinai and enlighten the editor, myself, and the producer of the video. We waited. He did not appear. A day passed. Two days. Still no Stallone. In the meantime, since the deadline was fast approaching, we continued to edit.

Then on the third day he appeared, with an entourage, of course, that included his manager, his personal producer on *Over the Top*, and a covey of assistants. I'll never forget what he said when he walked into the editing room. It was a good line: "Here I am, Sergio Einstein." We all laughed and started schmoozing. Or at least the producer of the video, Alexis, and I followed the advice I give above and turned on the charm, trying to defuse the adversarial lead-up to this editorial post-mortem. I remember we talked about Jane Fonda's politics — all of us trading quips at her expense. After that, we went through the video once and Stallone made one change. I think we took out a piece of a shot of Sammy playing guitar because in the part we edited out you could see some finger and palm prints on the body of his guitar. That was it. All chuckles and grins.

Then Stallone walked out of the editing room with his entourage. Alexis, the producer, went with them. And, according to her, on his way to his car, Stallone turned to his manager and producer and said, "That guy, Bettman, get rid of him. He's history." This was also said for Alexis' benefit. Stallone wasn't firing me off the video I had just directed, the video for *Winner Takes All*, since that video was going on MTV in a couple of days and so was virtually history. What I was being fired off of was the next video that was going to be made in support of *Over the Top*. This was a video for a song by Kenny Loggins. Alexis was going to produce this second video and I had been hired to direct it. But now, as Stallone had decreed, I was "history."

All of which goes to prove that actors can be temperamental. A director's relationship with his actors is an affair of the heart. As in love, there is no certain way to control the outcome. Sometimes you can truly act like a prince and get treated like a dog. And sometimes you can act like a dog and get treated like a prince, or at least that's what I have heard. I really wouldn't know, because that's not my style, but some directors do get into mind games and manipulation with their leading actors. This is the kinky school of directing in which the director seduces his actors into giving him what he wants much as a pimp seduces his string of girls.

Hearsay has it that this was how Roman Polanski handled Faye Dunaway on the set of *Chinatown*. The story is that Polanski and Dunaway had a huge fight on set right before Dunaway was going to do the famous scene in which Jack Nicholson slaps her around and gets her to admit that she was raped by her father, and so the young girl that she is hiding and protecting is: "My sister." SLAP! "My daughter." SLAP! "My sister." SLAP! "My sister and my daughter... you figure it out. You're the detective!" Apparently, just minutes before she was supposed to do this scene, Polanski picked a fight with his leading lady that culminated in his calling her, "a c---." Strange as it may seem, this was just the kind of abuse that Faye Dunaway needed to get her into the mood to deliver her Academy Award-winning performance. And even more surprising is that, somehow, Polanski sensed this. Again, this story is just hearsay, so I make no claim to its authenticity. And I would not recommend that you try something like this unless you regularly use Polanski's brand of reverse psychology to bend your friends and loved ones to your will.

Your goal should be to have a genuine human relationship in place with each of your leading actors before you embark on shooting the scenes in which they will have to shine. Given the day-late-dollar-short constrictions of a typical break through film, it will be almost impossible to achieve that goal. With a tight casting budget, the casting process will continue right up to the minute you start shooting. You will be trying to get A-list actors for B-list prices or B-list actors for C-list prices. So there will be an endless poker game going on between the actors' agents and your producer. Everybody will be jerking everybody around and the end result is that you will not have your cast until the last minute. Then you will be insanely busy trying to secure locations, finesse the shooting schedule, and get your camera-blocking homework done.

Still, you must try to socialize as much as possible with your cast. Make the time to do this. Get less sleep. Turn your back (temporarily) on your loved ones, friends, and family, and hope they understand. You always have to give something up to get something, and if you want to succeed on your breakthrough, you are going to have to be ready to make sacrifices when it comes to personal relationships.

The reason you must establish some sort of human connection with each of your leading actors is because this will provide you with a little reservoir of good will —

just a dab of the human lubrication you will need to squeeze through when you get into a jam with one of your leads. This is going to happen. Given the nature of the director-actor relationship and the inherent stress of filmmaking, it is inevitable that in the midst of shooting you will have at least one colossal disagreement on a very important point with each of your leading actors. The actor will absolutely insist on doing something that you the director are 100 % certain is out of character for his role or — and this happens much more frequently — the actor will absolutely insist on doing something in front of the camera that will force you to completely rethink your camera blocking plan at a moment when you simply do not have the time to do so. And after discussing it for a reasonable length of time, you, the director, will pull rank and make the actor do it your way.

This is the moment when you need to have some sort of relationship in place. Because if the actor genuinely likes you and respects you as a human being, then he will put his heart into his performance and you, the director, will not only get what you want, you will get it good. On the other hand, if you have no relationship to fall back on at such a moment of confrontation, then when you pull rank, you will get it your way — but the chances are that the performance you get won't be worth keeping in the film. You will have won the battle and lost the war because, either consciously or unconsciously, the actor will not give you his best stuff.

An established director can always fall back on the respect he commands when he ends up in a jam and has to force an actor to do something he doesn't want to do. The actor will do as the established director insists, because he looks up to the director very much as a child looks up to a parent and so does not want to displease him. The first time director cannot hope to command such respect.

The actor does not have to actually love the director like a parent, a best friend, or a significant other. He just has to like him enough to not want to piss him off. A little bit goes a long way here. If the actor just cares a little bit about how the director feels about him, this will motivate him to get over his anger or disappointment. Of course, this does not apply to all actors. Some are just too hard-hearted or perverse and don't value or respond to the human connection. But these are rare.

Some people will disagree with me that it is so important for a first time director to endear himself to his leading actors. There is a school of thought that says that catering to all the actors' whims is counter-productive. This school says that actors should do their jobs and behave like professionals. The director should be able to treat them like any other principal collaborator on the set. If he gives them all the information they need to do their job well in an easy to understand, businesslike manner, that should be enough. No hand holding is necessary. Some directors with this attitude have had very successful careers. And many of them are quite outspoken in their contempt for the Method and the image of the director as a sort of modern-day Svengali who can get into any actor's head and transform him into an Academy Award-winning performer.

These directors succeed in spite of their inability to harness the Method and interact extensively on a human level with their leads. They succeed as directors because they are either extremely gifted as screenwriters or as visual storytellers. They have had the great good fortune to be able to rely exclusively on their preternatural gifts in these areas to launch their careers. Then, once they are in the forefront of working directors, they are guaranteed casting budgets sufficiently ample to hire only the best actors, who can do it all on their own without the help of a director. If you are 100% certain that you are as good a writer as James Cameron or as a good at visual storytelling as Steven Spielberg, then you can ignore my advice. If you are not that good, make a point of trying to nurture a genuine friendship with each of your leads.

Admittedly, this may not be easy. Actors tend to be more eccentric as a group than people in other professions. If they have achieved a degree of fame and fortune, they will have attracted lots of sycophantic hangers-on. This gives them the freedom to indulge themselves in all kinds of eccentric behavior. The way Stallone fired me for no apparent reason is a good example of incomprehensible behavior on the part of an indulged star.

I am convinced that we all share something in common. To get through to a hard case or an eccentric like Stallone, you have to discover what you share in common and break bread over it. Again, if you start by focusing on something that you truly like and respect in the actor, the chances are good that you will find something in common with them. Once you have found it, try to bring the conversation around to this common ground every time you interact with them. This will enable you to discover still more commonalities and topics that you can freely discuss. In the best-case scenario, without even having to make a conscious effort to get through to them, you end up having lively spontaneous interactions that you both actually enjoy. If this happens, you might develop a real friendship and start spontaneously seeking out each other's company for the duration of the shoot. That would be hitting a home run. You don't always do that. But just pounding out a single is good enough. Any human connection or vestige of friendship is far better than none at all.

For example, with Stallone, my point of departure would have been my respect for him as a screenwriter. On the day of the *Winner Takes All* shoot, when I told him exactly why I thought his script for *Rocky* was groundbreaking and a milestone in the genre of sports films, we got into a decent conversation on the topic of sports movies, which led to conversation about film in general. I remember we discussed the works of some of the classic American directors and discovered that we both admired the work of Billy Wilder and Frank Capra. That was a good start. If I were hired to direct a film starring Stallone, I would propose that we have lunch or dinner together. Dinner is better because dinner will most likely include a bottle of wine and that helps loosen the tongue. Chances are he would accept the invitation, because a little socializing prior to shooting is customary in the film business. As soon as possible, I would steer the conversation back to those classic American filmmakers, Wilder and Capra. Ideally, this would lead to other topics that I am well informed on and passionate about — such as changes in the American film industry that have made it impossible or difficult to make the kind of films Capra and Wilder made.

The goal would be to find a topic that both you and the actor know a lot about and are passionate about. It doesn't have to be esoteric or intellectual. If I got nowhere with any of the above with Stallone, I would switch the topic to sports or women. Most men can talk passionately and knowledgeably about sports and women.

The objective here is twofold. First, you want to connect with each other as human beings. All this requires is that you feel a bit of a kindred spirit. If you share some passions — whether for redheads, the Cincinnati Reds, or the sex life of red ants — it doesn't matter. You do not necessarily even have to agree. You can agree to disagree. You just have to enjoy each other's humanity and company for a few moments; all that requires is that you both get passionate and real about the topic of conversation. The second objective is to express some opinions or reveal some knowledge that impresses the actor. You want the actor to be just a little in awe of your command of the subject.

When you achieve the first objective and connect with the actor, you make the first step towards a friendship. This friendship, no matter how tenuous, will be the source of that little bit of good will you, the director, will need to draw on each time you piss the actor off by bending him to your will. The stronger the friendship, the deeper the reservoir of good will, the easier it will be for the actor to submit to your putdown and go on to deliver his best performance.

If you achieve the second objective and impress the actor with your command of a subject that he is passionate about, you will also make it easier for him to accept your direction. You want him to be able to trust your judgment when you tell him how to improve his performance. If you were an established director — if you were

Martin Scorsese — and you told an actor to change his objective and suggested that he try playing "to get him (the other actor) to leave the room" instead of "to humiliate him (the other actor)," he would do it in a New York second, because he would implicitly trust Scorsese's ability to determine what was lacking in his performance and to come up with the best way to fix the problem.

As a first time director, you cannot expect the actor to accord you the same trust. A secure actor will give you the benefit of the doubt. He will trust you until you give him a good reason not to. But most actors are not very secure, especially on the set on a day when they have to do a scene that can make or break their performance in a film. This is when you, as a first time director, will need to have already struck up a relationship with the actor — a relationship that has provided you with opportunities to win the actor's trust. The more good direction you give him, the more trust he will accord you. To attain these two objectives — to win the friendship and secure the trust of your leading actors — you must start socializing with them as soon as they are cast.

During Production – On the Set

Every film set works at a hurry-up-and-wait pace. The only people that work continuously on a film set are the director and the 1st AD. The actors, in particular, have substantial amounts of waiting to do. They get called to the set hours before the crew goes to work on their first scene, and even if the company is working on a scene that they are in, they have to wait between the walk-through for camera and when the set is lit. Given that the first time director on his breakthrough film will have no rehearsal time prior to shooting, or extremely limited rehearsal time, these blocks of time provide him with his first and last opportunity to improve his actors' performances. When the director walks on the set at the call time, the 1st AD is usually right there to get in his face with a million fires that need to be put out. And guess what? There will be a million fires to be put out every minute that the director is on the set, because the director is responsible for everything, even that which he has no control over. So if you are smart, you will perform triage. You will handle that which absolutely has to be taken care of right at that moment, you will put off everything that can be put off, and you will delegate to someone else everything that can be delegated, and then you will go off and find those actors with whom you have had the least rehearsal time and you will start rehearsing with them.

Ironically, the actors will probably be a little taken aback that you've come looking for them, intent on rehearsing. This is because 1) most directors on the set allow themselves to get sucked up into all the minutia of mounting the production and forget that the production is just a frame to put around the script and the performances, and 2) in the post-Spielbergian era, most filmmakers have become overly preoccupied with the visual aspect of filmmaking. In addition, I suspect the biggest reason your insistence on rehearsal will be a surprise to your actors is because the ambiance of the set is not at all conducive to rehearsal. Right up until the moment the AD calls "Lock it up," the set is a rowdy workshop full of cowboys, carpenters, and costumers. The din is horrendous. Those that are working are shouting and those that are schmoozing are shouting to be heard above those who are working. Loosely controlled anarchy holds sway in every quarter. The lowest guys on the totem pole — the grips — pick up lights on three-pronged stands and charge across the set with the prongs out, shouting, "Hot points, coming through!" fully expecting the head of the studio to dive out of their way. But the grips are no worse than everybody else on the set, since to a man, everyone on the crew acts as if whatever they are doing is the absolute top priority until someone tells them otherwise. On a big-budget set the air of anarchy tends to be jolly. On a day-late-dollar-short shoot the anarchy is rife with fear and loathing.

As a first time director I have found it quite pleasurable to play the role of captain of the ship and swagger around reigning in as much of the chaos as I could. Actually, that is the 1st AD's job. The first time director needs to tell the 1st AD that you want the actress playing Jane and the actress playing Mary out of make up and hair for rehearsal in Jane's trailer in 20 minutes (or however long it will take you to put out all the fires that absolutely must be put out).

If you know that you need a lot of rehearsal time with a specific actor or actors, have them called to the set early. This means you will have to get less sleep and get to the set early enough to get them up to speed. But remember, sleep is for beginners. If you call the actors to the set early or keep them late for rehearsal, you better put in enough time with them to get them to break a sweat. Most actors enjoy rehearsing on the set. They are a little nervous and glad for a chance to work the kinks out off camera. But they hate sitting around looking at walls while waiting to go on. That leaves them completely at the mercy of their need to be brilliant and their fear of failure. If allowed to ricochet between the two for a couple of hours, actors can be reduced to Jell-O or tie themselves in knots. Don't risk it.

The rehearsal should be held in the quietest place you can find that is still close enough to the set so you can be fetched back quickly. On big budget sets, the lead actors all have motorhomes or at least a portable dressing room in a trailer or the honeywagon. Any of these will do quite nicely for a rehearsal. Low budget productions often skimp on such amenities, which forces a director to get creative (which should come naturally to him if he is any good). I have held excellent rehearsals in restrooms. They all come with a lock on the door for privacy and, with the seat down, the commode serves nicely as a prop chair. Even a parked car with the windows rolled up and the AC on will suffice.

You should rehearse the actors on the set using the same step-by-step procedure I laid out in Chapter 7. Simply stated, first you have them run the lines without feeling, to make sure they are 100% off book. Once they are off book, have them do it for feeling. Fix one part of the performance at a time, starting with the part you like the least. On a day-late-dollar-short production, it is always best not to get overly ambitious. If it ain't broken, don't fix it, especially in the middle of shooting. If the actor is playing it a little differently than you imagined, but his performance is at least credible, let it be.

If for various reasons you have a little extra time before the first setup of the day is ready — you may be moving into a new location or setting up for a night shoot — try to take the performances up a notch or two using objectives and adjustments as I describe in Chapter 7. Time will be short, so you are going to have to always go for the quickest fix. If during the first rehearsal on the day of the shoot, the actor gives you a good performance, just try to fine-tune it to your taste using adjustments. Save the three silver bullets — ultraplayable objectives, physicalizing the objective, and improv — for the rehearsal that you will squeeze in while the set is being lit, after the walk-through for camera. During this last rehearsal before you go on camera, try to make the good performance great by applying one of the three silver bullets. Use your instinct and judgment to determine which of the three to try.

If during the first rehearsal on the day of the shoot the actor's performance lacks credibility, don't wait. Trot out the heavy artillery and try to fix it by giving the actor an ultraplayable objective and/or getting him to physicalize the objective. This leaves an improv — your most powerful weapon — for the rehearsal after the walk-through for camera, right before the actor goes on. If all goes according to plan, in the first rehearsal you make it credible, and then right before he goes on you make him do the improv — and that helps him take it up a notch.

If in this first rehearsal you fail to make the performance credible using ultraplayable objectives and physicalization, don't hold the improv in reserve. Hit him with it and see if it works. The improv you have prepared may not fix the problem. It might not make the performance credible. You need to find that out right away, so you have enough time before the actor goes on camera to devise an improv that works.

On the Set in front of the Camera and Crew

In the worst-case scenario, you go before the cameras with an actor or actors that have not yet been able to deliver a credible performance. When this happens, you have to pray that you can give the actors an improv to do in front of the cameras that will get them into the moment. Work out a hand signal that will cue camera and sound to start rolling and let everyone know that the take will be slated at the end. Tell the actors to start the improv and go into the scene when you clap your hands. Ideally, the improv will get them into the moment. When you sense this, you give the hand signal. Camera and sound start rolling. When they are up to speed, clap your hands. The actors will do the scene and then you have to remember not to say "Cut" until the camera assistant has had the time to slate the take. If that doesn't make it real, you can try to alter the improv or come up with a whole new improv, and then repeat the same drill where you start the improv, then roll the camera and end slate the take.

Sometimes even that doesn't work. Usually your airtight schedule and budget will allow for no more than 10 takes. Stanley Kubrick has been known to do 60 takes, but the first time director is advised to cut his losses much earlier than that. If you get stuck with an actor who can only say his lines, without breathing life into them by backing them up with real feelings, then your last resort is to hope you can cut around him and keep him off camera as much as possible. This will minimize the damage he does to the credibility of the film. It also makes it easier to redo or replace his performance with ADR lines. To do this, you simply have to make sure that every time the offending actor speaks, you have another angle to cut to that he is not in, so you can keep his lines off camera. On the TV series *BJ and the Bear*, we called this "cutting to the monkey." When we got stuck with an actor who couldn't act, and if Bear, the chimpanzee who played BJ McKay's sidekick was in the scene with the offending actor, we always made sure to shoot a single on Bear. Since Bear never spoke or complained about how he looked in his close-up, this was the simplest cutaway we could come up with. Fifteen seconds of film of the chimpanzee silently reacting to what the offending actor was saying would guarantee that we could "cut to the monkey" every time the actor who couldn't act tried to act.

One absolute truth about directing actors for camera is that each actor is different; what works great with one, won't work at all with the next. This is because as human beings we are vastly complex. Every actor works differently and every actor will react in his own unique way to you as a director. You must keep your radar on and rely on your knowledge of human nature to tell you when you are getting through to your actors and when they are rejecting your direction, and adjust accordingly. Two stories I have heard from name directors about working with name actors come to mind.

The first was told by Randa Haines when she spoke at the School of Film and Television at Chapman University, where I teach. Randa is so skilled at working with brilliant but difficult actors, she actually did two films back to back with William Hurt: *Children of a Lesser God* and *The Doctor*. I asked her to come to Chapman to talk with a class of my directing students and to screen a film she made with another brilliant but extremely independent actor, Robert Duvall. The film, *Wrestling Ernest Hemingway*, is really a piece of filmed theater portraying a tempestuous friendship between two characters — one played by Duvall and the other by the brilliant British actor, the late Richard Harris. Duvall's reputation is that he mostly directs himself. He goes to great lengths preparing for each of his roles, and since he is always excellent, if not brilliant, on screen, he must feel that he has a mandate to shape his performance on his own, his way, without any tampering by any pipsqueak director. Certainly he would take direction from Francis Coppola or another director of that stature. But the word is that unless you measure up to that standard, you should be grateful that he is in your film and not get between the master and his canvas. This did not daunt Randa Haines. She established a good working relationship with Duvall and did not hesitate to offer him suggestions as to how to approach his character. However, in her own words, she would do it by "throwing a crumb over the wall, and then seeing how he reacted. If he did not object, then another crumb would go over the wall." Randa is about as poised and diplomatic as is humanly possible. She obviously manages to work successfully with actors who regularly bite other directors' heads off much as a lion tamer works with a lion — by staying cool and self-assured but keeping a respectful distance.

This obviously contrasts sharply with how writer-director Brad Silberling found it most efficacious to work with Dustin Hoffman. Silberling came to Chapman to screen his film, *Moonlight Mile*, starring Dustin Hoffman, Susan Sarandon, and Jake Gyllenhaal. After the screening there was a Q & A during which Silberling told the students present that Hoffman sought him out for directorial input at least once a week during preproduction and up to a dozen times a day during shooting, depending on how many scenes he was in. Obviously Hoffman is an extremely hard-working actor, who, like Duvall, goes to great lengths to take on the persona of the character he is portraying. But he is as open to directorial input during this process as Duvall is suspicious of it.

As a first time director without a reputation, you have to move very gingerly. Delicately probe each of your leading actors and try to discover how they like to work. Think about what they tell you and come up with a game plan for how you will interact during the production. Then go back and discuss it with them. Agree on how you will proceed together, but remember, this is just a point of departure. Actors, like every other human, don't know themselves inside and out. They can think they want to work a certain way, or be treated a certain way, yet they react very poorly when treated that way. You just have to keep your radar on and rely on your knowledge of human nature to tell you when you are getting through to your actors and when they are rejecting your direction, and adjust accordingly.

One of the greatest challenges a first time director will have to face is deciding when to allow his lead actors to change the script at the last minute on the set and when to insist that they play it as written. It is inevitable that on a regular basis your leads will get hit by inspired ideas for how to reinterpret their role right before they go on camera. They will just be brimming with excitement at their insight, and absolutely certain that if you just let them change these lines, or just zig when the script says they zag, it will enable them to deliver a brilliant performance. Actors love to do this. I found out why when I became a parent and got to listen to my two kids doing make-believe routines together. Kids love to do this for the same reason that actors like to act. They create fantasy roles for themselves in which they enjoy being a different person in a fantastic situation.

In a rehearsal prior to the start of shooting, such improvisation or reinterpretation should be welcomed. If the actor wants to change his lines or give another actor in the scene a Dutch rub, even though that's not in the script, so long as it doesn't alter the logical sequence of the story, the director should encourage such invention. The actors are helping themselves by making the fantasy they are projecting themselves into that much more delicious and wonderful to act out. But they are also helping the director if by so doing they manage to bump their performances up a notch. Remember, there is no such thing as a performance that is too convincing. Even if the idea sounds a little bizarre, try it — you may like it. Many actors work instinctively. Some of them have woefully limited verbal skills. Even if the idea doesn't sound great, that might just be because they cannot describe it accurately. Let them act it out. Even if it is a little off, you can adjust it, or it may inspire an even better idea in you. Bottom line, as much as you want your leads to shine, they want to shine for you more than you can imagine. You should encourage and empower their every effort to do so. At rehearsal prior to shooting, you have nothing to lose and everything to gain by letting them act out their ideas.

On the set, it is another matter, especially right before the camera rolls or even worse, between take one and take two. Such last minute changes may require rewriting some other actor's lines so that all the lines flow together naturally. Or it may require you to rethink your camera-blocking plan. Such adjustments take time. If your actor waits until after the set is lit to make his suggestion, he really is putting you between a rock and a hard place. You want to empower him and help him improve his performance, but if the set is lit then everyone in the crew will have to stand around and wait while you readjust the camera blocking or come up with some new lines. Every minute you spend doing that is a minute you fall behind schedule, and on a day-late-dollar-short production you have very few minutes to spare. Under these circumstances, I would try to implement the last-minute change only if it strikes you as a great idea, or if very little has to be adjusted to accommodate the change.

There is no guarantee that the actor's last-minute inspirations will be an improvement over the existing script. They can be fool's gold or the real thing; the director's true talent will be revealed in his ability to distinguish between the two. This was one of the lessons I learned while listening to John Badham discuss many of his films when he was the Filmmaker-in-Residence at Chapman.

Badham gave most of the credit to actor John Travolta for the performance that made Travolta a star: his depiction of Vinnie in *Saturday Night Fever*. According to Badham, for the most part all he did as a director to assist Travolta was "get out of the way." This is not surprising. Travolta came into *Saturday Night Fever* as an immensely gifted actor with great instincts, who had yet to prove to the world what he could do. He knew that the role of Vinnie was perfect for him and could make him a star. So he worked his ass off, not only training as a dancer, but also creating shtick for his character. Badham said Travolta came to the set everyday with a half dozen little improvements on the script for his character. They were not all great, but most were. Badham obviously had the directorial genius to distinguish between the two, and so what you see on film is a magnificent performance. If you have never seen *Saturday Night Fever*, or if it's been a while since you last took it in, rent it and study Travolta's performance. He is a great actor, and this is obviously the role in which he spread his wings and sailed to the heavens.

Badham also confessed that he willingly gave Emelio Estevez permission to rewrite almost all of his scripted dialogue on the set or between shoot days throughout the filming of the movie *Stakeout*. This was because Badham got a little too creative during the casting of *Stakeout*. Richard Dreyfuss, an old Badham favorite, had been cast in the lead as a Seattle police detective. At the last minute, Badham cast Estevez as his partner, despite the fact that Estevez was in his late twenties and the role he was cast to play had been written for a crotchety old lady kind of cop who was about to retire. The first day on the set, Badham and Estevez agreed that the scripted lines did not work coming out of Emelio's mouth. At that time, Estevez already had several produced feature films to his credit as a screenwriter. So, according to Badham, he gave Estevez carte blanche to rewrite his part, and he did. This meant that much of Dreyfuss' dialogue had to be rewritten as well, so that it worked with Estevez's new lines. As a result, the scenes between Dreyfuss and Estevez, which comprise at least half of the film, were not scripted until right before the cameras rolled. It is a tribute to Badham's self-assurance and adaptability as a director that he was able to come to the set everyday not knowing exactly what he was going to shoot, and then bring it all together and make it work at the very last minute.

Badham was so well established as a top director when he made *Stakeout,* he knew that, within reason, the studio was going to give him all the time and money he needed to get the movie made properly. The first time director will not have that latitude. He should not undertake a rewrite as comprehensive as what Badham pulled off on the set of *Stakeout.* He runs the risk of blowing his schedule and budget. But the first time director should study the scenes between Estevez and Dreyfuss. They are lively, fresh, and funny, and they obviously contributed substantially to *Stakeout's* remarkable success at the box office. And, by and large, they are the product of two leading actor's last minute inspirations. They are a perfect example of the real gold that leading actors can contribute to a film and that the director can take credit for in the final analysis — provided he remains open to suggestions on the set, has an ear for good dialogue, and an infallible story sense.

Like John Badham, the first time director has to be able to reject the bad ideas his leading actors are more than capable of coming up with. Badham told us that on the film *Drop Zone* he had to give Gary Busey a lecture to keep him in line. Busey's offenses were many, but one that Badham specifically mentioned was his constantly wanting to rewrite his part, generally for the worse. Yet if you watch the film, what comes through in Busey's performance is the incredible zest and rambunctious joy he brings to the part. He plays the lead bad guy and he delivers a great performance. He is convincingly cunning, violent, and completely unpredictable, all of which make him exciting to watch and a very worthy adversary for the hero, played by Wesley Snipes. The lesson here is: When the director shoots down an idea his leading actor is in love with, he must do it in a way that does not intimidate, anger, or frustrate his lead. In the words of the agent Mark Lichtman, he "gives good 'No.'" This is never easy. Badham made it clear that Busey was very hard to deal with. I have dealt with difficult, demanding actors who, like a child who is being a brat, you just want to slap. Don't give in to this very natural impulse. You could end up with a sulking actor who is going to walk through his part to get even with you. Don't risk it. Give good "no" and move on.

Collaborating with Your Lead Actors
During the First Walk-Through for Camera

The first walk-through for camera is a moment of truth for the director and his leading actors, in much the same way that it is a tense moment between the director and the cinematographer. Prior to the day of the shoot, the director has done his necessary homework and come up with a camera-blocking plan for every moving master that he will shoot on that day. The camera-blocking plan is dependent on an actor-blocking plan, so the director has to also come up with a complete actor-blocking plan — which is to say he knows exactly where and in what manner he would like the actors to hit their marks and say their lines. But the actors do not have a clue about how the director wants to block them, unless the director has had the luxury of some rehearsal time.

Most professional actors will, with a minimal amount of questioning, do as the director tells them to do when it comes to blocking. This is a good thing, because it will be difficult for the director to work extensively with his leading actors on whatever objections they may have. But not all actors can be counted on to hit their marks and say their lines exactly as they have been instructed. Some very good actors, as soon as they hear the word "Action!" try to lose themselves in the character and try to think only as the character would think. This means they cannot act and think about blocking at the same time. Zemeckis told me that on one occasion while shooting *Back to the Future*, Crispin Glover got so into being George McFly that the only way they could get him to follow the path he had to follow to hit his marks was to put sandbags down on either side of that path, so if he veered off course he would trip over the sandbags. This is the extreme example. But the point is that Method acting encourages the actors to think and feel as the characters they are portraying would think and feel. This makes it difficult for some actors to hit their marks and say their lines as the director would like them to.

After a couple of days on the set, the director will be able to figure out which actors are going to object to his actor blocking and which are going to promptly do as he asks them to. The director then has to work to adjust all of his actors' blocking so that the actors who are prone to reject his blocking are unknowingly led to follow it by the actors who are always willing to do just as he asks. For example, if the director wants the leading man to take the leading lady's hand on a certain line — and he knows that the man will not do it on a specific line, but will insist on doing it only when he feels it, the director just tells the leading lady to offer her hand on a certain line; nine times out of ten the Method actor will, unthinkingly, take it. Actors generally play scenes with other actors. Since the hard cases who systematically reject the director's instructions on actor blocking are in a minority, the director can usually control those cases by using the cooperative actors to herd them around.

When this tactic does not work, the director has no choice but to enter into a discussion with an actor about why he would execute a specific piece of blocking on a specific line. In these instances, the director must simply sweet-talk them into it, as quickly as possible. Don't spend a lot of time debating it, because the actor can always trump your best logical argument by saying he just can't do as you ask and make it real. Time is precious, so before spending five or 10 minutes debating it, spend the time rethinking your camera blocking so that it works with the blocking that the actor insists on.

Before the shoot day, when you are planning your camera blocking, you will also be preparing your actor blocking, because about 90 % of your camera movement is externally generated. Avoid giving any subtle actor blocking to those actors who are inclined to resist specific instructions to make a subtle move on a specific line.

For example, if you were planning your actor blocking for the master from *What Lies Beneath* discussed in Chapter 5, the camera had to rotate clockwise about 90 degrees from a tight two-shot (Figure 4.13 – page 97) of Claire (Michelle Pfeiffer) and Norman (Harrison Ford) to a the reverse two-shot (Figure 4.14) on Warren Feur (James Remar) and Mary Feur (Miranda Otto). This rotation was accomplished by having Harrison Ford deliver his first line in the scene while taking a big step to camera right towards Feur. He is apologizing for Claire's having just loudly accused Feur of murdering his wife. He takes the step toward Feur as if to make an apology sotto voce. The camera had to pivot to camera right to keep him in frame. This takes it most of the way through the 90-degree clockwise rotation.

What essentially is happening here is that Harrison Ford, by making a subtle move on a specific line, is steering the camera from a two-shot to the reverse two-shot. This tricky little bit of actor blocking eliminates the need to cut between the two reverse two-shots, and therefore enables director Zemeckis to make it half way through the bravado camera blocking needed to shoot the whole scene in one shot. Zemeckis, no doubt, first decided to shoot the scene in one shot and then devised an actor blocking plan that would allow him to do so. Next he gave all the crucial little bits of actor blocking to those actors who he knew would be 100 % cooperative and open to making subtle little gestures on specific lines — especially Harrison Ford. There is nothing in the script that necessitates that these little gestures be made. You can argue logically that it would be out of character for Norman to make such a gesture, and you can almost be certain that those actors who are not inclined to accept the director's camera blocking will confront the director with these arguments if asked to perform such gestures and movements. Time is too precious on a day-late-dollar-short production to be wasted on arguing fine points of blocking with prickly actors. Therefore, make every effort to avoid giving them blocking that is not necessitated by the script, and never do it if your camera blocking is dependent on their actor blocking.

Some actor blocking is practically necessitated by the script and can be safely assigned to actors who are inclined to reject the director's blocking suggestions. A good example of such inarguably logical blocking is Michelle Pfeiffer's blocking in this same scene. The script requires that her character, Claire, enter the lobby where this scene takes place, rush (because she is being chased) up to where Feur is standing, and accuse him of murdering his wife. So Claire's blocking is determined by Feur's position in the lobby. Zemeckis put him in the middle of the lobby with his back to the door through which Claire enters. Therefore the actress playing Claire, without the director necessarily having to even suggest that she do it, will rush up to where Feur is standing and reach out and tap him to turn him around. Zemeckis' camera blocking plan was dependent on Michelle Pfeiffer doing this, which she did without hesitation. Michelle Pfeiffer is a consummate professional, and one would assume she would hesitate before challenging a director as acclaimed as Zemeckis. But even the biggest pain-in-the-ass, contrarian actor could be trusted to do just as Michelle Pfeiffer did and Zemeckis intended. This bit of actor blocking is so necessitated by the script it is practically automatic. Reserve this sort of actor blocking for the actors who make a habit of challenging you.

Harrison Ford is so sensitive to the needs of the directors he works for, he actually volunteered to make the step towards Remar to bring the camera around before Zemeckis even suggested that he do so. Zemeckis told me that, among the actors whom he has worked with, the two who are the very best at helping the director out in this way are Jodie Foster and Tom Hanks. "And you know why they're so good?" he quizzed me. "Because they've been there. They've both directed, and they know how hard it is."

The first walk-through for camera is the director's first and last opportunity to achieve the hoped-for mind meld with his DP. Those actors who seem to appreciate this and do not make the first walk-through for camera more stressful by doubting or refusing to accept the way the director blocks them for camera are an extremely welcome asset on the set.   The implication of Zemeckis' observation that actors who have directed do not question the way the director blocks them is clear. They have stood in his shoes. They know how much the director has riding on the work he is doing with the cinematographer during the first walk-through. Realizing that, they are not going to add to his burden. They do everything they can to help him out.

There is only one more thing to say about collaborating with your leading actors during the first walk-through for camera. If you have laid out your actor blocking as I prescribe — giving the subtle gestures and moves to those actors who are inclined to help you and making a point to give the actors who have a penchant for challenging you only those pieces of blocking that are necessitated by the script — then, ideally, the actors will almost be able to block themselves and you will have to give them only a few crucial pieces of blocking. The key word here is *almost*. You should be prepared to give some guidance to the actor who is driving the scene and the other actors can usually key off of him. Generally, if the blocking is necessitated by the script, any experienced actor, once on the location or in the set with the other actors on their marks, will only need to be given a starting mark. He can deduce the rest.

For example, in the scene from *What Lies Beneath*, Michelle Pfeiffer's character is driving the scene up to the moment she accuses Feur of murdering his wife. During the first walk-through for camera, Zemeckis began laying out his blocking for his leading actors by placing Feur where he wanted him in the middle of the lobby, and then giving a starting mark to Pfeiffer. He showed her where to stand so she would be just out of frame on the other side of the lobby, ready on "Action" to break the frame and start her move to Feur (Figure 4.12 – page 94). He did not say anything to Harrison Ford or James Remar. He was too busy working with Don Burgess, the cinematographer, on the dolly move that would cover Pfeiffer as she charged into the center of the lobby. In fact, he did not initiate any conversations with any of the actors about their blocking until he told Miranda Otto (Mary Feur) to exit the ladies room on a certain cue (Figure 4.20 – page 103) and to deliver her line as she glides up alongside James Remar (Figure 4.14). He did not even bother to give Harrison Ford his blocking for when he takes over driving the scene after Michelle Pfeiffer finishes her opening block of dialogue (Figure 4.16). Ford was watching the camera and knows enough about directing to anticipate what Zemeckis was going to ask him to do when he delivers a line to James Remar apologizing for his wife's behavior (Figure 4.18). Like a student who wants to answer the professor's question before it is asked, Ford was volunteering to make the big step towards Remar that comprised the second key piece of actor blocking in this scene. All that Zemeckis had to do to complete his actor blocking for this scene was to instruct Remar to lean forward with concern toward Pfeiffer (Figure 4.14) when he implicitly questions her character's sanity in his final line of the scene. Remar's lean-in brings the camera around to Ford (Figure 4.15); again, when Ford felt the camera on him, he suggested moving from camera right of Pfeiffer to camera left of her (Figure 4.23 – page 97) before leading her toward camera left, out of the lobby.

So for the entire scene, Zemeckis only had to share his thoughts on blocking three times with the actors. He gave Pfeiffer her starting mark. He gave Otto her starting mark and cue line, and he asked Remar to lean forward with concern when he delivered his final line. The rest of the time his actors were able to figure out what he wanted them to do by keying off the other actors and the camera. This is ideal.

It allowed him to focus most of his time and energy during the first walk-through on working with Don Burgess to resolve the many unforeseen problems brought about by attempting to shoot the whole scene in one continuous master. So the bottom line on blocking your actors is that less is more. Give the obvious blocking to the difficult actors, the subtle blocking to the cooperative actors, only instruct the actor who is driving the scene — and ideally the actors will be able to fill in the blanks. Whenever they look lost, step in and lend them a hand.

Taming the Actors Who Chew the Scenery

Some experienced actors who know they are good cannot resist strutting their stuff in front of the camera. A talented, experienced actor can easily fall into the trap of working in a vacuum, independent of the director and the other actors. This is human nature. Most of us are a little insecure and cannot resist showing off a bit of the things we do very well. But if an actor gets too caught up in himself and his ability to evoke powerful and real feelings on cue in front of a camera, he ends up looking like he is acting in a different movie. What he is doing bears no relation to what the other actors are doing. This makes the scene seem a touch unreal. In real life, most people play off of each other. Those individuals who walk down the street having loud conversations with themselves do not seem very normal. Somebody screaming into a cell phone will turn heads in alarm. As a director, you do not want performances that stick out like this in your breakthrough film. Some actors, like Gary Oldham, are notorious for pushing their excellent interpretations up to an ostentatious level where the performance does not seem in keeping with what the other actors in the scene are doing. In the business this is known as **chewing the scenery**. When Gary Oldham does it, it's not ideal, but he is such a good actor he can often get away with it — as over the top as he may be, he usually seems to be driven there by very real emotions.

It is unlikely that you will be working with actors of Gary Oldham's caliber on your breakthrough project. If one of your actors starts chewing the scenery, chances are he is showing off doing something that he thinks he is really good at, but actually is not. This is bad. One of the best ways to control this problem is by giving the actor a get-from or do-to objective, which should force the actor to play off the other actors in the scene. If the other actors are playing the scene on a realistic level, it should bring his performance down to that level. If he is determined to chew the scenery, the best quick fix available to the director is to remind the actor to play the objective. If he continues to chew the scenery, the director can resort to a little humiliation. Often actors who like to show off are especially sensitive to being humiliated. A little humiliation, judiciously applied, can motivate them to stop showing off. To do this, the director can ask for another rehearsal, ideally in front of all the crew. Loudly, he can remind each actor what his objective is, and then warn each that if he doesn't see them convincingly going after the objective, he will say so. As soon as the show-off actor starts to chew the scenery, the director should restate the objective out loud. If that does not tone the actor down, then the director can continue to call out, "I don't see it. I don't see it. I don't see you... *trying to make her laugh*" or whatever the objective is. If this does not work, then the director has to change the objective, in such a way that the new objective will lead the actor to be less ostentatious. For example, if initially the objective was *to make her laugh*, then the director could make it *to make her smile* or even *to amuse her*. The director can also help the actor stop chewing the scenery with an adjustment or a battery of adjustments. So combined with a change of objective, the direction would change from *to make her laugh by clowning around* to *to make her smile by teasing her*. But it makes little sense to even start working with adjustments unless the change of objective succeeded in bringing the ostentatious actor's performance in line.

Collaborating with Yourself

About the time that Lance Armstrong starting winning the Tour de France bicycle race, and it started getting much more coverage in the American press, I read an article on the sports page of *The New York Times* that explained why this race is probably the most physically demanding athletic event on the planet. The article stated that each leg of the Tour — that which the riders cover in one day — is almost as demanding on the body as running a marathon. Therefore, competing in the Tour requires each contestant to run a marathon everyday for 21 days. It boggles the mind.

Pick any incredibly demanding job: preparing for your law boards, getting through tax season as a CPA, surviving a hurricane on a fishing trawler. Directing your breakthrough film will be to any of those tasks as the Tour de France is to any other sporting event.

I was raised to believe that illness was a state of mind. In my family, if you started feeling like you were coming down with anything, the only acceptable therapy was gutting it out. You never took to bed. You kept on moving until you fell down. The logical extension of this thinking was that doctors were strictly for hypochondriacs. I adopted this mindset completely, but when I got done directing my first film, I went to see a doctor. I was sure that having endured the Tour de France of jobs, I had damaged my health. I was fine, but considering what I had put myself through, I had lucked out.

Anybody who has what it takes to make it as a director will kill himself trying to do the best job he possibly can on his breakthrough film. If he has the fire in the belly that he must have to make it, then he will push himself up that insurmountable mountain created by the fact that the director is responsible for everything — even that which he has no control over — until he collapses, hopefully just temporarily. If not, he is not a director. If you don't believe me, ask any working director.

Perhaps you will not ride yourself this hard if you are one of those rare individuals who is completely self-assured. The rest of us who doubt ourselves in some way will overcompensate for this doubt by pushing ourselves up to and beyond our limits. And why not? The chances are good that, unless you hit a home run this first time at bat in the majors, you won't get a second chance. When you sit back down on the bench, you'd better know you had given it everything you had. Everything — every last ounce of energy.

So, since it's a given that you are going to push yourself this hard, you are going to have to be your own best cornerman/trainer/guru/healer. If you can do a great job as your own support team, you might just make it through. As to exactly how you go about fulfilling that role, only you can tell. However you talk yourself down off the ledge when you hate yourself and want to jump, however you recharge your batteries when you are spent, only you know best. Just recognize that there is a law of diminishing returns when it comes to applying oneself 100% to any task. Eventually, you are so worn out, you are functioning counterproductively. Most of us know the signs, though they are different for all of us. Just make a mental note to respond to them when you see them, so you can recharge before you start working against yourself.

I happened to know one of the assistant directors who worked on *Jaws*. One day I ran into this AD on the lot. I immediately started quizzing him about Spielberg's directing style. I guess I hoped to pick up a few tips on how to become the next, hot, young thing. This AD was an Arthur Hiller type — a super bright, super mensch who excelled at getting ahead by getting along. He told me he didn't like working with Spielberg and ventured that the way that Spielberg interacted with the crew was actually counterproductive. I asked him for an example.

"Whenever the shit really hit the fan, he'd just walk away from it," he told me. "He couldn't be bothered."

"Like what?" I asked.

"Oh like, when we were out on the water and trying to fight through some big technical glitch, like getting one of the robot sharks to work, he'd just put on stereo headphones and read a comic book until it was fixed."

Amazingly, unwittingly, my acquaintance had just given me a tip on how to become the next hot young thing. Not that listening to stereo headphones and reading a comic book are guaranteed to make your first movie as good as *Jaws*. But Spielberg knew that to get through the stress of the production he would have to grab every opportunity to recharge his batteries, and do whatever it took to stay centered and at his best. This way, when the time came for him to seize the reigns, he could perform brilliantly. Find out what the equivalent of stereo headphones and a comic book are for you; keep them at the ready and apply them liberally whenever the opportunity presents itself — no matter what anybody thinks. If it works for you and you can squeeze it in, do so at every opportunity. You just might do more than survive your breakthrough gig, you might just ace it like Spielberg did. (Yes, I know his first theatrical feature was *Sugarland Express* and it wasn't the monster hit *Jaws* was. But, if your first feature is as good as *Sugarland Express*, you should be so lucky.)

CHAPTER 8 | SUMMARY POINTS

■ The director sets the tone on the set. If the director remains cordial and poised, his whole crew will do their best to emulate him.

■ You must never think out loud or seem unsure of yourself. You must perform credibly as the alpha dog, or the pack will turn on you.

■ It is a collaborative business. The director who is a gifted collaborator — who is truly open to suggestion — will, given luck and talent, go the farthest. Collaboration is a two-way street. You have to prove to your collaborators that you are open to their ideas before they will offer them to you, free for the taking.

■ If the 1st AD is experienced and good, he is probably more capable than the first time director of working with the crew to set up the shot. If the director lets the 1st AD work with the crew to set the shot, that frees the director to do what the 1st AD probably cannot do: work with the actors.

■ A good, clearly written shot list, or overhead, football-play type diagrams, can give a 1st AD almost all the information he needs to figure out what shots the director has in his mind.

■ Of all the director's responsibilities on the set, the first walk-through for camera is the most challenging. If the walk-through takes more than 15 or 20 minutes, it has taken too long. The first time director should think of the first walk-through as the moment when he puts his mark on the film.

■ On his breakthrough film, the first time director should put the DP's experience with camera blocking to work for him. The director should describe the shot as he envisions it and let the DP improve on his good ideas and replace his bad ideas.

■ The first time director is advised to be extremely aware of all of the emotional currents flowing between himself and his leading actors. In this arena in particular, the best way to get ahead is to get along. Your goal should be to have a genuine human relationship in place with each of your leading actors before you embark on shooting the scenes in which they will have to shine.

■ If you know that you need a lot of rehearsal time with a specific actor or actors, have them called to the set early. If there are no dressing rooms or trailers to rehearse in, then the rehearsal should be held in the quietest place you can find that is still close enough to the set so you can be fetched quickly.

■ If you get stuck with an actor who can only say his lines without breathing life into them by backing them up with real feelings, then your last resort is to hope that you can cut around him and keep him off camera as much as possible. To do this, you must make sure that every time the offending actor speaks, you have another angle to cut to that he is not in.

■ Delicately probe each of your leading actors and try to discover how they like to work. Think about what they tell you and come up with a game plan for how you will interact during the production. Then go back and discuss it with them.

■ Time is too precious to waste on debating the fine points of blocking with prickly actors. Avoid such confrontations by never giving such actors subtle moves that have to be made on specific lines, especially if such subtle moves are intended to trigger externally generated camera moves. Give them only the blocking that is practically necessitated by the script.

■ If you as a director have no choice but to enter into a discussion with an actor about why he would execute a specific piece of blocking, such as get out of a car on this line rather than that line, don't spend a lot of time debating it. The actor can always trump your best logical argument by saying he just can't do as you ask and make it real. Time is precious, so rethink your camera blocking so that it works with the actor blocking that the actor insists on.

■ The bottom line on blocking your actors is less is more. Give the obvious blocking to the difficult actors, the subtle blocking to the cooperative actors, or only instruct the actor who is driving the scene.

■ If an actor's performance is over the top — if he is chewing the scenery — giving him a get-for or do-to objective and forcing him to commit to it will usually bring his performance down to earth. If this doesn't work, change his get-from or do-to objective and make it less and less demonstrative.

PART FIVE:
POSTPRODUCTION

CHAPTER 9 | TO THE ANSWER PRINT AND BEYOND

Collaborating with Your Editor

All of the truths about getting the most out of your principal collaborators can be applied to having a successful working relationship with your editor. The best-case scenario is that your editor is truly gifted, so you can step back and let him perform his magic. Truly gifted editors are born, not made. What they have cannot be learned. These guys really are like magicians. They will take footage from before the slate and after the cut, or silent reactions and looks which you intended to be used at one point in the scene, and use them to save or significantly improve another part of the scene.

Before you watch the first assembly of your footage, you will have a pretty good idea of what it should look like. You've seen most of the footage on the monitor or in dailies. You should be a respectable editor yourself. If you got a lot of coverage and the performances were solid, it should look pretty good. If you ran out of time and did not get all the coverage you wanted, then usually you are just praying that the film will be okay. Not great. Just okay. A gifted editor can take your okay dailies and make them look great. He will take your good dailies and make them look spectacular.

On my second feature, *Never Too Young to Die*, the producer hired and fired two teams of editors who each did a cut. Neither team ever got the picture to flow, to feel like a movie. Yes, there were editorial problems. There have probably been editorial problems on every movie made since John Ford retired. Matt, total shoe-salesman-cum-producer that he was, had completely goofy ideas about how to improve the picture editorially. When he tried to force his ideas on the editors, they balked, and it was, "Off with their heads!" Then, we lucked out and got Bill Anderson to come in and re-cut. Anderson is as gifted as they come. He's from Northern Ireland but started his career in Australia, where he cut some of Peter Weir's and Bruce Beresford's best early films: *Gallipoli*, *Breaker Morant*, and *Don's Party*, to name a few. When he came in to save *Never Too Young to Die*, he was slumming because he had just moved to the States and did not yet have a green card. He got his green card and went on to cut all of Peter Weir's American films, including *Dead Poet's Society*, *Green Card*, *Fearless*, and *The Truman Show*. He also cut *Tender Mercies* and *Driving Miss Daisy* for Beresford. As his assistant, he brought along Paul Seydor, who shortly thereafter went on to cut *White Men Can't*

Jump, The Program, Cobb, Tin Cup, and a slew of sports movies. The day those two walked into the editing room of my little low budget action film was one of the luckiest days of my life. They politely closed the door to the editing suite and told us to come back in a couple of weeks. When we came back, the editorial problems had vanished — like magic.

Besides Anderson, I have been fortunate to work with several other gifted editors. I got well acquainted with Robert C. Jones when he was the Filmmaker-in-Residence at Chapman. Jones cut almost all of Hal Ashby's films, among them *The Last Detail, Shampoo*, and *Bound for Glory*. All these extraordinary editors share certain characteristics. First, they seem to be able to remember and recall every foot of dailies, or at least every good foot. (Anderson proved this when he pulled pieces of gold out of what had been discarded by the first editing team on *Never Too Young to Die*.) Next, they all like to work fast and then knock off. When they're hot, they're hot. When they're not, they're not — and they know it. Fortunately, with digital editing they can get even more done when they're hot. This leads me to believe that they work more on an instinctive level than an intellectual one. They are sensing and manipulating the rhythm of the film. Last, they usually like to be left alone when they work. Again I think this is because what they are doing is instinctive. Having to intellectualize what they are doing by talking about it with a co-worker or the director blocks them. Thinking for long about their cuts removes them from the instinctive source that informs their best decisions. When they are cutting, it must be like composing a song.

When working with truly gifted editors, I have always found that the best approach is to give them as much independence as they want. This approach works well with all of the director's principal collaborators because it empowers them, but it seems to work especially well with gifted editors because of the intuitive nature of their work. The way Bill Anderson likes to work is to do a cut of the whole picture entirely on his own, and then go to work on it section by section with the director. The director will give Anderson his ideas for changes, leave the editing room, and let Bill do them on his own. If after viewing the film again, the director is still not satisfied, Bill lets him into the editing room and they go through the film together and attack each problem area. They discuss each editorial solution. Bill implements the suggested solution while the director waits. If that doesn't fix it, they keep trying, working on it together in the room until they fix it or give up and move on. Leaving a sticky problem unsolved and coming back to it the following day is a wise practice. Usually you discover that you have fixed the problem, but were too obsessed with it to let yourself off the hook. When you look at it with fresh eyes, it's gone. If it's not, you go back to work on it.

Robert C. Jones likes working in much the same way as Anderson, as do about 90% of all the most successful professional directors and editors I know. There is no guarantee that you will be editing your breakthrough project with a truly gifted editor. Nonetheless, I would advise you to work in this same fashion with any editor, because I think this model, which gives the editor a lot of freedom, will bring out his gifts, whatever they may be. Over time, through trial and error, you and your editor will have to discover exactly what approach to collaborating works best for the two of you. I would advise starting with Bill Anderson's method, and then modifying it to accommodate you and your editor's work habits and eccentricities.

One mistake first time directors are inclined to make is to try to fit the movie they have shot into the template of the script. The script is a blue print. It is not the Bible. Good things happen during production that were not in the script. Actors get ideas and improvise, and sometimes go so far as to reinterpret their characters — as Emelio Estevez and Richard Dreyfuss both did in *Stakeout*. Stunt sequences are rewritten to work better on the location where they are shot. And bad things also happen during production that were not in the script. Actors misinterpret their roles. Actors who are supposed to like or love each other clearly do not, and the camera does not lie. The sun goes down before the director gets enough coverage to make a scene work. Stunt sequences end up looking very tame. Everything that happens during the production that was unexpected — good and bad — is not in the script.

Any director who deserves the title has studied his script hundreds of times before he gets into editorial. The result of all that studying is that the director creates a mental picture, based on the script, of what the finished film should look like. If in editorial he tries to make the film that he has shot look like that mental picture, he is making a huge mistake. He has to throw the script out. He has to look at the film that he has shot and make the best movie he can from that film. To do that while assembling his first cut, he has to use big chunks of the footage of the brilliant accidents that happened on the set, and he has to cut out everything that might have been good in the script but fell flat.

After he has done that, he has to step back and look at the film as a whole. And then he has to take out anything that does not improve the film. Often that entails cutting out good or even great sequences. The first time director must learn to have the guts and discipline to eliminate scenes that he has deprived himself of sleep, sex, and sanity to make good. He has to do what Zemeckis, quoting William Faulkner, urged me to do when I showed him my final cut of *Never Too Young to Die*: "Kill your little darlings." Less is always more in film. A perfectly good scene may throw the balance and the pacing of the whole film off. The scene may be really funny or really exciting, but the film may flow better and be a more satisfying experience without it.

If you get a truly gifted editor to cut your film, he can help you make these hard choices. He has not studied the script hundreds of times. If he is any good, he will look at the film that you have given him and judge it accurately and objectively. When he tells you a scene that you want in the movie has got to go, because, as good as it is, it throws off the pacing or the balance of the whole film, believe him. Do as he says. Your judgment is impaired. His is not.

After going through the entire film several times in the editing room to make it as good as they can, the director and the editor will screen the film together, and seeing it as a whole, will discover new problem areas that have to be worked on. After those problem areas have been addressed, they will look at the entire film again, and find more as yet undetected problem areas. This process will be repeated until both the editor and the director agree that they have done the best job they can with the film they have. Then the director will screen his cut for the producer or the studio. After that, the producer will create his cut, ideally collaborating with the director and the editor as a unit, just as the director collaborated with the editor. When the producer is satisfied that the film is as good as he can make it, it will be tested in front of an audience.

The scenario described above is the best-case scenario. It is predicated on the assumption that the producer and/or the studio or whoever those higher up than the producer might be have enough good sense to respect the director as a collaborator and an artist. Just as any good director gives his key collaborators all the rope in the world to hang themselves with, so those up the ladder from the director should give the same amount of rope to him. Often it doesn't happen that way, especially in the day-late-dollar-short world of breakthrough projects. On my first picture, Pedro, my Spanish shoe-salesman-cum producer, was so nervous about having sunk a half million dollars of his own money into *Crystal Heart*, he never let me in the editing room after the film was shot

In the end, he who writes the checks will get the final cut, unless he has surrendered that right contractually to the director or someone higher up. So, if he who writes the checks insists on changing the director's cut for the worse, the director can try to sweet-talk him or even deceive him into changing it back. If the director tries to fight more forcefully, he runs the risk of getting kicked out of the editing room. If that happens, he has cut his nose off to spite his face.

On *Never Too Young to Die*, Bill Anderson delivered his final cut to Matt, and Matt started spouting some goofy ideas about how he wanted to improve the film editorially. Rather than confront Matt, I suggested that we take the film out to Speilberg's Amblin Productions to screen for Zemeckis, who had his office there. After Bob had looked at it, Matt could try out his goofy ideas on Bob. Matt went for it. True Sammy Glick-wannabe that he was, Matt probably thought he could talk Zemeckis into directing one of the projects he was developing. No doubt, Matt fancied himself a sort of later-day Svengali, but Bob Zemeckis is the Svengali of Svengalis. The minute Bob shook Matt's hand, Bob had him under a spell. Matt sat silently and watched while Bob carefully went through the picture on the flatbed with Bill Anderson and they communicated genius to genius what could be done editorially to improve the picture. Bill went back to the editing room and made Bob's changes. Of course, they dramatically improved the picture. After that, all Matt could think and talk about was getting the picture into theaters so he could make millions. This is the kind of subterfuge or non-confrontational tactic that a director can adapt to influence a hardheaded producer.

Reshoots

Some of the improvements that Bob Zemeckis insisted that we make in *Never Too Young to Die* could only be done by going back into production and shooting some new, as yet unscripted, scenes. I would venture to say that there has never been a film made that could not be improved by shooting some additional scenes that are written only after the film has been fine cut and tested. Why? Because the process of production inevitably morphs the movie into something other than what was represented by the script. This new morphed movie is going to be missing a piece here and there, and the only way to fill in those missing pieces is to go out and shoot them. Zemeckis has done this on every film he has directed, except the first two, and the first two were the only ones that did not make money. Spielberg regularly goes back and shoots additional scenes after he has finished cutting and testing. Irving Thalberg made a practice of doing this when he was the boy genius of Hollywood in the '30s. I think if Zemeckis, Spielberg, and Thalberg all made a practice of doing something, it would be wise for the first time director to do his best to follow their example.

Unfortunately, in the day-late-dollar-short world of breakthrough directing, there is rarely money in the budget for such an indulgence. After the movie has been shot and the cost of the production has been paid, the higher-ups are usually completely crazed about saving money. They have a gargantuan case of what is referred to in the real estate business as "buyer's remorse." They have made a huge investment in something and, in spite of the fact that — before making the investment — they thought it through as carefully as is humanly possible, they are absolutely certain that they have made a huge mistake. Even good test results will not dispel this negative mindset. Only once the film has come out and is still a hit in its first *and* second week in the theaters will they feel reassured. In this frame of mind, it is unlikely that they are going to increase their production costs by an additional five or ten percent — unless your name is Zemeckis, Spielberg, or Thalberg.

In fact, the head of Fox was so totally out of his skull with buyer's remorse after Zemeckis had talked the studio into putting up an extra million dollars to go back into production and shoot some unscripted scenes on *Romancing the Stone*, he had Zemeckis fired off the next picture that he was signed to do — *Cocoon* — because it happened to be a Fox picture. *Romancing the Stone* cost a whopping $7 million to make (the bill for craft services on *Titanic* was probably $7 million). Zemeckis got that extra million out of Fox to shoot some unscripted scenes needed to make the female lead, Joan Wilder (Kathleen Turner), sympathetic and a worthy love interest for Jack Colton, the Michael Douglas character. The added scenes were cut in, but the picture did not go through the roof when it was tested. At that point, the higher-ups at Fox decided that the re-shoots were a waste and that Zemeckis had suckered them into throwing good money after bad. They were so incensed, they forced the producers of *Cocoon*, Daryl Zanuck Jr. and David Brown, to pay Zemeckis off. Ronnie Howard came in to do the picture. *Romancing the Stone* opened and was a huge hit. Zemeckis pocketed his six-figure salary for *not* directing *Cocoon* and went over to Universal, where he signed a deal to write and direct *Back to the Future*. And I am sure, dear reader, that of the three films mentioned in this tale, the one that you are the least likely to have ever heard of or remember seeing is *Cocoon*.

The first time director will be up against that sort of mindset when, after delivering his fine cut, he quickly asks for more money to shoot some new scenes that he is absolutely certain will take his film up to another level. So he should not be shocked when his request is denied. If re-shoots are so difficult to get approved, why do I even bring them up? Because on the off chance that they can be done, they should be. There is an excellent chance that they will make a significant improvement in the movie — an improvement that could turn out to be the deciding factor in the success of the film.

Take *Romancing the Stone* as an example. The new scenes that Bob talked the studio into letting him write and shoot after the picture was cut were, in my opinion, absolutely essential to the film's success. The Turner character, Joan Wilder, and the Douglas character, Jack, have a highly contentious relationship throughout the film. They never agree until the very end what should be done with "the stone," the huge emerald that they are both chasing. The added scenes were critical to establish a credible romance between these two adversaries. Most notable is the one in which Joan and Jack inadvertently get high together when they make a bonfire for warmth out of bricks of marijuana that they find in the wreckage of a drug smuggler's airplane. Without these added scenes, *Romancing the Stone* would have turned out to be yet another Hollywood movie in which the two leads fall in bed together for no good reason. Since the relationship isn't believable, a movie like this rarely becomes a smash hit.

Romancing the Stone was a huge hit. If it had not been a hit, it is doubtful Spielberg would have been able to set up *Back to the Future* for Zemeckis at Universal. There is a chance that Bob might never have been able to launch his brilliant career. So, as risky and as difficult as it may be to go back into production to shoot new material, it is an option always worth fighting for.

Inserts

Shooting as many inserts as you can is the next best thing to going back into production to shoot new scenes. An **insert** could be described as just about any shot that does not have an actor's face in it. Because actors are not involved, inserts can be shot weeks, months, or years after the completion of production, using extras along with wardrobe, props, and backgrounds that match the scenes that the inserts go into. Most commonly, inserts are a postproduction tool used to give the audience a closer view of something that played a crucial role in the story but was too small to be seen distinctly in the footage shot during production. For example: a treasure map, text on a computer screen, a snapshot, a fuel gauge, or an LED readout on a bomb. Those are the more classical kind of inserts. Since, in fact, an insert is any shot that does not have an actor's face in it, inserts can be used as a poor man's alternative to going back into production. With inserts a director can try to fix the same problems that added scenes are intended to address — namely, the problems that only become apparent after extensive editing.

If I had 10 dollars for every insert I shot as an associate producer overseeing the postproduction of every new Glen Larson television show that came out in the late '70s and early '80s, I would be a rich man today. On the two-hour pilot for *Switch* — a series starring Robert Wagner, Eddie Albert, and Sharon Gless that only lasted one season — I shot over two hundred inserts. As a writer-producer, Glen Larson could always spot the missing pieces in a TV episode after accidents on the set had morphed that episode. He was habitually profligate with the studio's money during production, so he was always over budget going into post. The guys that ran the television division at Universal at that time — first, Sid Sheinberg and then

264 first time director | *bettman*

Frank Price — would have put out a hit on Larson if he had tried to spend another dime of the studio's money by sending out a first or second unit to generate new footage. So Larson would send me over to the insert stage with some pieces of wardrobe and carpet and some extras who specialized in inserts. I would shoot the new sequences on the insert stage, doing everything that a first unit would do, but always shooting from the neck down. Larson would then get the series leads — Dennis Weaver, Lorne Greene, David Hasselhoff, Lee Majors — to record a bunch of new dialogue, **wild lines**, that would be edited in as if they were said, off camera, by the characters that I had shot from the neck down and, "Voila!" Larson had created the new scenes he needed to flesh out the new, postproduction story.

Admittedly, inserts work best if they are quick and tight and carefully composed, so they fit in seamlessly between two pieces of production. Mini-sequences comprised of inserts and wild lines look weird and start to call attention to themselves if they stay on screen too long. As soon as that happens, the audience has been thrown out of the story and the all-important illusion of reality has been destroyed. Larson regularly overused inserts and crossed that line. But inserts used judiciously, so that they go by without calling attention to themselves, can be an extremely valuable tool in postproduction. They can act like subtitles to convey data to the audience that helps fill in some of the unforeseen gaps in the story created by the production process. Look at any of the films that involve computer sleuthing and you will see dozens of important story points conveyed through tight inserts on computer screens. If the first time director cannot get back into production to fill those gaps, he can often do an adequate job of filling them by shooting inserts.

The power of an insert as a story-telling device is well represented by the inserts of the photograph of Marty McFly and his brother and sister in *Back to the Future*. These inserts were used to create suspense that was absolutely critical to the success of the story and the film. The entire movie, bottom line, was about Marty accidentally preventing his parents from meeting in 1955, and then having to struggle heroically and mightily to get them back together. To do this he had to make sure that they went to the high school prom, the "Adventure under the Sea Dance," where they shared their first kiss. If he fails to do this, his parents will never get married and never sire him and his two siblings, thereby preventing their existence. Every time Marty suffers a setback in his quest to get his parents back together, another piece of the image of himself, his brother, and his sister is magically erased off the photograph (Figures 9.1 through 9.4). The photograph therefore becomes a physical representation of the fact that time was running out for Marty and his siblings, and the results are a matter of life and death. In the entire film, there is no more graphic and accurate image representing the dire consequences should the hero fail to achieve his objective. Therefore, this little close-up insert of a 3" x 5" snapshot (Figure 9.1) becomes an invaluable device for generating much of the edge-of-the-seat suspense that made *Back to the Future* a movie franchise — conceivably just as valuable as other much more costly images, such as the shot of Doc Brown hanging from the clock tower by the hands of clock.

Inserts can also be extremely useful in building energy and intensity in action sequences. Montage generates energy. When shooting a high-energy action sequence, the more angles on that action which you can divide it into, the more energetic it will become when it is cut together. If you don't believe me, rent a John Woo film and count the angles when he does a big stunt like plowing a jet into an airplane hanger. John Woo has all the money in the world, so he uses the montage-generates-energy rule to make big expensive stunts like an airplane going into a hanger look powerful. By the same token, a first time director shooting stunts on a shoestring budget can use this rule to make his small, cheap stunts look powerful.

Figure 9.1

Figure 9.2

Figure 9.3

Figure 9.4

I used a series of inserts to this end in a stunt sequence from *Never Too Young to Die*. The stunt featured the female lead, played by Vanity, driving a Corvette under the trailer portion of a tractor trailer. She lays in wait there, under the truck, until two bad guys on motor cycles who are threatening the male lead, played by John Stamos, pull up alongside the truck (Figures 9.5-9.15). She then pulls a 357 Magnum out of the arm rest in the Corvette and blows away the bad guys (Figures 9.16-9.21). Months after we completed principal photography on this film, I went out into the parking lot behind the editing suite and shot the inserts of Vanity pulling the gun out of the arm rest and cradling it in her lap (Figures 9.16 and 9.17), as well as inserts of the Corvette's speedometer and Vanity's boots on the gas and break pedals (Figures 9.8 and 9.10). The reason I shot these inserts was not to solve the classic problem inserts are intended to address: giving the audience a sufficiently close look at something that they have to see up close to understand, but is too small in the footage shot during production. In fact, an audience watching this footage would have a very clear idea of what transpired in the stunt sequence and the story.

Rather, I shot these inserts to give my editor, Bill Anderson, more different angles on the same action so he could quick cut them together and give more energy to the sequence. These added angles often have as much visual impact as what was shot during the production, and can be generated at a fraction of the cost. In doing this I was copying the Australian director, George Miller, who, in the early '80s directed two stunning action films: *Mad Max* and *The Road Warrior*. Both of these films were made on budgets significantly under $1 million, yet in some ways they are more thrilling than contemporary action films which cost a hundred, if not two hundred times what Miller spent on his films. Rent them and watch them and you

Figure 9.5

Figure 9.6

Figure 9.7

Figure 9.8

Figure 9.9

Figure 9.10

Figure 9.11

Figure 9.12

Figure 9.13

Figure 9.14

Figure 9.15

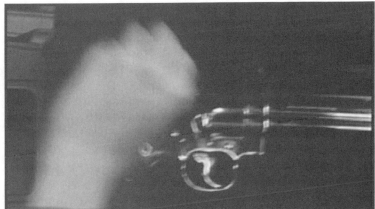

Figure 9.16

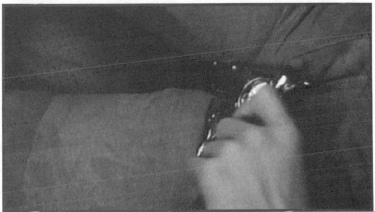

Figure 9.17

Figure 9.18

Figure 9.19

Figure 9.20

Figure 9.21

will see that Miller always peppered his action sequences with (cheaply produced) inserts that gave him more angles which he could use in editorial to heighten the energy level of his stunt sequences. The first time director would do well to do as I did and emulate Miller's example.

Post Sound – An Overview

Once the picture is locked, the next major undertaking in the completion of the film is the postproduction sound work: music scoring, ADR (automatic dialogue replacement), sound effects spotting and editing, and finally sound mixing. In my experience making three movies and working as a postproduction supervisor for six years for Glen Larson, I have seen the full spectrum of possibilities in postproduction sound. I have worked on TV shows and movies that had the best — and the worst — sound treatment you can imagine. At Universal when I was overseeing much of Larson's post sound on the shows he made there — *McCloud*, *Battlestar Galactica*, *Switch*, *The Hardy Boys*, *BJ and the Bear*, *Sheriff Lobo*, *Knight Rider*, and *Magnum P.I.* — a large percentage of the sound editors were alcoholics. Not all, but a lot more than you would encounter in most other lines of work. Universal paid its editors less than any studio in Hollywood. They hired the union editors that could not get a job anywhere else — the bottom of the barrel. Many of them were older men who had aspired to be picture editors, but never made it, and they soothed their angst and coped with the monotony of their drudge jobs with the bottle. Some of them also popped uppers to keep cranking the work out. Their work was at best, uninspired, and at worst, marginally passable. In contrast, I did the post sound for *Never Too Young to Die* at Saul Zaentz's Fantasy Studios in Berkeley, California. With the exception of one mixer, I had the same crew of sound mixers who won the Academy Award for *Apocalypse Now*. The head mixer, Mark Berger, had three Oscars in his trophy case. B. J. Sears, who worked as my head sound effects editor, went on to be the picture editor on *The Unbearable Lightness of Being* and *Storyville*. My entire crew had just finished doing the post sound on *Blue Velvet*. It was first cabin the entire way. How could a shoe salesman-cum producer like Matt, who intentionally bilked the production crew of *Never Too Young to Die* out of their last week's salary to save money, afford a classy outfit like Zaentz's? In order for Zaentz to keep his talented crew working for him in Berkeley, he had to keep them regularly employed. Since he made a movie under his own banner every couple years, the only way to keep his crew together was to rent the post sound facilities out at bargain-basement prices to low budget indie producers like Matt.

Having experienced both the world's best and worst postproduction sound, I can tell you that if you have a good film going into post, the worst treatment will not hurt you much, and if you have a mediocre film going into post, the best won't make it much better. There are really only two areas where a significant contribution can be made. One is the score. A great score can push a good movie into the realm of greatness. *Chariots of Fire* is the best example of this phenomenon. On the other hand, a great score will not make a mediocre movie much better than mediocre. The second area of post sound where a significant improvement in the film as a whole can be made is in **ADR** — automatic dialogue replacement — in particular, those instances when an actor's performance is completely dubbed or replaced. I did this several times for Larson on TV pilots he made. In both cases, an actress who looked the part but could not deliver a credible performance was cast in the pilot. Because any actor who cannot deliver a credible performance immediately destroys the illusion of reality as soon as he opens his mouth, it was decided that these performances had to be replaced in their entirety for the pilots to realize their potential. In both instances an actress named Lisa Eilbacher, who combined excellent acting skills with a flawless ability to hit sync in ADR, was hired to do the job. And when it was done, it radically improved the quality of the entire show.

Every brilliant performance in every Fellini and Antonioni movie was created on a dubbing or ADR stage. In the same way, a first time director can dramatically improve his film by excising a mediocre performance in its entirety and replacing it with a good, credible performance created on an ADR stage. Various financial and contractual obstacles will present themselves as soon as the director announces his intentions to re-voice an actor in this way. But these obstacles are not insurmountable, and a first time director should be prepared to move heaven and earth to get a bad performance out of his breakthrough film.

By the time the first time director starts to work on the postproduction sound, his opportunities to raise his breakthrough film to a level of excellence have pretty much passed. It would be wise for him to pull in his horns a bit, and try to get ahead by getting along. By nature, I am not the kind to pull in my horns, and so I have fought many bloody battles in the realm of post sound. Bottom line: It was never worth the fight *except* when it came to re-voicing a lousy performance or picking a composer.

The best way for the first time director to assure that his breakthrough film will get the best post sound treatment possible is to be as hands-on as his producer will allow him to be when hiring the key personnel. All of the key jobs in post sound require great technical competence and a special kind of genius. Just like great picture editors, great composers, sound effects editors, dialogue editors, and sound mixers are born, not made. What distinguished Mozart from Solari, as Solari himself was all too painfully aware, was a gift of the gods. Similarly, I am certain that it was not Lucas, but one of his sound effects team on the first *Star Wars* that came up with the signature sounds of the light sabers being unsheathed and slashing through the air — not to mention the distinctive chirps, whistles, and bleeps of R2-D2. Lucas probably initiated and guided their efforts, but I am sure that the real genius of creation lay with his head sound effects editor or a member of the sound effects team.

The best way to guarantee that your breakthrough film will get the best post sound treatment possible is to make sure that your producer hires the very best key personnel that he can afford. If he is open to your suggestions, you should absolutely make the time to canvass every director or producer whose judgment you can trust and milk them for the names of the composers and the post sound technicians that have delivered for them, and who will work for the money that your producer has allocated for their positions. If you are not already familiar with their work, go to Blockbuster and check out the films that they have contributed to. Once you have come up with your picks, turn on the charm and try to get your producer to hire them. Usually the post sound crew is hired during picture editing. As soon as you wrap, you will have few other demands on your time, so make the effort to participate in hiring them.

Spotting the Picture for Sound Effects and ADR

After the picture is locked, the director screens it with the head sound effects editor and head ADR editor and comes up with a game plan for all of the post sound — with the exception of the music. I personally like to run the picture once and talk only about ADR, and then run it again on a separate day and talk only about sound effects. I find that I do a better job if I am only listening to and thinking about dialogue or listening to and thinking about effects. Two separate screenings is an added expense that your producer may not be willing to treat you to. If that's the case, just go with the flow. It's not worth getting into a battle over post sound.

Probably the most important task in post sound — just as important as coming up with a great score — is the job of cleaning up or replacing bad dialogue. You can't make a good movie without a good script, and to a large extent the script is delivered to the audience in the dialogue. This is not to say that the audience has to be able to understand every single line. Some lines — in the script for flavor, not meaning — are intended to be garbled or marginally intelligible. Marlon Brando is famous for mumbling. He garbles many of his lines and renders them largely unintelligible, but such lines often add dimension to his performance. It varies

276 first time director | bettman

from film to film, but generally speaking, there are 50 to 100 lines in every movie that everyone in the audience absolutely must hear, otherwise they will be unable to follow the story.

When the director spots his picture for dialogue replacement and ADR, he consults with the dialogue editor and the head sound effects editor to identify those lines that are unacceptable because they are unintelligible. There are two ways they can be rendered more intelligible. One is to "clean up" the existing dialogue tracks. Essentially this involves putting each actor's lines on a separate dialogue track so when the final sound mix is performed, the sound mixer can treat each actor's lines differently — using dialogue enhancing technologies to render these lines more intelligible. There is a subcategory to cleaned-up dialogue: clean dialogue that was recorded for the same scene but as a different take. These lines are commonly referred to as **alternate takes**. If the sound is bad for the main character, "Rex," in the wide shot when he calls the heroine, "Glenda," "a lying bitch," perhaps this same line is clean in one of the close-up angles, and perhaps the line recorded for the close-up "fits" in Rex's mouth in the wide shot and so can be substituted for the unintelligible line. In many cases, marginally intelligible dialogue can be cleaned up by substituting alternate takes. The other alternative is to replace the marginally intelligible dialogue with ADR lines. This involves getting the actor to redo the unintelligible lines on an ADR stage where the conditions are ideal for recording dialogue.

Of the two alternatives, the first — cleaning up the existing dialogue — is by far the most preferable. The performances are inevitably better in cleaned up dialogue because these are the original performances recorded in the heat of the moment on the location where the actors were all assembled, putting their hearts into recreating the reality described in the script. Under these natural circumstances, the actors can buy into the reality and deliver their most credible performance. On an ADR stage, the actor recreates his performance one line at a time, working by himself in front of a microphone and a monitor. Under these circumstances, the performance inevitably suffers. So the best alternative is always to try to salvage the maximum amount of dialogue that was recorded on location. However, during the spotting session it is impossible to accurately determine which problematic lines of dialogue will be rendered intelligible after they have been cleaned up and treated on the sound mixing stage. Some original dialogue can be salvaged and some cannot, and there is no rock solid way to find out until the final mix. Therefore, as much as possible, all marginally intelligible dialogue should be both cleaned up and replaced with ADR lines. This way the director, working with the dialogue mixer on the sound mixing stage, can make a line by line determination as to which lines of original dialogue can be salvaged and which have to be replaced with ADR.

This is the best way to prepare your dialogue for mixing. But it calls for double work, and so is not financially feasible on some day-late-dollar-short productions. If a director is forced into an either-or decision between cleaning up original dialogue and ADR, he should get the sound effects and dialogue editors to venture their best guesses and then make a judgment call — always erring in favor of original dialogue, unless the lines in question are pivotal and must be understood in order for the audience to grasp the fundamentals of the story.

With that said, some actors are so good at ADR, they can always come very close to recreating their original performance, and in some cases even improve on it. By the same token, some very good actors are a disaster on the ADR stage. So the first time director is advised to hire a dialogue editor who has worked with most of his principal actors. An editor with this kind of experience can help the director factor in each actor's skill as an ADR artist when determining exactly how much of their marginally intelligible dialogue to replace with ADR. If for some reason the director must hire a dialogue editor who has never worked with his principal actors, then he is advised to get on the phone and hunt down a director or a dialogue editor who has worked with each actor and get the skinny on their skill as an ADR artist. Some excellent Method actors are a complete disaster on an ADR stage. They cannot hit sync, and even if they hit sync their performance is all wrong. Time on an ADR stage is expensive, so a first time director working on a day-late-dollar-short production should make every effort to minimize the number of lines of dialogue he attempts to replace when working with such an actor.

At the sound effects and dialogue spotting session, the director will also brainstorm with his head editors to determine which crowd scenes need to be augmented with supplemental wild lines provided by a **walla group**. Large crowd scenes often need more than such sound effects as cheering, booing, whistling, or unintelligible murmuring to come alive. This is because, even in a crowd, one hears words out of context and snippets of intelligible conversation. In *Titanic*, when the ship is sinking and the crew tries to prevent the immigrants in steerage from getting up on deck, in addition to the lines delivered by the principal actors and the roar of the crowd you can hear shouts of: "There are women and children here!" and "Let us pass!" These little bits of intelligible dialogue are created by bringing a walla group of 10 to 15 actors onto an ADR stage and recording them as they watch the picture and ad lib appropriately.

When it comes to walla, more is more. The first time director should err on the side of caution. In every instance when he suspects that a specialized walla is needed to enhance a crowd scene, he should arrange for the walla group to meet that need. Of course, he has to make sure he stays within his producer's budget.

But it is better to come to the sound mixing stage with more wallas than you need than to discover that a scene in your film falls flat for want of some specialized walla.

When it comes to spotting sound effects, here again the best rule to follow is that more is more. Better to come to the sound mixing stage with more good effects than you need crammed into the effects reels, and throw some out — rather than come to the stage and find that some scenes just do not come alive for want of a few crucial sound effects or a big enough wall of sound. Generally, the big action sequences or crowd sequences are the ones that need the most sound effects. Most crowd and action sequences are shot **MOS** (without sound), using multiple cameras. If sound is recorded during production, it is usually only intended as a **guide track** — a template that the sound effects editors can use to determine where the sounds of cracking bones, bullet hits, squealing tires, shouts, screams, and explosions should go. All the sound has to be manufactured or dug out of a library and cut in, sound effect by sound effect. In a big action sequence such as the Normandy Invasion scene in the opening of *Saving Private Ryan*, the sound effects editors built dozens if not hundreds of sound tracks with separate effects on each track — bullet hits on bodies, bullet hits on sand, bullet hits on water, bullet ricochets, small arms fire, carbine fire, machine gun fire, mortar fire, howitzer fire, etc., etc. The quantity and the intricacy of the work that goes into building the effects for a big action sequence are absolutely mind-boggling. In such instances, the director cannot guide all the work. He has to communicate his overall vision of how the action sequence should sound to his head sound effects editor and then trust the editor to successfully render that vision.

Science fiction or fantasy movies are similarly demanding and complex; they require the director to give his effects editor some good visionary ideas as a guide and then allow the editor to fill in the details on his own. In science fiction or fantasy, many of the sounds have to be invented. Lucas could not tell his effects editor to cut in the effect for a light saber being unsheathed. He had to describe it in words or approximate the sound using his mouth as a sort of sound effects duplication instrument, much the same way that kids playing with toy guns mimic gunshots. This is no time to be embarrassed by doing something that might seem slightly childish. If the director has a sound in mind and can almost duplicate it using his mouth, then he should do so. This will take a significant amount of the guesswork out of the task for the sound effects editor, and enable him to manufacture the sound that much more rapidly and effectively. I learned this lesson while doing the postproduction sound supervision on *BJ and the Bear*. The "Bear" was a pet chimpanzee who accompanied the series lead, truck driver B. J. McKay, on his various travels and adventures. The chimp was in most of the scenes that were played for laughs, and the scenes could be made much funnier if the sound effects editors cut in additional cackles, screeches, growls, and howls to cover the chimp expressing himself. I quickly discovered that the fastest and most effective way to communicate to the editors exactly what kind of chimp-speak I wanted cut in was to mimic the chimpanzee. I had to get over my initial embarrassment, but it was the best way to get the job done.

Even if your movie is not set in outer space or in the future, it is always best to use your imagination and push the limits of credulity when building sound effects. When it comes to sound design, it is self-defeating to be constrained by reality. Film is fiction. So it is best to think of sound effects as another kind of music that plays along with the picture to amplify the drama that is unfolding on screen. I learned this early on while working as postproduction sound supervisor on the Universal lot. Spielberg was doing the sound mix on *Jaws* and all the top sound editors whom I never got to work with, but whom I knew by reputation, were running around knocking themselves out to make the boy wonder happy. Like all good film technicians, they took pride in their work and were happy to describe it to a curious wannabe director such as myself. What I learned was that Spielberg decided he wanted a sound effect for the moment when the shark lifts its head out of the water and spreads its jaws. Of course, in reality, there is no such sound. The sound effects editors tried to create an appropriate fictitious sound by pushing a basketball underwater and releasing it and recording the sound. This did not sound quite right, so they got creative and discovered that if they played it in reverse at a slower speed it seemed to work. Spielberg liked it and so it made it into the final mix.

There are two important lessons to be learned from this little story. Number one: When it comes to sound effects in particular and post sound in general, even a genius like Spielberg is only as good as his technicians. The director may have the vision, but his vision will never make it into the final film unless his producer provides him with technicians who have what it takes to turn his ideas into sound effects that can be recorded. All the more reason why the first time director should do everything in his power to help his producer track down the best sound technicians who will work for the money in the budget. Number two: A little imagination goes a long way when it comes to sound effects. The sound that something actually makes does not necessarily make the best sound effect. Films are best if they are bigger than life, and the same can be said for the sound effects that go into films.

This second lesson — to get creative with the sound effects — should guide the first time director when he brainstorms with his sound effects editor to come up with the sound design for the important dramatic scenes in his film. The rule that more is more applies to all sound effects. One should always come to the sound mixing stage with more than you need. With action sequences and crowd scenes, this is of paramount importance. But with dramatic sequences, you can often succeed without having every logically conceivable sound, provided you have a few good imaginative choices. It is far more important to have the few sounds or just the one sound — the slap of small waves, kids voices on a playground, bed sheets on a clothesline flapping in the wind, the drone of hot weather insects — that captures and amplifies the dramatic essence, the mood of the scene.

On the ADR Stage

ADR is unbelievably tedious, but the first time director should be on the ADR stage when his leading actors do their ADR. If at all possible, he should be there for every actor's ADR session, as well as when the walla group comes in to do their wallas. Why? Because in ADR you are replacing dialogue, which is to say you are redoing the performance. Nothing is more important than the script and the performances, so during the ADR sessions that which is of paramount importance is on the line. A good performance is gold. It is money in the bank on the way to a hit film that will launch your career. If that good performance has to be replaced using ADR lines, the director should be there to do everything in his power to make sure that the quality of the performance in each line is maintained. His dialogue editor, as experienced and knowledgeable as he may be when it comes to ADR, cannot be expected to help the actor match the quality of the original performance.

Before the ADR sessions begin, go over the schedule with the dialogue editor. Scheduling is particularly important because you do not want your leading actors to be kept waiting before they do their ADR. You should be ready for them when they get there. You need to keep them fresh, so they can deliver their best performances. Scheduling is tricky because some actors are very fast at ADR and some are impossibly slow. Ideally, your dialogue editor has worked with most of your leads on an ADR stage in the past. This should have been an important criterion for his selection. If not, he must be prepared to do the research necessary to find out specifically the speed at which each of your leading actors works. Have your ADR editor make up a preliminary schedule, but make sure that he does not book your leads back to back. As much as possible, spread out the times at which your leads come in to do their ADR. Fill in the time between their sessions with the secondary characters' sessions. This way, if you fall behind, you can rush through some of the secondary characters' sessions and get back on schedule by the time the leads come in. Absolutely err on the side of caution when calculating how long it will take to do each session. You and the crew will do a better job if you have five or 10 minutes of down time between sessions. This will cost more money, but it is money well spent.

Come to the ADR sessions with the leads, ready to help them recreate their performances. Get your script breakdowns out and study them. Before the actor starts his ADR session, the director should discuss the scene with the actor and, without hammering on it, remind him what the most playable objective and the ultra-playable objective were. Hopefully, when you start to discuss the scene in general, he will already have some ideas to get his juices flowing so he can go back to the place in his head where he was when he did the scene during production. If you have broken the script down according to my instructions, you should have every change or adjustment noted. If the actor's performance seems to be falling short of what he did on the set, supply him with the adjustment to his objective that he is playing in that specific line or lines. If this does not bring the level of performance up to where it was on the set, stop the ADR session and do an improv. You can use the same improv that you prepared for the shoot. Even if you are not a trained actor and feel silly doing an improv with your lead, get over it. If you are serious about succeeding as a director, you have to be ready to do anything and everything to preserve whatever was good about the actor's original performance. The quality of your movie is on the line. Hopefully, the improv will enable the actor to summon up the feelings he needs to deliver the lines credibly.

Even if they do not admit it, most actors love the sound of their own voice and are captivated by every good thing they do on screen. Work hard during ADR to fan these narcissistic fires. When each line is played during the ADR rehearsal, if there is anything complimentary that you can say about the line, say it. If the line is good or great, celebrate it. Make the actor feel like each line is precious and sacrosanct and get him to give his all to replicate it. The actor will inevitably tire of the ADR process. Be sensitive to this. Cheer him on as long as you can. As soon as it seems that his ability to match his performance is slipping, call a break. Try to give him whatever he needs to revive himself: a nap, a cup of coffee, a phone call, some stretching or yoga, etc.

If an actor gave a performance that lacked credibility during the production, it is unlikely he will be able to improve on that performance during ADR. The sterile environment of the ADR stage, the way the performance never flows but must stop at the end of each line, the nerve-racking difficulty of hitting sync — all conspire to make it hellishly difficult to improve a performance in ADR. By the same token, nothing is more important than the performances. So if you are not satisfied with a performance an actor delivered on the set, and it turns out the actor must come into ADR to redo the performance because the sound quality was unacceptable, then you must try to do everything you can to improve the performance in ADR.

Because ADR is monotonous and difficult, everyone wants to rush through it. You must buck this trend. Do not accept a line in which the performance is wanting or the sync questionable. Keep working on the line until you get it right or the actor begs you to stop. If you have to give up before you get it right, come back to it later in the session, or later in the day, or some other day. But do not go onto the mixing stage with an ADR line that is unacceptable because the performance is lacking or because it is out of sync. Stay on the ADR stage and keep working with the actor until you get it right, or until your producer throws you out. If you do not have the will power to persist in this fashion, you do not have what it takes to be a director.

I have found that there is only one absolutely surefire way to be certain that when you go into the final mix all the ADR lines will sync perfectly. Every time your dialogue editor tells you that the actor has delivered an ADR line that will sync, keep working until he is sure that you have a second line that will sync. If you have two choices for each ADR line, in the end, they will all sync. Your actors and your dialogue editor will probably object to this and try to convince you that you are being overly cautious. And following this practice will lengthen every ADR session, so your producer may disallow it. But, to my mind, it is worth it. All it requires on your part is will power. The alternative is to cave in, be a nice guy, and end up on the mixing stage with a couple of out of sync ADR lines. When this happens, the dialogue mixer usually spends a lot of very expensive time on the mixing stage making the production dialogue work. In the end, this costs more and the result is never 100% satisfactory. To my mind, you end up with a better dialogue track and save money if you simply go the extra mile when recording the ADR.

When the walla group comes into ADR to create the wallas, the director should be there to insure a successful result. A significant chunk of the film budget goes into the crowd scenes. Those scenes will never play properly unless they are backed up with good walla. To make sure that this money is well spent, the director needs to go to the walla sessions to be certain the walla group is coming up with the right kind of ad lib dialogue. He will not be able to hear the finished crowd effects until the final mix, because the crowd backgrounds are made up of multiple walla tracks and general crowd effects like cheering or screaming or booing — all mixed together. So when it comes to determining if the wallas are technically acceptable, the director will have to rely on the judgment of the ADR mixer and his head dialogue editor. What the director can judge on his own is if the ad lib lines that the walla group is coming up with are right for the scene. If the producer has done his job properly, he will have hired a walla group that is experienced and well trained. If this is the case, the walla group — without the director's guidance — will get the walla about 90% right. As clever as they may be, the walla group cannot understand the essence of each crowd scene as well as the director; in the end, he will have to skew their interpretation slightly so that it is spot-on. This does not take a lot of effort. The director can sit in the booth with the engineers, and after a couple of takes he can use the intercom to talk to the walla group in the studio and get them to alter their approach slightly. This little bit of guidance will go a long way. If the director fails to attend the walla session, he can be certain that when he gets to the dubbing stage all the wallas will seem a little off. Then it is likely he will keep telling the dialogue mixer to play them softer, in which case the money that was spent on them will have been wasted, and the crowd scenes will not seem as vibrant.

Hiring a Composer

The first time director should knock himself out to find the best composer possible for his breakthrough film. If he has made a good film from a good script with good performances, he can actually bump it up another notch if he can find a composer who will write a great score for it. The problem is that most great composers charge prices that are out of range for a first time director's production. Therefore, the director must discover a composer who is on the cusp of greatness.

This is not as hard as it seems. As in all other competitive job fields, for every talented working individual in the film business, there are about 10 equally talented individuals who are not working. The director has to trust that he has a good ear for film music and then scour the business for demo tapes of film score composers who have done a couple of scores, but are not yet hot and charging top-drawer prices. There are a number of agencies in Hollywood that specialize in handling composers. They will gladly send the director and his producer tapes of all their clients who will work for the money in the budget.

The first time director should also get on the phone and call anyone and everyone who has recently gone through the process of hiring a composer. That's how I got a recommendation for Mason Daring when I was looking for a composer for *Never Too Young to Die*. Since 1985, when I was shopping for someone good to score my film, Mason has broken through as a composer for TV movies and good little independent films. But at time, for the most part, all he had done was score movies for John Sayles.

To my ear, Mason was an excellent composer, but I could not talk Matt into hiring him. Matt had never heard of John Sayles. On top of that, the minimalist, low-key, intellectual vibe of Mason's music went completely over Matt's head. I did not protest too vehemently because about the same time I suggested hiring Mason, I also suggesting hiring Trevor Jones — and Matt told me we would get Trevor to do the score, which thrilled me. Trevor Jones is now a big-name composer. At that time, all he had done was score some low budget, indie films in England and write the score for *Runaway Train*, by far the best film ever turned out by Cannon Films. It was made for a very modest budget and yet was a big hit in the theaters. As soon as I saw the film and heard the magnificent score, I called Matt and told him we had to hire Jones. Matt was all for it, but Trevor passed on our offer. Supposedly it was because we did not offer enough money, but I am certain it was because he decided that writing a score for our goofy little action film would do nothing for his ascending career, and he was probably right. Even though Jones eluded us, I would urge every first time director to emulate everything I did to try to get him to score my film — namely, sample every recent film with a budget comparable to the budget for your film, and go after the composer of every score that you like.

I have found that when it comes to film scores there is one tried and true rule to follow: The only effective way to make any decisions regarding film scores is to make those decisions while listening to a piece of score playing against the picture. This seems self-evident, but much time is wasted trying to do otherwise. When the first time director goes about trying to discover a composer on the cusp of greatness to score his breakthrough film, he can only effectively gauge these prospective composers' talents if he can listen to the previous scores they have written playing against the appropriate piece of film. Listening to a soundtrack album or a sample tape is not an accurate way to judge the quality of the score. The music may sound great on its own, but it is worthless as score if it in any way weakens the intensity of the scene it is intended to play behind.

Working with the Composer

Usually the composer is hired when the picture-editing process is winding to a close. The director, film editor, and composer should all watch the film together and discuss in general terms the kind of score that would work best for the film. Since editors, like musicians, work instinctively, most have great insights in the realm of film scoring. Their artistic decisions are made on an intuitive, gut level. Your editor, if he is gifted, may have a better feel for the dramatic rhythms of your film than you do. These rhythms must be amplified by the score, so your editor's judgment about the film score is invaluable.

Fortunately, because of the preview process, most picture editors cut a temp music track to accompany the film. For the first time director, this is very good thing. The **temp track** will allow the first time director to immediately engage in a meaningful dialogue with his composer about the score before a note is written. Some composers will refuse to look at your movie with the temp track playing. Their complaint is that hearing the temp music will squelch their creativity, because when they go to write a piece of original score to replace the temp, they will inevitably mimic the temp track. Before you hire your composer, make sure that he will not raise this objection. Every creative person is certainly entitled to do whatever he has to do to summon his muse. But to my mind, you and your composer must watch your movie with the temp music playing against it several times over — because words are entirely inadequate to describe music. Watching the picture without any music playing against it and verbally communicating to your composer what kind of music you hear in your head for the places where you want music, is like trying to fill a swimming pool with an eye dropper. It can be done, but it's not worth the effort. The only effective way to make any decisions regarding film scores is to make those decisions while listening to a piece of score playing against the picture.

When you, your composer, and the film editor run the temp music against the picture, you and your editor can tell the composer what you like about each temp piece and what you don't like. This is by far the most effective way to get the composer to hear the ideal pieces of score that you hear playing in your head. You and the editor can also tell the composer exactly what you like and don't like about the **spotting** (the start and end point of each cue) of the temp track. You can tell the composer that he should start the cue that he will write to replace the temp music a little sooner or a little later. And your composer can object to anything you and the editor tell him about the way the score should sound or where it should start and stop. He can do so most effectively using the temp track as a point of departure.

The director should insist that the composer include him in the creative process. This is the best way to ensure that when the score is finished and recorded, the director will be completely satisfied with the final result. Make sure that the composer you hire has a sequencer program set up in his studio, so he can play easily modified versions of the score against the picture as he completes them. Even better, he should have you over to his studio on a regular basis to listen to key melodies and themes played against picture, even when they are incomplete. This is the most effective way to work.

Using words to describe music and how it will play against a scene is comparatively futile, because that is how it was done when I started in the business. This antediluvian method of working resulted in various horror stories describing how a director rejected a composer's complete score after it had been written and recorded. A Bob Zemeckis' protégé, Howard Franklin, did this on his breakthrough film, *The Public Eye*. Universal Studios paid Oscar-winning composer

Jerry Goldsmith top dollar to write and record a score for this film, but when Franklin heard it playing against the picture he was certain it would ruin his movie. This kicked up a huge amount of Sturm und Drang, heartache, and tsuris — all of which can be avoided today thanks to digital technology and sequencers. If, as soon as Jerry Goldsmith had hit upon a musical idea for the score of *The Public Eye*, he had been able to call Howard Franklin over to his studio and had played the music that he heard in his head against the picture for Franklin, then Franklin could have compared that music to the music he heard in *his* head, and they would have had something substantive to discuss. Franklin would have been able to successfully communicate to Goldsmith how to modify each cue so that it would turn out to be just what he wanted. Then when Goldsmith stepped up to the podium on the scoring stage and started to guide the full orchestra through the final score, everything Franklin heard would be music to his ears.

This is the best-case scenario. If on the other hand, it developed that Franklin and Goldsmith had fundamental artistic differences about the way the score should sound, this would have become apparent early on. Then an amicable and not so cataclysmic and costly parting of the ways could have been arranged.

The most important musical idea the composer and the director should get in sync on as soon as the composer comes on board is the musical theme of the movie. Comedies generally do not have a theme. But a great theme can add a tremendous amount of power to a dramatic film. The themes to *The Bridge on the River Kwai*, *The Great Escape*, *Doctor Zhivago*, *Love Story*, *Chariots of Fire*, and *Titanic* are all equally memorable and all helped these films win multiple Oscars and set box-office records. When a great theme is playing behind the dramatic high points of a great film the level of excitation — the rush — that the audience is made to feel exceeds the highest high points of real life. To my mind, few movie moments compare to when, at the end of *The Great Escape*, a defiant Steve McQueen is marched by his German captors back to his cell to the tune of Elmer Bernstein's uplifting, catchy theme, or at the end of *Doctor Zhivago* when Yuri watches Komarovsky take Lara away from him forever while the haunting zither theme, *Lara's Song*, plays. Much of the power of these moments can be attributed to the musical theme playing against the picture. A first time director can instill some of this same movie magic in his own little breakthrough film if he can get his composer to write a theme that even comes close to matching the greatness of the musical themes of any of these films. When it comes to a musical theme you should aim high. You might just hit your mark.

Student directors would do well to try to match the coup young student filmmaker Bob Zemeckis pulled off when he talked Elmer Bernstein into letting him use the theme to *The Great Escape* as the score for *Field of Honor*, the film he made as a senior at USC. *Field of Honor* is a good film, but the score clearly helps it rise to the level of greatness. It might well have been the deciding factor that moved Universal bosses Sid Sheinberg and Ned Tannen to agree to let Zemeckis direct his first studio film for Universal, when his only other directing credit was for that student film.

Sound Mixing or Rerecording

When the ADR is all recorded and cut, all the sound effects reels built, the location dialogue tracks cleaned up, the score recorded, and the source tracked into place, then you take the film to a rerecording or dubbing facility and do the final sound mix. In describing the essence of sound mixing, I am always reminded of a sure-fire way to find out if pasta is al dente. You throw it against the wall, and if it sticks, it's just right. That's how sound mixing works. You mix all your sounds together and play them against the picture. What's good sticks, and what's not is dropped out. The only difference is that it's a lot easier to get pasta to stick. Sound mixing is a lengthy, tedious exercise in trial and error. In the beginning, the pasta keeps falling off the wall.

Before you are ready to do the final mix, the sound effects, dialogue, and music editors cut together from 100 to 200 (if not more) total tracks of sound effects dialogue and music to be run in sync with the picture. Three sound mixers — one each for dialogue, effects, and music — cannot mix that many tracks at once. You must boil them down so they can be mixed together. Those are the **premixes**. The main premix categories are Dialogue, Music, and Effects. You would further subdivide these categories into stems such as foley, ADR, etc., to retain a certain amount of flexibility and control over the tracks during the final mix.

Nothing costs more on an hourly basis (with the exception of large crowd or action sequences) than sound rerecording; on any production with less than an unlimited budget, time on the dubbing stage will be limited. Your producer will give you a certain number of days to get the mix done, and you have to do the best job possible in the prescribed amount of time.

Unfortunately, sound mixing by nature is time-consuming and inefficient because it is a process of trial and error. You have to hear the sound mixed and playing against the picture to know if you like it, and if you don't like it and correct it, you may decide you still don't like it. Then you have to try to correct the correction, or give up, start from scratch, and rethink your approach. Therefore the time-consuming, inefficient part of sound mixing is best done before the project hits the dubbing stage. The first time director on his break-through project must make sure that some individual on his editing team has the know-how and the equipment to do pre-dubs and sample mixes using Pro Tools. In addition, the post schedule has to be laid out so there is adequate time between when the picture is locked and the start of the final mix to allow the head sound editors and the director to go through all the reels and have them rebuilt more than once. Since this digital option is now available, the first time director will be able to try out more of his ideas for the final mix without incurring much expense. It should follow that in the end he will be more satisfied.

One of the mixers, usually the dialogue mixer, is the head mixer. If you are to have a successful experience on the dubbing stage, you must forge a good working relationship with the head mixer. As in your relationships with your other key collaborators, the secret to developing a good working relationship with your head mixer is to empower him by giving him a lot of rope to hang himself with. To do this you have to be patient and trusting. He will want to try things — to do it his way — and he won't be able to play it for you to judge right away. You are going to have to hope that he's onto something good and wait minutes, maybe hours, for him to figure out exactly how the tracks are built, and then rehearse it and finally mix it before you can hear it mixed his way. Then comes the moment of truth. Because after all that waiting around (whether it is five minutes or five hours, it always seems like forever), you may not like it. My advice: As a first time director, unless you hate it, don't shoot him down. Buy it.

There are two reasons for this. Reason One: Unless you are a first time director with extensive experience in post sound, he's probably right. Most head sound mixers on any professional rerecording stage are damn good. There are not that many top-drawer rerecording stages in business in this country; the guys who run them are the best of the best in the world of sound. They make more money than any other sound technician in the film business, with the exception of some of the very best production sound mixers.

All the same, the head mixer could be technically right, but his taste may differ from yours. So on aesthetic grounds, you may have every reason in the world to shoot him down. You may be an artist and he might be getting in the way of your freely expressing yourself. Still, I am certain that it is wiser for you to accept what he has done unless you really hate it. This is because of Reason Two: It's not going to make or break your movie. Some things are worth going to the mat over: the script, the cast, or a good performance. These components of your film will ultimately determine its worth. I guarantee you that nobody on the planet will have either a positive or negative response to 99 % of whatever you and the head mixer disagree on. So, unless you really hate it, buy it.

If you do as I suggest, and thereby validate and empower your head mixer, he will put all his energy and talent to work on the sound design of your film. He will also exhort and bully his co-mixers into doing the same. Even more important, he will demand the most of all the dialogue, sound effects, and music editors, even when he knows they are fed up with changing and re-changing their work as you go through the lengthy and tedious process of fine-tuning the sound design of your film.

Sound mixing is hard work. It requires tremendous patience and obsessive attention to detail over long spans of time. If you accept your head mixer's judgment most of the time, he will gladly do the very hard work required of him to mix your film well. In addition, if when he asks, you let him do it his way, then he will return the favor, and when you ask, he will do it your way — even if he doesn't like it.

In the late '70s when I was a postproduction supervisor/associate producer on the Universal lot, the top dubbing mixer was a brilliant, outspoken, iconoclastic curmudgeon named Robert Hoyt. He was the head mixer on *Jaws, The Breakfast Club, The Lonely Guy, Walk Proud, Slap Shot,* and many of the major movies that were made at Universal at that time. Universal had a very favorable program for employees to acquire MCA stock. Hoyt wisely took advantage of it throughout the '50s and '60s, so by the '70s he had a big pile of MCA stock. Throughout the '70s, MCA stock doubled in value and split three or four times, leaving Robert Hoyt a very wealthy man. He did not have to work. He loved to ski all over the world, but when he wasn't skiing in Idaho or Switzerland, he ran Dubbing Stage 3. He ran it absolutely his way. Because if it wasn't going to be his way, it was going to be the highway or the jet-way to retirement on the ski slopes.

In the early '80s, Marlo Thomas (Danny Thomas' actress-producer daughter) did a remake of Frank Capra's classic, *It's a Wonderful Life,* for Universal. She mixed it with Hoyt. Marlo had a reputation for being a bit of a brat. Hoyt told me one day how he cured her of that. He said he was sweetness and light until the first time she got surly with him and then he turned to her and said, "Marlo, ordinarily I am the nicest guy in the world. But you know what?" He then tore a piece of paper off a note pad, held it out and, pausing dramatically, added, "I can change, just like this." With that, he dropped the paper to the floor. She was smart. She never snarled at him again. Take Robert Hoyt's advice and get ahead by getting along with your sound mixer.

Apart from that, the only rule to follow on the rerecording stage is to rely on your own judgment and not settle too easily. Keep cooking the spaghetti until it really sticks to the wall. Dubbing is so tedious and detail driven, there is a natural tendency to quit before you have exhausted all the alternatives. So keep bouncing the reels and brainstorming with the editors and the mixers for ways to rebuild the tracks, so that when they are mixed they will sound better. At some point your budget will dictate that you must start laying down finished tracks. But until that time comes, keep trying to improve the finished sound.

It is also wise to remember, as stated earlier, that the audience only needs to understand about 85% of the dialogue to fully appreciate a movie. So you do not need to hear every line. Some lines are just there for flavor. Do not make the dialogue mixer play them at an absurdly loud level so they can be heard clearly.

And during a big action sequence, if you have got a good piece of score to play, you do not have to make every single tire squeal, hoof beat, fist sock, glass break, etc., poke through the music. The audience isn't even going to notice if the odd sound effect here and there gets drowned out by the score. If the story is good, and the action is good, and the music is good, and the sound effects are adequate, the audience will be so full of terror and elation — feelings that the music taps right into — they will not be able to focus on details like missing sound effects. In this case, you should definitely not sweat the small stuff.

The two simple rules for mixing will help you work more efficiently to create a good sound design. The chances are there will only be enough money in the budget for an efficiently rendered sound mix. When, like Doug Liman, you graduate from *Swingers* to *The Bourne Identity*, you can take all the time you need on the dubbing stage to create a world-class sound design. Until then, get the maximum bang for your buck and recognize that, in the interest of working efficiently, you can do without hearing some lines of dialogue and some of the sound effects. Certainly, if your producer is breathing down your neck to work at a faster pace, learn to mix according to the two rules. If you and your producer have come this far together and you are still on good terms, do not blow your good working relationship over a couple lines of dialogue or some sound effects.

Promotion

A certain, sad irony holds sway over the final stage of your breakthrough venture. What you have already accomplished is remarkable. The fact that you have come this far is a resounding affirmation of your abilities as a director. Yet, now, at the very end, what may well determine the success or failure of your film — the campaign to promote it — is wrested from your control. Only huge directors like Spielberg or Zemeckis or Scorsese have any say in how their films are promoted. Almost universally, those who put up the money to make films, from the most lowly independent producer to the richest studios, like Sony or Paramount, are so conscious of the difficulty of luring a film's potential audience into the theaters to see it, they are loathe to entrust this crucial task to anyone other than the most exalted film-marketing guru — or, at least, the most exalted film-marketing guru that they can afford. The director is kindly requested to butt out, or, at best, to offer polite suggestions, and then retire back to the trenches on the dubbing stage or the ADR stage or wherever else he is slaving away to complete the film.

This is like having your baby ripped away from you just as it exits the womb. Almost every working director I know complains bitterly about this systematic usurpation of the director's control over the destiny of his work. And with every passing day, they complain more vociferously, because this trend of creative usurpation is becoming more pronounced as the cost of making films continues to be pushed up by the studios' blockbuster mentality. The more films cost to make, the more is spent on promoting them — the expense of the former being used to legitimize the expense of the latter. The huge sums being poured into promoting and distributing films make it less likely that the director will be given any say in shaping the promotional campaign. Even if you successfully bamboozle your rich parents into paying for some or all of your first film (as the Coen brothers did) or emerge from the bayou to triumph at Sundance (like Steven Soderbergh), you probably will have to make a deal with a distribution company to get your film into theaters, and the distribution company will almost always make you sign away your right to have any real say in shaping the campaign to promote the film. Then, just to add insult to injury, only one film in five really clears a profit, and only one in 10 is a true hit, so when it comes to the bottom line, most promotional campaigns fail. Yet the exalted marketing gurus tell you to back off while they work their magic, which, in fact, succeeds in producing a hit movie 10% of the time. Truly, the business of promoting and distributing films is brutal in the extreme.

The best way to deal with these hard truths is to confront them with an extremely positive attitude and try to make the best of an awful situation. Try to win over the marketing gurus with enthusiasm about their proposed campaign. Every director I have ever spoken to who fought to get an ad campaign changed or thrown out, lost the battle. But Ron Yerxa, who with his partner, Albert Berger, produced Alexander Payne's second feature, *Election*, told me that he, Berger, and Payne were always upbeat and just tried to make helpful suggestions on Paramount's campaign to promote the film. Paramount actually did not see much market potential in the film after it was completed, and so did not bring it out in a wide release supported by an expensive advertising campaign. To their surprise, the film took off on its own, fueled by strong reviews and, one would presume, good word of mouth. After that, Paramount put more money into promoting the film. What I think this story shows is that Paramount was going to distribute and promote the film the way they saw fit, no matter what Yerxa and his partners said or did. But by not fighting the studio, they kept the lines of communication open and so, when the film started to make money, the studio's marketing people were that much more influenced by their suggestions — to whatever extent they were susceptible to being influenced at all.

The key to luring a film's audience into the theaters — that which is sought after by all marketing campaigns — is to find the essential image or series of images which will show the target audience that if they go see the film, they will get something very much worth $10. If your film is a comedy, an action film, a horror movie, or a sci-fi film that is intended for the masses, the most crucial piece of the marketing campaign is the 30-second TV spot. Bob Zemeckis told me that, to his mind, the 30-second spot for *Romancing the Stone* was what established him as a bankable director. It convinced the target audience for that film to pony up their money to go see it in sufficiently large numbers to make it a big hit. The 30 seconds that went into the spot were lifted from the mudslide scene during which the Kathleen Turner and Michael Douglas characters get introduced to each other in the most unconventional way imaginable. They are walking through a torrential rainstorm along a goat path in the mountainous jungles of Columbia when the path collapses beneath them, sending them ass over teakettle in a mudslide down the side of the mountain. Turner hits the bottom first, landing on her back with her legs splayed open wide, and Douglas comes in right behind her, burying his head in her crotch. To Bob's mind, this scene captured the essence of *Romancing the Stone* in that it contained 1) good stunts/action, 2) sex/romance, 3) comedy, and 4) the star of the film, Michael Douglas, doing what he does best — acting sexy, hard-assed, and witty. After they hit the bottom, Turner lies there gasping in shock, whereas Douglas immediately lifts his head from her crotch and announces, "What a ride, huh?"

If your film has any artistic pretensions, then reviews, trailers, and the one sheet or poster are the crucial instruments of the marketing campaign. Again, if the campaign is to succeed, the trailer and the poster must contain the most appealing central element of the film. The marketing campaign for *American Beauty* was certainly one of the most successful in recent years. Most of the posters simply displayed the midsection of a beautiful naked woman holding a single rose. The trailers, for the most part, focused on the essential hook of the film: that it was about a beaten down, demoralized, average American, middle-class male (played by Kevin Spacey) who suddenly falls in lust with an alluring, blonde teenager (Angela, played by Mena Suvari) and throws all caution to the wind as he relentlessly pursues her. The campaign made it clear to the potential audience that for the price of admission they would get to see Spacey as Lester Burnham go ape in suburbia. One has to assume that the goal was to make the slightly lurid, central conceit of the story — the seduction of a teenager by a married, middle-aged man — as charming and acceptable as possible. The poster did this by evoking Lester's romantic, idealistic flights of sexual fantasy that focused on a naked Angela covered only with rose petals. The trailers did this by emphasizing that it was the always likeable Kevin Spacey doing the seducing and doing it in sort of mad, almost clownish way to escape the worst kind of middle-class conformity. This makes Lester Burnham empathetic and his story somewhat heroic, not only to widest possible audience, but also to the critics who can be counted on to always champion non-conformity.

It is a little too easy to look at the marketing campaigns for *Romancing the Stone* and *American Beauty* and say that all you have to do is duplicate their approach. Both these campaigns triumphed, but hindsight is 20-20. No doubt, given the steep odds against the commercial success of any film, there are numerous examples of marketing campaigns for good films that theoretically did everything that a marketing campaign should do except turn the film into a box-office success. As important as film marketing may be, more often than not, it is completely ineffective. When they are instructed to butt out of marketing campaigns, directors should try to take some comfort in the irony of this cold, hard truth.

With that said, when the studio or the distribution company starts to work on the campaign, I would advise the first time director to enlist his producer's help and seek to identify the quintessential moment or moments in your film — such as the mudslide scene from *Romancing the Stone*. If you can join forces with your producer and present a united front to the marketing people, your suggestions will be taken more seriously. It also would be wise to study the advertising campaigns of all recent box-office hits that resemble your film. Try to glean what the campaigns for these films have in common and try to identify that similarity in your film. Then go back and re-determine the defining moments of your film, factoring in this new data.

Next, set up as many meetings as possible with the marketing gurus. At these meetings, join forces with your producer and advocate centering the advertising campaign on the quintessential moment or moments. Argue your point as forcefully as possible, always bearing in mind that you are suggesting rather than dictating. Be grateful if the marketing people use any part of any of your ideas, and don't even make a tiny fuss if they don't do anything you suggest. You aren't Spielberg yet.

To the Answer Print and the Sweet Hereafter

After you have weighed in on the marketing campaign, your work, for the most part, is done. You want to assist your DP in getting the answer print timed properly. Unless you are an experienced cinematographer, your input on how to best correct the timing of the answer print will be minimal. Your cinematographer will have a very precise idea of exactly what each scene should look like in terms of contrast, color balance, and diffusion, and he will work very hard with the technicians timing the answer print to make sure that the film comes as close as possible to that desired look. I defer to my DPs in these matters and limit my role to acting as a good sounding board for their ideas.

Signing with a Manager/Agent

After this, all you have to deal with is the success of your film or the lack thereof. There are many different levels and varieties of success. And success has practical ramifications as well as purely psychological or emotional consequences. Regardless of whatever kind or level of success you achieve, you have to parlay that success into getting signed by the best manager/agent you can attract. Managers have now taken over as the key player in launching a director's career. When I was breaking in, it was the agent. All my advice on this subject relates to my experiences with agents. So in the pages that follow, when I refer to an agent or agents, it should be read as manager/agent or manager.

You cannot establish yourself as a bankable, working director on your own. Most directors will tell you that — thanks to their breakthrough film — they landed an agent. But then they did all the hard work hustling up their critical second or third directing job and the agent just came in at the end and negotiated the deals. This is generally true because all agents work hardest selling directors that they know they can make their 10 % on. Until you become the next Doug Liman or the next Rob Cohen, that ain't you. After an agency signs you, they will put some effort into shopping you around. The extent of that effort is directly proportional to the amount of profit your breakthrough film makes. Every producer with a good script and any real funding has 10 solid, bankable directors to choose from. The odds that your agent is going to talk that producer into choosing you, instead, are slim. Even if you have made one successful film, unless it was a huge success, the producer will have other directors to choose from who have had more and bigger successes than you. This is why most agents do not work long enough or hard enough to find their newly signed directors a second film to direct.

Still, you must have an agent because when you, working on your own, succeed in getting someone truly interested in hiring you to direct your second film, the first question out of that person's mouth is, "Who's your agent?" If you can say, "Jeff Berg" (who is the president of ICM), the prestige accompanying the fact that Berg is your agent might be the deciding factor in your landing the gig. If you can only answer, "I don't have an agent. I don't believe in them," or words to that effect, your credibility as a viable director will be fatally damaged or perhaps destroyed.

So when your film is ready to be screened, you have to do everything in your power to get prospective agents to see it and sign you. If your film is accepted at one of the top festivals — Sundance, Toronto, Chicago, New York, etc. — agents will see it, and, if they like what they see, you will be hearing from them. If your film is a more commercial release, it will not be shown on the festival circuit, so the first opportunity for agents to see it would be at press screenings, or cast and crew screenings. The same holds true if it is neither commercial nor accepted at major festivals. Whenever possible, try to get prospective agents to come to a cast and crew screening. The cast and crew are usually an enthusiastic, receptive audience. The pleasure they take in watching the film will make a good impression on a prospective agent. Most agents will probably tell you to send over your resume along with a DVD of your film, but this is the least preferable of all alternatives. If your film has magic, that magic is most likely to come across on the big screen with a responsive audience.

If your first film is a commercial success, you will be courted by any number of agents, big and small. Since the odds are against your hitting a home run your first time at bat, the most likely scenario is that you may hear from some agents, but ultimately you will have to go after the agents you want and convince one to sign you. After I made *Never Too Young to Die*, there was a little heat on me because of a minor buzz about the movie and the success of my rock videos — in particular, the video I made for Sammy Hagar, *I Can't Drive 55*. I got David Gersh of The Gersh Agency to come to a cast and crew screening of *Never Too Young to Die*. He came out very eager to sign me. We had a lunch meeting with my lawyer at which Gersh promised that he could get me quality projects to direct. But I stalled going with Gersh, because Zemeckis had advised me to sign with his agent, Jack Rapke of CAA.

Being represented by a top agent at CAA to my mind seemed comparable to dying and going to heaven. At that time (in the late '80s) CAA was undisputedly the most powerful agency in Hollywood, and Rapke was a top agent specializing in directors. Besides Zemeckis, Rapke represented Ronnie Howard, Martin Brest, John Hughes, Chris Columbus, Harold Ramis, and Joel Schumacher, to name a few. That kind of client list gave Rapke immediate access to every top producer and studio executive in the business. In addition, CAA, being a major agency, represented a big chunk of the very best above-the-line talent in the film business and enhanced the salability of their clients by packaging them together — attached to scripts turned out by the best writers in the film business, most of whom were represented by CAA. I sent a 35mm print of my film over to CAA and waited. While I was waiting, Gersh got impatient and pressed me for an explanation as to why I had not signed with him. I made the mistake of telling him the truth. Then Rapke passed on handling me, and when I went back to Gersh, Gersh passed as well. I went back and shopped around for agents. Lucy Fisher, a Senior VP at Warners, whom I used to go skiing with when we were both undergraduates at Harvard, recommended that I sign with Dick Sheperd of The Artists Agency and I followed her advice. Sheperd was a classy guy who had once run MGM, and, before that, had produced some classy films, among them *Breakfast at Tiffany's*. He and his cohorts at The Artists Agency shopped me around for about a year. After that, they pretty much gave up trying to find me work.

In retrospect, I think it is clear that I should have immediately signed with Gersh. The Gersh Agency has a long and distinguished record of finding good projects for good directors. They are a boutique agency as opposed to a major agency like CAA, William Morris, or ICM. This is to say they have about a dozen agents, whereas the major agencies have hundreds. Boutique agencies usually specialize in representing specific kinds of **above-the-line** personnel: directors, writers, producers, actors, or any combination of the above. Some boutique agencies specialize in **below-the-line** talent, such as editors, art directors, and graphic designers. Gersh would have been just about the perfect fit for me. They have a reputation for being smart and hardworking in lining up intelligent projects for intelligent, if not edgy, directors. Penelope Spheeris (*Wayne's World*; *The Beverly Hillbillies*; *The Little Rascals*; *The Decline of Western Civilization, Parts I, II & III*) is a very smart, hardheaded businesswoman, as well as a talented director, and she has stuck with Gersh for most of her career.

Even if CAA had wanted to sign me, I doubt if they would have worked very hard for me. The major agencies handle almost all the A-list directors working in film and television as well as the B-list directors. They have a shocking overabundance of excellent, proven, talented directors to promote, most of whom are much more likely to land a job and return the crucial 10% than a director with just one or two films to his credit — unless those films were hugely successful. If Rapke had called Zemeckis and said he wanted to sign me, and Bob had made Rapke promise to beat the bushes until he found me a second film to direct, then it would have made sense to sign with CAA. Then Rapke would have had something very real to lose by not finding me work: the trust of a top client. Short of a commitment like that, it seems inevitable that a director with one or two marginally successful films to his credit will fall between the cracks at a major agency.

A boutique agency cannot do everything that a major agency can do for their clients. Unlike a top CAA agent, a boutique agent like David Gersh is not going to have all doors in town open to him. And boutique agencies generally do not package their clients with scripts. The Artists Agency was a boutique agency. Dick Sheperd was a lovely human being, but he never packaged me with a script, and, in fact, he never got an assignment. While I was represented by Sheperd, Zemeckis got me a deal to develop a film at Universal. I found the story and I wrote the script with a friend of mine, Michael Auerbach, who had some professional writing credits. Zemeckis insisted that I write and direct because, to his mind, that was the only way I could get a good script to direct. "All the good scripts are written by the good writers at CAA, ICM, and William Morris," he told me. "And they go straight to the top directors at those agencies." This is another part of the downside of signing with a boutique agency. But boutique agencies survive because they recognize and sign breaking talent that then breaks big and stays with them out of loyalty. It simply stands to reason that the only way a boutique agent like David Gersh can compete with the major agencies is by signing unproven talent that he believes in — and then continuing to knock on doors to find that talent work, even after he has been repeatedly rebuffed and long after the point when a major agency would have abandoned the search.

The difficulty of making a rational, informed choice of an agent is complicated by the fact that agents and agencies take full credit every time a client lands a job on his own or lucks into one. Personalities and chemistry also play a role in how well the agent/client relationship works; after you have met with an agent only one or two times, it is hard to judge how well your personality and your agent's will mesh over the long haul. The important lesson to be gleaned from my experience with CAA and Gersh is that even though you must use your friends for access to agents and agencies, it is unwise to take their recommendations of agents at face value. Jack Rapke would have been the best agent for me if I had been the next Bob Zemeckis. I wanted to believe that I was. I should have been coldly analytical and realized that I was not.

When trying to select the best agent, a first time director is advised to research agents and agencies extensively, and find the agent who recently did the best job breaking a client whose talents and disposition most resemble your own. Then go after that agent and try to get him to represent you. This sounds easy, but it is a difficult and time-consuming venture. All of the factors in the equation will be very hard to accurately determine. Selecting an agent is a decision that can make or break your career. So put every ounce of time and energy you can summon into making this choice. As a rule, what you put into it will equal what you get out.

Signing with a Publicist

You are also going to need to line up the right publicist. I never even thought of having a publicist until I directed my second film. But the fact is that we have now progressed from the atomic age into the information age, and media hype has become absolutely crucial for success in almost any field. It used to be that only name actors needed publicists to plaster their face on the covers of every magazine in the checkout line and get them on every television talk show. But after Robert Rodriguez made *El Mariachi*, suddenly you saw his handsome mug in the check-out line and on Oprah and Larry King, and to some extent that helped make him both a household name and a successful working director. Every first time director should try to hype himself as successfully as Robert Rodriquez did. To do that, you need the best publicist you can get.

Almost everything I've said about agents and finding the right agent applies to publicists — with the important exception that, if a publicist takes credit for a good publicity campaign, the chances are that he did most of the work and the director had very little to do with building his own hype. This makes it easier to pick a publicist. To a large extent, what you see is what you get. Research publicists and publicity agencies extensively and find the publicist who recently did the best job hyping a client whose talents and disposition most resemble your own. Then try to talk that publicist into representing you.

Don't be so naïve as to think you are an artist and above needing to be hyped. Tina Brown succeeded as the editor of *The New Yorker* because she understood that what *The New Yorker* lacked was subject matter that was hot, or had "buzz" because it was being hyped. She introduced buzz to that august bastion of the literary arts, and in so doing retooled it for success in the information age. Even if your life's ambition is to make the 21st-century version of *Last Year at Marianbad*, you won't be able to do it without a good publicist.

Coping with Success or the Lack Thereof

If you aspire to become a successful working director, there is no such thing as too much success. You will need all the success you can get. Again, as I was told by Bob Zemeckis, the film industry in the United States is like a very exclusive private club. It is extremely difficult to get into the club, but once you are admitted, it is pretty hard to get kicked out. Those from outside the industry are always amazed at how studio executives, producers, and directors who have some cachet and so are in the club, can churn out one bomb after another without losing their jobs or their ability to get films financed. There are many reasons for this, but the most relevant one pertaining to directors is that aforementioned statistic: about only one film in 10 is a real hit. Therefore, it is only reasonable to expect that a director's big success will be followed by a number of failures before he can turn out another winner. Every producer who hires a director and every studio executive who gives him a green light is gambling (they are all riverboat gamblers at heart) that this time when he rolls the dice, he will make the point. It doesn't matter if he has been crapping out for years and his last movie was a colossal bomb. It doesn't matter if he has made two or three or four big losers in a row. What matters is that he had that one big hit somewhere back there, so he must have another one in him. And a producer or a studio head or a nut-and-bolt manufacturer from Taiwan who wants to make movies will feel better hiring this three- or four-time loser director than the hottest young thing on the block with the best agent and the most eye-popping demo reel in the history of Hollywood. So as they are striking the release prints for your first feature or getting ready to air it on network or cable, say a prayer, or chant, or sacrifice a goat, or pull whatever strings you've got with the forces that control the universe. If Janis Joplin could beseech the Lord to deliver her a Mercedes Benz, then you can ask him for a hit movie. Because if He comes through, you will damn near be set for life.

If your first film is not an unqualified success, do not let it faze you. As Smashmouth sang, "Take your knocks; dust 'em off; you're gonna take 'em again." Because so few films are hits, there should be no shame in making one that is not. As objectively as possible, and perhaps relying on the judgment of those you respect and trust, scrutinize your film and honestly identify its every flaw and shortcoming. Take responsibility for all the flaws that were your fault and decide exactly what you should have done to prevent them. If you can make this effort, you will have profited from the experience of making this first film and will be able to put it behind you, knowing that you have used it to grow as a director.

Zemeckis' first film, *I Wanna Hold Your Hand*, was a box-office dud, as was his second, *Used Cars*. Both of these failures must have been doubly painful because Zemeckis co-wrote both movies (with Bob Gale) as well as directing them. After *I Wanna Hold Your Hand* had been pulled from release without making much money, Lew Wasserman, the Chairman of the Board of MCA, the parent company of Universal Pictures (which released the film) got Zemeckis on the phone. "Don't jump off The Tower," Wasserman counseled Zemeckis. (The Tower is the

15-story MCA world headquarters that dominates the Universal lot.) "Drink some whiskey," Lew told him. "You made a good movie. We believe in you."

Wasserman at that time was the most powerful man in Hollywood. His words were fraught with meaning and wisdom. Meaningful because if anyone could have guaranteed to Zemeckis that his breakthrough film's failure at the box-office was not going to be held against him, that, if anything, he was now more bankable as a director after having made this loser, it was Lew Wasserman. If Wasserman had determined that Zemeckis was bankable, then it was more than likely that his projects were going to be green-lit.

There was wisdom in what Wasserman was telling Zemeckis, because as Wasserman correctly assumed, Zemeckis wanted desperately to make a hit movie and was worried about the consequences of not having done so. What Zemeckis needed to hear, and what Wasserman told him, was that he had made a good film that admirably showcased his talents. To a certain extent, that was good enough. Wasserman wanted to assure Zemeckis that there were people with clout who could appreciate what he had accomplished in *I Wanna Hold Your Hand* and, based on that, would be willing to green-light his second film. So for a first time director, there can be life after a breakthrough film that doesn't make money.

And Wasserman was proved correct when Frank Price, who then was the head of Columbia Pictures, gave a green light to *Used Cars*, Bob's second film. When *Used Cars* did not make any money, Zemeckis had a deeper hole to dig himself out of and it took him five years to do it. But to prove Wasserman right, yet again, Michael Douglas had the savvy to look at *I Wanna Hold Your Hand* and *Used Cars* and see two well-directed films rather two box-office duds. *Romancing the Stone* was a big hit and that put Bob in the club. Since every film he's made subsequently, with one exception, has been a big hit, he is in that club for life.

Unfortunately, there are fewer and fewer producers and studio executives who have the good gut instincts about filmmaking and filmmakers that Frank Price or Michael Douglas have. The blockbuster mentality is taking over Hollywood. If Zemeckis were starting out today, there is a good chance he would not get a third chance after two duds. Price made a living as a TV scriptwriter and Douglas as a TV actor and producer when they started in the business. They are both artists as well as businessmen. More and more so, the people with green-light power in Hollywood were never artists. They have only been businessmen, and they are less inclined to give a second, much less a third chance to a young filmmaker who makes films that are not commercially successful. It's gotten tougher since Zemeckis broke through. It would be dishonest of me to say otherwise.

Still, to a limited extent, the wisdom of Lew Wasserman continues to hold true. How did *My Big Fat Greek Wedding* make it to the big screen? Because someone who was an artist first and a businessman second — Tom Hanks — provided the clout to get it made. So even if your breakthrough film is not an unqualified hit, you have got to assume that to whatever extent you are blessed with directorial talent, it is on display in your film. If it is, then take heart in the wise words of Lew Wasserman: "Don't jump off The Tower. Drink some whisky." You have showcased your directorial talents and that's good enough. Think positively. Get your manager/agent to start beating the bushes for you and tell yourself that sooner or later your Frank Price or your Michael Douglas will recognize your talent and give you your next shot.

And whenever your confidence falters, remind yourself that you have actually directed a feature film. That means that you are made of some very strong stuff. Think of the physical and emotional strain you have endured. How many of the people you know could go back, day after day, as you did all through preproduction, production, and postproduction and face that strain? How many of your friends would be willing to chew glass, as you would gladly do, to repeat that grueling experience? Take pride in being a glutton for punishment.

George Lucas once compared making a film to climbing Mount Everest. In his mind, here's how they equate. You have to hustle and prove your mettle just to get selected to do it. When you first find out that you will get to be one of the chosen few, you're elated. Then you start the climb and it gets harder and harder, and just when you think you cannot take another step, it gets even harder. There you are stuck in a blizzard in a place where no man was ever intended to set foot. You are physically and psychologically drained. You are absolutely miserable, more miserable than you have ever been in your entire life, and you wonder, "Why did I ever undertake this impossible mission?" You resolve that it was the stupidest decision of your life. You will never do it again. Then, somehow, you get to the top. You did it. You survived. You come down off the mountain, and about a month later you are planning to do it again. Nothing else compares to the challenge of climbing that mountain. Existentially, you have never been more alive in your life than when you were in the middle of that hell. And so you must go back and do it again. How many people have that kind of drive in them? Life is about the journey, not the destination. If you can make your journey, the journey of a film director, the journey up Everest, you will lead a remarkable, rich life. Compared to that, in the big scheme of things, whether or not your film made money is insignificant.

CHAPTER 9 | SUMMARY POINTS

■ Try to find a truly gifted editor and then give him as much independence as he wants. Because of the intuitive nature of his work, an editor is best left in the cutting room working by himself. Even if your editor is not immensely gifted, work according to this model, because it will bring out whatever gifts he may possess.

■ The director creates a mental picture, based on the script, of what the finished film should look like. If in editorial he tries to make the film that he has shot look like that mental picture, he is making a huge mistake. He has to throw the script out. He has to look at the film that he has shot, and make the best movie he can from that film.

■ Be prepared to "kill your little darlings." A perfectly good scene may throw the balance and the pacing of the whole film off.

■ Zemeckis and Spielberg, like Irving Thalberg before them, almost always shoot additional scenes for their films to fill in holes in the story that only become apparent after the film has been cut and tested. Such reshoots are critical to the popular success of their films. The first time director should do everything in his power to emulate their example.

■ An insert could be described as just about any shot that does not have an actor's face in it. Inserts, carefully composed and used judiciously so that they fit in seamlessly between two pieces of production footage, can be an extremely valuable tool in postproduction. They can convey data to the audience that helps fill in some of the unforeseen gaps in the story created by the production process.

■ Inserts can be extremely useful in building intensity in action sequences. Montage generates energy. Inserts provide an editor with more different angles on the same action that he can quick cut together in order to give more energy to the sequence.

■ Once the picture is locked, the next major undertaking in the completion of the film is the postproduction sound work: music scoring, ADR (automatic dialogue replacement), sound effects spotting and editing, and sound mixing.

■ There are really only two areas of postproduction sound where a significant contribution can be made to the film. One is the score. A great score can push a good film into the realm of greatness. *Chariots of Fire* is the best example of this phenomenon.

■ The second area of postproduction sound where a significant improvement in the film as a whole can be made is in ADR. A first time director can dramatically improve his film by excising a mediocre performance in its entirety and replacing it with a good, credible performance created on an ADR stage.

■ All of the key jobs in postproduction sound require great technical competence and a special kid of genius. The best way for the first time director to assure that his breakthrough film will get the best post sound treatment possible is to be as hands-on as his producer will allow him to be when hiring the key personnel.

■ In many cases, marginally intelligible dialogue can be "cleaned up" and rendered intelligible by replacing it with an alternate take or isolating it on a separate track so it can be specially treated on the dubbing stage. These alternatives are generally preferable to substituting ADR lines because the performance in the original dialogue is generally better than in an ADR line.

■ When it comes to sound design, it is self-defeating to be constrained by reality. Film is fiction. So it is best to think of sound effects as another kind of music that plays along with the picture to amplify the drama that is unfolding on screen.

■ The crowd scenes in the film will never play properly unless they are backed up with good walla. With walla, "more is more."

■ When it comes to spotting sound effects, more is more. Better to come to the sound mixing stage with more good effects than you need and throw some out, than to come to the stage and find that some scenes do not come alive for want of a few crucial sound effects.

■ Because performance, along with script, is of paramount importance, the director should be on the ADR stage for every lead actor's ADR session to help the actor match or improve on his original performance.

■ A significant portion of the film's budget goes into the crowd scenes. To make sure that these scenes come to life, the director should be on the ADR stage to guide the walla group.

■ The first time director should knock himself out to find the best composer possible for his breakthrough film. If the first time director is working on a day-late-dollar-short production, he must discover a composer who is on the cusp of greatness.

■ The only effective way to make any decisions regarding film scores is to make those decisions while listening to a piece of score playing against the picture.

■ The first time director and his editor should run the picture with the temp music track for the composer, and tell the composer exactly what they like and don't like about each piece of temp music.

■ The composer should have the director over to his work space on a regular basis and use his sequencer program to demo all his musical ideas against the picture.

■ The most important musical idea the composer and the director should be in sync on is the musical theme of the movie.

■ There are two good reasons to accept your head mixer's judgment over your own: (1) he's usually right, and (2) it won't make or break your film. Furthermore, if you defer to him in this way, he will gladly do the very hard work required of him to mix your film well.

■ The first time director must make sure that some individual on his editing team has the know-how and the equipment to do pre-dubs and sample mixes using Pro Tools.

■ The huge sums being poured into promoting and distributing films make it less likely that the director will be given any say in shaping the promotion/marketing campaign.

■ If the campaign is to succeed, the 30-second TV spot and/or the trailer and the poster must contain the most appealing central element of the film. Join forces with your producer and advocate centering the advertising campaign on this quintessential moment or moments from your film.

■ Regardless of whatever kind or level of success you achieve, you have to parlay that success into getting signed by the best manager/agent you can attract. You may hear from some managers/agents, but ultimately you will have to go after the manager/agent you want and convince one to sign you.

- When trying to select the best manager/agent, a first time director is advised to research managers/agents and agencies extensively, and find the manager/agent who recently did the best job breaking a client whose talents and disposition most resemble your own.

- You need a publicist. Don't be so naïve as to think you are an artist and above needing to be hyped.

- Even if your breakthrough film is not an unqualified hit, you have got to assume that to whatever extent you are blessed with directorial talent, it is on display in that film.

Gil Bettman is a director and an Associate Professor in the School of Film and Television at Chapman University in Los Angeles. He studied creative writing with Robert Lowell at Harvard and, in 1970, was awarded the Harvard Prize for literary excellence. Bettman has directed three feature films: *Crystal Heart, Never Too Young to Die*, and *Night Vision*, as well as multiple episodes of the television series *BJ and the Bear, The Fall Guy*, and *Knight Rider*. He has also directed numerous rock videos for a variety of artists including Chicago and Sammy Hagar. He has just completed *The Long Road to Cabo*, a feature documentary for Hagar that was released in September, 2003.

More information about Gil Bettman is available under "faculty" at *http://www.ftv.chapman.edu/faculty/*

DIGITAL FILMMAKING 101
An Essential Guide to Producing Low-Budget Movies

Dale Newton and John Gaspard

The Butch Cassidy and the Sundance Kid of do-it-yourself filmmaking are back! Filmmakers Dale Newton and John Gaspard, co-authors of the classic how-to independent filmmaking manual *Persistence of Vision*, have written a new handbook for the digital age. *Digital Filmmaking 101* is your all-bases-covered guide to producing and shooting your own digital video films. It covers both technical and creative advice, from keys to writing a good script, to casting and location-securing, to lighting and low-budget visual effects. Also includes detailed information about how to shoot with digital cameras and how to use this new technology to your full advantage.

As indie veterans who have produced and directed successful independent films, Gaspard and Newton are masters at achieving high-quality results for amazingly low production costs. They'll show you how to turn financial constraints into your creative advantage — and how to get the maximum mileage out of your production budget. You'll be amazed at the ways you can save money —and even get some things for free — without sacrificing any of your final product's quality.

"These guys don't seem to have missed a thing when it comes to how to make a digital movie for peanuts. It's a helpful and funny guide for beginners and professionals alike."

> — Jonathan Demme
> Academy Award-Winning Director
> *Silence of the Lambs*

Dale Newton and John Gaspard, who hail from Minneapolis, Minnesota, have produced three ultra-low-budget, feature-length movies and have lived to tell the tales.

$24.95 | 283 pages | Order # 17RLS | ISBN: 0-941188-33-7

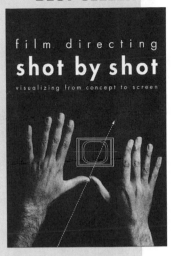

DIGITAL MOVIEMAKING
2nd Edition
All the Skills, Techniques, and Moxie You'll Need to Turn Your Passion into a Career

Scott Billups

This book is geared to professional-minded people who have hopefully had prior experience in some aspect of production and who understand the fundamental difference between a hobby and a career. It's about how to be successful at making movies by taking an opportunity to experiment and demonstrating your abilities.

Scott Billups' goal is to kick your professionalism, your toolset, and your image quality up a notch so that you can compete in the real world of cinema. There are no simple solutions, secret tricks, instant remedies, or gizmos that will turn you into a moviemaker. In fact, the odds are against you. But Billups promises that by the time you've finished this book, your odds of success will have improved.

"If you are in or entering the new world of digital filmmaking and you want to know everything about everything... read this book by Scott Billups. You'll be sorry if you don't."

— David Lynch, Director

"An individualist in a town where conformity can be a Zen-like state of grace, Billups is not afraid to lock horns with mainstream studios as he seeks to invent 'the new Hollywood.'"

— Paula Parisi, *Wired Magazine*

Scott Billups is an award-winning director/producer who has produced, directed and written countless feature films, television programs, and commercials.

$26.95 | 300 Pages | Order # 107RLS | ISBN: 0-941188-80-9

SCREENWRITING 101
The Essential Craft
of Feature Film Writing

Neill D. Hicks

Hicks brings the clarity and practical instruction familiar to his students and readers to screenwriters everywhere. In his inimitable and colorful style, he tells the beginning screenwriter how the mechanics of Hollywood storytelling work, and how to use those elements to create a script with blockbuster potential without falling into clichés.

Neill D. Hicks' screenwriting credits include *Rumble in the Bronx* and *First Strike*.

$16.95 | 220 pages | Order # 41RLS | ISBN: 0-941188-72-8

MYTH AND THE MOVIES
Discovering the Mythic
Structure of 50
Unforgettable Films

Stuart Voytilla
Foreword by Christopher Vogler
Author of *The Writer's Journey*

An illuminating companion piece to *The Writer's Journey*, *Myth and the Movies* applies the mythic structure Vogler developed to 50 well-loved U.S. and foreign films. This comprehensive book offers a greater understanding of why some films continue to touch and connect with audiences generation after generation.

Movies discussed include *Die Hard*, *Singin' in the Rain*, *Boyz N the Hood*, *Pulp Fiction*, *The Searchers*, *La Strada*, and *The Silence of the Lambs*.

Stuart Voytilla is a writer, script consultant, and teacher of acting and screenwriting and the co-author of *Writing the Comedy Film*.

$26.95 | 300 pages | Order # 39RLS | ISBN: 0-941188-66-3

FILM DIRECTING: CINEMATIC MOTION
A Workshop for Staging Scenes

Steven D. Katz

Over 30,000 Sold!

With this practical guide to common production problems encountered when staging and blocking film scenes, directors can better develop a sense of what is the right solution for any given situation. Includes discussions of scheduling, staging without dialogue, staging in confined spaces, actor and camera choreography, sequence shots, and much more — with hundreds of storyboards and diagrams.

Some of the staging examples are technically simple, others require substantial choreography. The underlying assumption for all is that the filmmaker wants to explore the dramatic potential of the camera to the fullest, within the day's shooting schedule.

Contains illuminating interviews with these well-known professionals, commenting on the practical aspects of production: director John Sayles (*Eight Men Out, Sunshine State*), cinematographer Allen Daviau (*ET, Bugsy*), visual effects expert Van Ling (*Doctor Doolittle, Inspector Gadget*), art director Harold Michelson (*Catch-22, Terms of Endearment*), producer Ralph Singleton (*Clear and Present Danger, Juwanna Mann*), and key grip Dusty Smith (*Rounders, Cop Land*).

"The art of staging movie scenes hasn't been written about very extensively, so the best way to learn is by watching others at work. *Film Directing: Cinematic Motion* provides a better idea with complete illustrated staging techniques and storyboards."

— *Millimeter Magazine*

Steven D. Katz is a writer/filmmaker. His work has appeared on *Saturday Night Live*, in feature films, and in numerous film festivals around the world. He is also the author of *Film Directing: Shot by Shot*.

$24.95 | 294 pages | Order # 6RLS | ISBN: 0-941188-14-0

24 HOURS | **1.800.833.5738** | **www.mwp.com**

ORDER FORM

TO ORDER THESE PRODUCTS, PLEASE CALL **24** HOURS - **7** DAYS A WEEK
CREDIT CARD ORDERS **1-800-833-5738** OR FAX YOUR ORDER **(818) 986-3408**
OR MAIL THIS ORDER FORM TO:

MICHAEL WIESE PRODUCTIONS
11288 VENTURA BLVD., # 621
STUDIO CITY, CA 91604
E-MAIL: MWPSALES@MWP.COM
WEB SITE: WWW.MWP.COM

WRITE OR FAX FOR A FREE CATALOG

PLEASE SEND ME THE FOLLOWING BOOKS:

TITLE	ORDER NUMBER (#RLS _____)	AMOUNT
_____		_____
_____		_____
_____		_____
_____		_____
_____		_____
	SHIPPING	_____
	CALIFORNIA TAX (8.00%)	_____
	TOTAL ENCLOSED	_____

SHIPPING:
ALL ORDERS MUST BE PREPAID, UPS GROUND SERVICE ONE ITEM - **$3.95**
EACH ADDITIONAL ITEM ADD **$2.00**
EXPRESS - **3** BUSINESS DAYS ADD **$12.00** PER ORDER
OVERSEAS
SURFACE - **$15.00** EACH ITEM   AIRMAIL - **$30.00** EACH ITEM

PLEASE MAKE CHECK OR MONEY ORDER PAYABLE TO:

MICHAEL WIESE PRODUCTIONS

(CHECK ONE) ____ MASTERCARD ___VISA ____AMEX

CREDIT CARD NUMBER _____

EXPIRATION DATE _____

CARDHOLDER'S NAME _____

CARDHOLDER'S SIGNATURE _____

SHIP TO:

NAME _____

ADDRESS _____

CITY _____ STATE _____ ZIP _____

COUNTRY _____ TELEPHONE _____

ORDER ONLINE FOR THE LOWEST PRICES

24 HOURS | 1.800.833.5738 | www.mwp.com